Paradise and Other Hells

Paradise and Other Hells
Published by phipl
an imprint of flipped eye publishing | www.flippedeye.net

All Rights Reserved

First Edition
Copyright © José Eduardo Agualusa

English translation of each piece is copyright © the respective translators, 2020. See page 395 for individual credits.

Jacket design by D237 | www.d237.com

No part of this publication may be reproduced, stored in or introduced into a retrieval system or transmitted in any form or by any means (electronic, mechanical, photocopying, recording or otherwise) without the written permission of the individual author, except for the quotation of brief passages in reviews; nor may it be otherwise circulated in any form of binding or cover other than that in which it is published and without a similar condition including this condition being imposed on the subsequent purchaser.

ISBN-13: 978-0-9563188-0-0

This book is typeset in Book Antiqua and Palatino Linotype
Printed and bound in Great Britain.

Paradise and Other Hells

José Eduardo Agualusa

Translated from the Portuguese by Rahul Bery, Daniel Hahn, Andrew McDougall, Victor Meadowcroft, Robin Patterson and Francisco Vilhena

For Yara, from whom I have been learning how to travel through time; for Lula Arraes and Vanessa Riambau Pinheiro, who have helped me to understand Brazil; and for Sérgio Guerra, who made it possible for me to think and write about Angola.

All ending is contemporary with all beginning.

It is only our eyes that come later.

Agostinho da Silva

Contents

Note	17
Wednesday, 20 August 2014	19
Cataloguing monsters	20
Dead poets' island	22
All poetry aspires to be song	24
Sunday, 19 May 2013	27
Thursday, 4 September 2014	29
Friday, 5 September 2014	31
Monday, 8 September 2014	33
My daughter's hair	34
Friday, 12 June 2015	37
The oldest tree in the world	39
An unlikely reader	42
A false blonde angel	45
Thursday, 28 April 2016	47
Thursday, 5 May 2016	49
Conviction and skulduggery	51
Tuesday, 12 September 2006	54
Tuesday, 22 June 2010	55

Monday, 1 June 2015	56
Tuesday, 5 November 2013	58
Black people in blackface	60
Death according to Sacks	62
Literature and identities	65
A toy for creating marvels	68
God is sick	71
In praise of strangeness	73
Friday, 25 September 2015	76
On race and justice	78
The nakedness of authors	81
Thursday, 25 June 2015	84
Friday, 3 July 2015	86
Thursday, 30 July 2015	88
Sunday, 2 August 2015	90
Saturday, 26 September 2015	92
Love letter to Luaty Beirão	94
The thinker's silence	97
Wednesday, 14 October 2015	99
Thursday, 15 October 2015	100
Thursday, 29 October 2015	102
The convulsive solitude of our days	104
On untranslatability	107
An unintentional anarchist	110

The extinction of unicorns	113
The Bar Oficina	116
The beautiful useless things that save our lives	119
The death of Cecil	122
Book of titles	125
A dead boy on the beach	128
Monday, 31 August 2015	131
The awareness of evil	134
Monday, 21 September 2015	137
The intelligence of life	140
Saturday, 3 October 2015	143
Starting again	146
On drugs and literature	149
The boy who walked through walls	152
A river's lament	155
Books burn well	157
Black power (or the power to be black)	160
Beware of the clown	163
The light of our language	166
The boys of Porto Mosquito	169
Non-places, non-people	172
Saturday, 16 January 2016	175
Thursday, 21 January 2016	178
From magical to autophagic realism	180

Tuesday, 9 February 2016	182
Private drama, public comedy	184
Monday, 15 February 2016	186
Something maybe like a forgiveness	189
That precise instant of glory	191
Lynchings	194
Mad not to dream	197
The zombie's bite	200
Trained not to smile	203
Towards an ethics of spitting	206
In case of emergency, use poetry	208
The magicians' reawakening	211
Before there was blue	214
Sunday, 15 May 2016	217
Monday, 16 May 2016	218
The writer who beat me	219
Wednesday, 6 July 2016	221
The flooded airplane	223
Paradise and other hells	226
Saturday, 24 June 2016	229
A whole host of whites	231
Keep calm: it isn't the end yet	234
Two views on Brazil	236
A ghost ship	239

Magnificent losers	242
Crazy season	244
Life's Vanquished, under the sun of the tropics	246
Castaways in the city	249
Uninventing the enemy	252
Almost immortals	254
The useless beauty of giraffes	257
Manoel and me	259
The day the Virgin Mary lost her head	261
The cruel months	264
A strange fruit	267
Cannibalism, expanded	270
A garden of memory	273
What is truth for?	276
My new obsession	278
He's back	281
Muhamed's choice	283
After the end	286
Wonderful cultural appropriation	289
While the earth shakes	292
Tiradentes' lice	295
Thursday, 4 May 2017	298
Sunday, 7 May 2017	300
The European explorer financed by an African king	302

The ideal kleptocracy	305
The end of miracles	308
Monday, 19 June 2017	311
Wednesday, 21 June 2017	312
Secret authors	317
Neural lace	320
Improbable happiness	323
The art of falling	326
The secret poetry of chance	329
Tuesday, 18 July 2017	332
The book thief	335
The language of the alchemists	338
Three divers and a dwarf	341
A wondrous discord	344
The Doomsday Clock	347
The curtains of censorship	350
A wolf in the mirror	352
Fear of nudity	354
The elegance of silence	357
On books and revolutions	359
The gold of the islands	362
Hero and traitor	365
Bantu Spring	368
Brave new world	371

The December sky	374
When the lion builds its own cage	377
The sceptical palm reader	380
A Swedish Hell	382
The Queen's blue-collar accent	385
The moon is not for everyone	387
The Macua samurai	390
Afterword	393
Translator Credits	395

Note

The reflections, observations and recollections in this book are based on columns published in the Brazilian newspaper *O Globo* and the Angolan e-newspaper *Rede Angola*. I have also included many entries from a diary that I have been writing for more than thirty years. All these texts, with only a few exceptions, were written between 2013 and 2018. They are not organised in chronological order. The Portuguese I have used is Portuguese in its entirety – global Portuguese, spoken in Angola, Brazil, Portugal, Cape Verde, São Tomé and Príncipe, Guinea-Bissau, East Timor, Galicia or Goa. It is my language.

Wednesday, 20 August 2014

The evening stretches out over the veranda. August spreads across the world like an epidemic. I have read in the newspapers that in Gafsa, in the Tunisian desert, a lake has appeared. In Siberia, on the Yamal Peninsula, in an area known as "the end of the world", the land collapsed suddenly, creating three deep craters. Twenty people suffering from Ebola ran away from a clinic on the outskirts of Monrovia, the Liberian capital, after the place was attacked by protestors. The protestors refused to believe the epidemic was real. The sick people are still on the run, contaminating others.

I close my eyes, listening Anouar Brahem's lute. Music does not defeat entropy, but it does postpone it.

Cataloguing monsters

I have been thinking a lot lately about a novel by the Portuguese writer Clara Pinto Correia, called *Os Mensageiros Secundários*, a lovely title that comes from biology. 'Second messengers' are molecules that transmit signals within cells. Clara Pinto Correia, who, incidentally, is a biologist with a long research career, recalled writing the novel after finding in some archive or other dozens of leaflets published in Lisbon in the months that preceded the great earthquake of 1755, dealing with sightings of monsters and freaks. The novel's narrator, a North American university professor named Chuck, believes said monsters to be messengers of sorts, proclaiming great disasters. Studying the leaflets, Chuck realises there is a correlation between the sightings and the earthquake. The monsters walk towards the city as the day of earthquake approaches.

At that time, there was an extraordinary variety of monsters in the world: mermaids, griffons, giants, Amazons, cannibals, Cyclopes, Arimaspi and Blemmyae – the latter headless men with a mouth and eyes embedded in their chests. I particularly like the monopods, beings with just one huge foot that they held up to protect them from the sun, and the astomoi, mouthless men with bodies covered in hair, that fed on odours and could die if the smell was too intense.

The monsters of our time are very different. They are not marked by any physical anomaly, nor by strange abilities or powers, but by their extreme moral deformity. Unlike monopods or astomoi, they have not a photon of poetry, nor the remotest trace of humour. Where there is humour, where there is poetry, there is always humanity. I see more humanity in an astomos than in certain world leaders.

These 'new monsters' call to mind the film of the same name (*I nuovi mostri*, 1977) directed by Dino Risi, Ettore Scola and Mario Monicelli and made up of fourteen brief stories, each one presenting a different kind of moral monster. I saw it as an adolescent, but I have never forgotten some of those monsters – such as the cruel son who has his elderly and naïve mother interned in a sinister asylum, or the mother who sells her youngest daughter to the pornographic film trade.

The new monsters walk among us. Some move with subtle discretion; others are public figures, respected and highly influential. Some are trivial; others are so bloated by moral deformations that they are transformed into a sort of supermonster. The impression I have is that this latter type is spreading at an unprecedented and alarming rate.

Thinking about Clara Pinto Correia's novel, I began to study the newspapers, noting down in one column tragedies caused by human action – wars, school shootings, fires, massacres, terrorist attacks – and, in another, great natural disasters: hurricanes, earthquakes, droughts, tsunamis. On the wall of my office, I put up a huge world map that I had bought, years ago, at the Altaïr bookshop in Barcelona. On it I mark the presence of supermonsters and the occurrence of catastrophes. I realise, horrified, that Chuck was right. Some time from now I shall be able to predict where and when the next earthquake will happen; where and when the next pandemic will emerge, just by the spread and progress of supermonsters.

The good news is that Angola, Brazil, Portugal and the rest of the Portuguese-speaking countries, seem, for the time being, to be relatively far from the supermonsters' main routes. That is not to say there are no monsters among us. There are, but they seem to be, in general, small, wayward, clumsy monsters, without conviction or seriousness. I reckon some of them to be clearly imitation horrors, fantasy frights; if you just gave them a shake, their false teeth and makeshift claws would fall out.

So one may assume that we shall be safe, at least in the short term, from earthquakes, hurricanes, plagues and epidemics. Still, it's best to be forewarned. I keep mapping incidents, cataloguing monsters. The advice I give you, dear readers, is to avoid the big cities. The end of the world will begin on asphalt. Remote settlements, beaches surrounded by palm trees and solitude, are completely off the supermonsters' routes. I have chosen my beach. It is on an island, far south, where everyone knows each other by name. The end of the world will never get to somewhere like that.

Dead poets' island

Small islands tend to be places far removed from the world, and are therefore fertile ground for the unexpected – for adventure. I read Stevenson's *Treasure Island* as a child, and then spent years searching for it. Eventually, I found it. My Treasure Island is the Island of Mozambique, also known as Muhipiti. The treasure is the island itself, the whole island, with its old colonial houses, churches, mosques and ancient matriarchs dressed in coloured fabrics, in whose veins runs blood that is European, African and Asian.

I returned to Muhipiti and its abundant tranquillity to finish a novel, and three days later I was already thinking about abandoning that one and beginning another in which the island itself would be the protagonist.

As I write this text, sitting at the table of the Café-Restaurante Ancora D'Ouro (where, as recounted by my Portuguese editor Francisco José Viegas in one of his pieces, Rui Knopfli saw Jorge de Sena write – on some sheets of Olympic Airways paper – the poem "Camões on the Island of Mozambique"), I see a group of joyful girls leaving the church opposite, singing in praise of Our Lady. Far off I can hear the muezzin's call to prayer. Nearby, you can visit an ancient Hindu temple, topped by two swastikas.

Just 3 km long and 300 metres wide, the Island is a UNESCO World Heritage Site. When Vasco da Gama landed on these beaches of white sand and coral in 1498, the Island was already an important settlement, with a strong Arab and Swahili presence, under the Sultan of Zanzibar. The Arabs are still here, although in smaller numbers, and Vasco da Gama is too – in his case, in the form of a statue that contemplates, with infinite tedium, the turquoise-blue sea. Also still on the Island, also fashioned from stone – unfortunately not very smoothly – is the poet Luís de Camões. Indeed, the Island has always attracted poets. Aside from Camões, who lived here for two years, and Knopfli and de Sena, the following have also passed through this city, and in some cases left descendants: Tomás António Gonzaga, Bocage, Miguel Torga, Alberto de Lacerda, Mia Couto and Nelson Saúte. What saved the Island was neglect. The first big blow came from the abolition of the slave trade; the second, the transfer of the capital to Lourenço Marques, now Maputo, in 1898. Prolonged abandonment, accentuated by independence and the violent civil war, explains the preservation of a relatively unchanged architectural style that combines Portuguese and Arab traditions.

So Mozambique began here. It was a happy beginning. If the whole country had followed and expanded upon this tiny island's long tradition of *mestiçagem* – the mixing of races – and peaceful cultural and religious coexistence, perhaps it would be in a better state today.

Tomás António Gonzaga arrived on the Island in 1792, at forty-eight years old, exiled for ten years for his involvement in the Minas Gerais Conspiracy. It did not take him long to forget Marília, or rather, Maria Doroteia Brandão, whom he had met in 1782 when she was sixteen and he thirty-eight. In 1793, the poet married a Mozambican girl, Juliana de Sousa Mascarenhas, daughter of a wealthy slave trader. Juliana may not have inspired his poems; however, she gave him two children. The poet's descendants now run into the dozens, scattered across various countries. Of all these descendants, just two, Dona Flora and Dona L. M., remain on the Island. The former is an affable woman who enjoys talking about the city's history and runs a small hotel in one of the large houses inherited from her family.

The past is so alive in the crooked streets of the old town that there are those who have settled into it and will never abandon it. Dona L. M. is one of those people. I saw her a few days ago, talking animatedly with someone in this very café where I now write. She was sitting at one of the tables. There was no one in front of her. Noticing my surprise, she explained: "I was just saying to Rui Knopfli here ..."

Knopfli died in 1997. It was explained to me later that Dona L. M. continues to meet not only with Knopfli but with many other figures who walked the city in colonial times. I like the idea of these figures, especially the poets, continuing to wander the city, even if only a few of us – very few – have the privilege of seeing them and talking to them.

All poetry aspires to be song

Last week I met Maria Bethânia in Maputo. She told me that Angola had made a good impression on her, and explained why: on landing in Luanda, she had found a large individual waiting for her, handsome, dressed impeccably in white. The man introduced himself: "I'm your driver. My name is Jesus of Nazareth."

In Maputo, Maria Bethânia did not have the good fortune of having Jesus of Nazareth as her driver, but, on the other hand, she found a city that was much breezier, greener, cleaner and more easy-going – despite the political situation, which was somewhat tense, and which has been affecting Mozambicans in recent months. Bethânia brought a beautiful poetry collection to Maputo, in which verses by African, Brazilian and Portuguese poets are bound together with a certain ingenuity and such naturalness that someone not familiar with the authors could be led to believe it is a single work.

Bethânia sings verses by Fernando Pessoa as much as she recites Caetano Veloso, and in doing so shows how artificial the boundaries are between poetry and what are conventionally known as "song lyrics". It was this, ultimately, that the Swedish Academy wished to highlight in awarding the Nobel Prize for Literature to Bob Dylan, songwriter. More than just honouring Dylan, the Swedes were recognising songs as words.

Last year, the ever-bolder Swedish Academy surprised the world by giving the Prize to a journalist, the Belarussian Svetlana Alexievich. The award was an opportunity to discuss what distinguishes journalism from literature. The answer – and it is enough to read Alexievich's astonishing and terribly harrowing *Voices from Chernobyl* to reach this conclusion – is that we should not impose boundaries. A report can be literature, and of the best kind, without ceasing to be journalism. There is good journalism without literature, good literature in bad journalism and great journalism that is excellent literature.

Caetano Veloso could present himself as a poet; Chico Buarque likewise, as could Ferreira Gullar or Eucanaã Ferraz. I enjoy listening to Leonard Cohen a lot – that husky voice full of shadows and omens. The poems he sings, moreover, do not lose the strange light that illuminates them if we happen upon them in the pages of a book, stripped of their melodic wings. And what is one to say of Jacques Brel?

All poetry aspires to be song; when it does not, it is probably not poetry. The thing is, sadly, most poets cannot sing.

We could, then, dispute the name of the awardee, but I do not think it fair to call for the prize to be differentiated for a writer of songs.

The indignant clamour that sprang up all around the world upon discovering the Swedish Academy's decision would likely not have happened had they recognised not Bob Dylan – whose lyrics are more often banal than surprising (or rather: than poetry) – but, for example, Leonard Cohen. Dylan is an excellent songwriter who happens, now and again, to be drawn to poetry. Cohen, on the other hand, is a poet the whole time.

The best part of the whole episode was the humour on social media. "I love Bob Dylan," commented the Portuguese writer João Tordo, "I've got all his books." An outraged editor added: "Dylan was always ahead of the game: for example, he started writing audiobooks before the concept of audiobooks even existed."

Returning to Mozambique, I remembered that Bob Dylan came here in the euphoric time of the revolution – in 1975, I believe. From that brief visit there is a song, "Mozambique", whose lyrics (may the Swedish Academy forgive me, but in this instance I cannot quite say "poetry") celebrate the beauty of Mozambican beaches and the girls who frequent them. Oddly, there is not the slightest reference to the revolutionary process that, at the time, was attracting intellectuals from around the world. Here are some lines:

> *There's lots of pretty girls in Mozambique*
> *And plenty time for good romance*
> *And everybody likes to stop and speak*
> *To give the special one you seek a chance*
> *Or maybe say hello with just a glance*

"The Girl from Ipanema", we can agree, beats Bob Dylan's girls from Maputo hands down, and this is no fault of the girls of Maputo. (Vinicius de Moraes, incidentally, deserves all the literary awards.)

Sunday, 19 May 2013

The boy is surrounded. He falls to the floor. He makes no attempt to defend himself. A man brings straw and old newspapers to cover his body. Around them, people comment on what is happening with a kind of distant curiosity. The man covers the boy's body with straw, pours petrol over him, lights a flame and moves away. The curious observers retreat as well, unhurriedly, while the fire spreads and grows. Then the boy jumps, covered in flames, shouting, and that is the only moment when the tragedy seems real – or rather, that is when it seems like something we see in films.

A video showing the episode described above has circulated in recent days on the social media networks used by Angolans. It did not cause much outrage. The comments from those who watched it, moreover, did not seem much different from those of the witnesses on the ground.

The worst horror is not the horror itself, but the silence around it.

The hardest part to accept is not the gas chambers destined to exterminate the Jews, but the ease with which the German engineers designed and built them. That, or the nightmare-less sleep of the pilots who dropped the bombs on Hiroshima and Nagasaki, and their chuckles as they thought up amusing names for them: "Little Boy" and "Fat Man".

That, or the adverts, in nineteenth-century newspapers, offering rewards for those who informed on escaped slaves. *Et cetera*.

If I sometimes have doubts about the fate of humanity, it is not so much to do with the displays of violence and folly I keep witnessing as with the indifference towards them. I regain my faith, thanks – so often – to simple acts, such as seeing a young girl crying over the image of an injured child at the World Press Photo 2013 exhibition in the Museu da Electricidade.

In the case of Angola, my hope is reborn daily, thanks, above all, to the non-conformity, generosity and talent of a new generation. The democratic movement that emerged in Luanda in 2010, inspired by the revolutions in North Africa, involved figures linked to popular music right from the beginning. Over time it has matured and expanded into new cultural and civic projects. Among these, a small group of singers and composers known as Geração 80 (Generation 80) stands out. The most remarkable voice of this group is that of a twenty-four-year-old woman called Aline Frazão. Born in Luanda, Aline studied in Lisbon before moving to Barcelona and then Santiago de Compostela. The person who first told me about her – with an enthusiasm that, at the time, seemed excessive – was António Zambujo. As soon as I heard her sing, however, I understood Zambujo's enthusiasm. With Aline it is not simply the voice – sweet, warm, sensual – that surprises. It is, more than that: the intelligence of a project that has no qualms about mixing the best and most sophisticated sounds of Angolan urban popular music (which is to say, all the inheritance left by the master Liceu Vieira Dias and his N'Gola Ritmos) with the best of Brazilian popular music. Besides, if anything can explain the vitality of African music, it is the voraciousness and joy with which it devours and incorporates other traditions. In 2011, Aline released her first album, *Clave Bantu*, consisting entirely of her own songs, plus one with lyrics by me and another by Ondjaki.

Aline's second album, *Movimento*, launched a few days ago in Lisbon (where, in the meantime, she has settled) confirms the young Luandan's immense talent. "Kalemba", perhaps the most striking song on the album, is a cry of faith in the movement for change:

Heard it coming from the beach
after the despair
the whole sea rising
in the kalemba *of change*
(. . .) And when the wind turns, turned
which side will you be on?

In another song, she warns: *Don't look, see!*
Anyone with ears should listen.

Thursday, 4 September 2014

Last night I dreamed about people who turned into donkeys and tried to eat me. In the afternoon I was interviewed by a Brazilian television channel for a documentary about happiness. We all want to be happy; rarely, however, do we stop to think about what brings us joy, or unhappiness.

In recent years, observing the rapid money-making of a small sector of Angolan society, and rubbing shoulders with some of that new bourgeoisie, I have been able to check how much truth there is in the old cliché that claims "money can't buy happiness". Talking about happiness, there are those who find it in adventure, others in repetition. Banality can be as cosy as an old sofa.

I have lost count of the number of times I have heard these *nouveaux riches* nostalgically recall their childhood, which, though they were not poor (poverty certainly does not bring happiness), was also not spent in a golden cot. Back then, happiness was a second-hand bicycle. Happiness was lunch in the backyard, listening to your elders tell stories of long ago. Happiness was whirling about on the dirt floor. Happiness was hearing Ruy Mingas sing "Morro da Maianga". Happiness was your grandmother's fried fish after a night out.

In the meantime, the years passed and the humble children grew up and got rich. Times have changed, they say. They buy the latest Ferrari, seeking to reproduce the glorious feeling they experienced when racing downhill on a go-kart, headed towards the cool flow of a river. It doesn't work.

Many of our *nouveaux riches* did not struggle to become rich. They did not wear themselves out. Now, however, their richness does tire them. It erodes. Imprisons.

As for myself, I have always had a certain knack for happiness. More so than for football, anyway. I live with little. I keep myself free.

Very young writers go for the easy tricks. The overuse of adjectives, for example, is a juvenile literary illness. Later, as they grow up, writers learn to cut. From a certain point onwards, we understand that simplicity is the key. It is the same in life. Cutting out whatever is artificial, we become freer and, perhaps, closer to happiness.

Friday, 5 September 2014

I travelled this morning from Rio de Janeiro to São Paulo d'El Rei, with a driver dressed like a lawyer – with that cold sharpness of lawyers – who later confided that he often worked for ministers and other important Angolans. As well as being a driver, Ubiratan raises and sells parrots, macaws and other more exotic, and more expensive, birds.

At one point we passed a place called Quissama or, rather, Quissamã. A few minutes later I saw a group of ostriches, dishevelled and flustered. They were more surprised to see me than I them, as I know ostriches are in vogue; I have been coming across farms of them all over the place. In Budapest, for example, years ago, I dined in a restaurant that only served ostrich meat.

Returning to Angolan toponymy in Brazil, I recall having been in Cadete (Rio de Janeiro), Caxito (Rio de Janeiro), Massangano/Massangana (Pernambuco), Luanda (Pernambuco), Caconda (São Paulo), Cazenga (Minas Gerais) and Mutamba (Formosa do Rio Preto), in Bahia. Sometimes you get the feeling the whole map of Angola was transferred to Brazil, and here it expanded and spread out.

Brazil's Angolan origins are evident in its toponymy and, more so, in the number of Bantuisms, principally originating from Quimbundo, Quicongo and Umbundu, that remain in the vocabulary of Brazilian Portuguese. The writer, composer, singer and essayist Nei Lopes has published various works on this theme, among them a delightful lexicon: the *Novo Dicionário Banto do Brasil*.

It would be interesting to study the inverse situation; that is, to examine what remained of Brazil in Angola, one land feeding another. Angola's development ran parallel to Brazil's. It being the case that Angola shaped Brazil, it is no less true that Brazil helped shape Angola. Some Angolan governors came from Brazil. In the seventeenth century, the Dutch who took Luanda had come from

Pernambuco, and they brought Brazilian Indians to Angola. Later, the armada that departed from Rio de Janeiro to fight the Dutch, captained by Salvador Correia de Sá e Benevides, included black soldiers under the famous Henrique Dias and Indian soldiers under the no less famous Filipe Camarão.

I have often heard the improbable legend according to which the ancestors of our Vieira Dias family are direct descendants of the bold Henrique Dias. I write "improbable legend" because Henrique Dias never visited Luanda. I am not aware, however, of whether or not relatives of his will have done so.

Mossâmedes and the plateau of Huíla received settlers who had departed from Pernambuco in the mid-nineteenth century. Descendants of these Pernambucans can still be found in the region. And the Indians? Likely there will be Angolan families, in Luanda and other cities, descended from those Tapuia and Potiguara fighters whom the wild twists and turns of history dragged to Angola.

Ubiratan, the driver, tells me that one day an Angolan minister ordered fifty blue macaws from him – a magnificent bird, already on the list of endangered species. The minister wanted to take the macaws to one of his properties, in the south of the country.

"My wife likes blue birds," the Angolan minister told Ubiratan.

Ubiratan did not sell him the birds.

Monday, 8 September 2014

Rio de Janeiro. I went to visit Juliana Luna, in Santa Teresa. The entrance consists of an iron door, in a road far below the land where the house stands. The door opens onto a sort of vault. There are some cement stairs, poorly made, barely illuminated, that rise up to the property. I followed her glorious hair, trying not to trip on the steps, and then continued to follow her through a courtyard shrouded by twilight and neglect.

Luna's hair is a flag. An affirmation of the power of black women.

Luna had a dancing pole put in the middle of her room, opposite the bed. She showed me how to use it. It did not seem at all easy. We then went to an old cinema, a short distance from her house, to re-watch *The Grand Budapest Hotel*. We had dinner at the Sobrenatural.

I arrived home very late. My phone rang. It was Vanessa da Mata, insisting that I accompany her to a party at Paula Lavigne's house. I went. Djavan, Otto, Eminem and a bunch of other singers and musicians were there, playing and singing. I saw two more girls with hair like Luna's. Using hair as an affirmation of identity is nothing new. I can clearly remember my adolescence, around the time Angola became independent, and the craze of the *jimis*, which was the name given in those days to those voluminous hairdos, in homage to Jimi Hendrix. Everyone with appropriate hair had a *jimi*, including one of my cousins, who gave shape and volume to his *jimi* very skilfully, with an iron goad. These days my cousin is almost unambiguously a white person. Back then, he was mulatto – something all white youths aspired to, but only rarely achieved. The mulattos, of course, wanted to be black. Likewise, few managed it.

My daughter's hair

I am the father of two gorgeous creatures. I'm not saying that in order to boast; I know they got their beauty from their mother. I have to deal on a daily basis with the surprise of people I meet: "Your children are beautiful! How did you manage that?!"

Some people avoid the *how is this possible?*, but I can read the incredulity in their eyes. Then I show them a photo of the children's mother and they calm down a bit: "They look just like their mum, both of them. Black, is she?"

That depends. In Angola she's a mulatta. In most other African countries, too. She's black in Brazil, in the United States and in Sweden or Denmark. In India, in the United Kingdom or in South Africa, she has been Indian. As for me, I'm half-Indian in India, half-Malay in Malaysia, of indecipherable race in the US, and totally Arab in any country in North Africa, Belgium, France, Germany or Sweden. When I travel around Europe, I'm almost always very Arab.

In Sweden, as in the rest of Europe, it's hard to be an Arab nowadays, at least on working days. On Saturday and Sunday (which are days that don't rush, they sprawl), the Swedes drink. You know when a Swede has had a bit too much to drink when they hold out their hand without having been introduced and start to chat. One night in Stockholm, I was in a bar along with an Angolan friend when a Swedish man held out his hand. It was a Saturday.

"*Salaam aleikum!*" the Swede greeted us. "I feel really sorry for you, you Arabs. You've suffered so much."

We thanked him. At first, we tried to correct the mistake. The Swede ignored our protests. "Oh, yeah, you've really suffered!" he insisted, hugging us. He was crying. "I'm so sorry for everything the Europeans have done to make you suffer."

He ordered beers for the three of us. "*Salaam aleikum!*" he shouted, raising his glass. Then, right away, he realised he'd committed a terrible gaffe, apologised and asked to have the beer replaced with tea.

My friend, annoyed, refused the exchange. *"Aleikum salaam!"* he shouted, and we all drank.

But back to my children. The oldest, a boy, is now more than 1.88 m tall, and he studies in Brighton, in the UK. He's a sweet boy who never gave us any worry, except when he was a baby, in Luanda, during the war. He used to cry a lot at night. There was nothing that could calm him down. His screaming upset the dogs. One dog would respond, howling, and then another in a nearby yard would join the first ... and then another ... and yet another. Three minutes after the start of the crying, we would hear a gunshot (some neighbour alerted by the barking of the dogs), and then a whole firefight would begin. Each time the boy cried, the war would come back.

The girl, Vera Regina, has an incredibly beautiful head of hair, long and curly. I divorced when Vera was still very small. The hardest thing, whenever I was alone with her, often for several weeks, was maintaining the radiance of that magnificent mane. I remember some end-of-the-year holidays I spent with Mia Couto and his family, on a remote beach in Mozambique. I chose to let the kids run free. I thought it cruel to subject Vera Regina, every night, after a prolonged period of swimming in the sea, to the painful ritual of reordering her hair. After three days, Vera already sported some solid dreadlocks – enough to make any Rastafarian die of envy. A week later, when we returned to the hotel in Maputo, her hair was an impregnable forest. I took her to the hair salon in the hotel and explained to the proprietor of the establishment, a taciturn Russian with angular features and prominent cheekbones, that I needed to return the girl to her mother the following morning, and I needed her back in shape. The man gave me a hard stare.

"Are you still together, you and the child's mother?"

"No!" volunteered the girl. "They're speculated."

"Separated," I corrected her. "She means separated."

"Naturally," said the Russian, icily. "I hope your ex-wife has you killed. If I were her, I'd kill you myself with my bare hands."

I didn't laugh. The man wasn't joking.

When I returned three hours later, I found my princess sitting in one of the chairs, very upright, very serious, while four pretty young assistants finished untangling her hair. The operation went on for another hour.

"This girl is a heroine," murmured the Russian, when he finally returned her to my hands. He looked at me with contempt. "Let's see if you might learn to deal with her hair yourself."

I did learn. I am proud of her hair. It always surprises me when I read about girls being hassled in Brazil – the country with the greatest number of people of African origin in the world outside Africa – for wearing their hair with its natural curls. There is nothing lovelier than beautiful curly hair. I'm not talking here about using hair as a banner of Blackness, or of feminism, or anything like that. I'm just talking about beauty. Pure beauty.

Friday, 12 June 2015

The Lisbon Book Fair will be drawing to a close in two days' time. This afternoon I'll head back to Parque Eduardo VII to sign my books. I imagine that, as on previous weekends, and as in previous years, I'll be met by a tightly packed crowd, noisy and celebratory, wandering between stalls, leafing through books, talking to writers.

I enjoy the ritual of book signings. It's one of the few opportunities a writer has to talk to his readers. The Lisbon Book Fair is particularly interesting for me, because I always discover so many Angolan readers. These are people of all different ages – some on brief visits to Portugal, others having already lived here for many years. Young people stop by, asking me to read the novel they've just finished writing. They want my opinion. They would like, above all, for me to help them find a publisher. There are readers who come to share a story. These tend to be family sagas, with complex plots involving sudden twists and the discovery of unexpected blood ties, like in soap operas. On other occasions, they are tales of war or political persecution. I've heard some extraordinary stories.

There are also those who come to ask me questions about my novels. Some of these questions are so good that I'm unable to provide an answer. The best questions, in fact, are almost always those for which we don't have answers. They leave us with a sense of unease. Good readers help us discover our own books.

I remember a woman from Benguela who came to tell me how much she'd enjoyed *O Vendedor de Passados* (*The Book of Chameleons*). Aside from the story, she'd been delighted with the narrator, a gecko who is able to laugh like a person. "I really liked that," she said, "because in my house I have a gecko who sings to me – and no one believes it!"

I believe her. I really did meet a laughing gecko – it happened in the Taman Negara rainforest, in Malaysia, many years ago. I fully accept the existence of singing geckos. But they don't sing for just anybody.

Finally, there are the characters. I remember one very elderly man who stood before me, perfectly straight, hat on head, skimming through my latest novel, *A Rainha Ginga e de Como os Africanos Inventaram o Mundo* (Queen Nzinga, and How the Africans Invented the World), before putting the book down, and – having explained to me that he was also Angolan, from Luanda, a contemporary of various celebrated figures from the nationalist movement – issuing the savage verdict: "Pile of shit!"

"My novel?"

"Your novel, and all the rest. All you Angolan writers, you're all a right pile of shit!"

I tried to argue with him. We have a number of writers we can be proud of, names such as Luandino Vieira, Ruy Duarte de Carvalho, Ana Paula Tavares, Pepetela. The man interjected gruffly, decisively: "All a pile of shit! All of them! Angolan literature hasn't produced anything interesting since António de Assis Júnior."

I conceded. It could have been worse. He could have said António de Oliveira Cadornega, who died (still Portuguese but already definitively Angolan) way back in 1690.

Tonight, we celebrated the festival of Santo António, the patron saint of Lisbon. I had dinner with Kalaf Epalanga and Pedro Hossi at Le Chat, then we went on to a Red Bull party in Largo do Intendente. We found Namalimba Coelho, lighting up the party as always, accompanied by a group of Angolan artists. Suddenly, a young woman fainted and collapsed right at my feet. As she fell, having tripped against a stone bench, the wind raised her dress up to her waist so that she was left almost naked, lying there in black knickers, to our collective astonishment. Then she opened her eyes and smiled: a smile of complete happiness. Two young men appeared – I'm not sure where from – helped her to her feet and then vanished with her.

"These things only happen when you're around," said Kalaf, shaking his head. And that's sort of true. I have a talent for attracting bizarre events and characters.

The oldest tree in the world

A few years ago, on a visit to Sweden, I heard about Old Tjikko, a European Spruce (*Picea abies*) said to be more than 9,500 years old. I was expecting to come across an enormous vegetable mass with broad twisting boughs, thick roots pushing up through the ground, its bark craggy like – I presume – the skin of a dinosaur. In short, a whole green, leafy universe, unfolding before my astonished eyes. But instead I was met by a sad, stunted-looking trunk with bare, sunken limbs, which I would never have noticed if I'd been travelling on my own.

The extraordinary is often discreet, sometimes invisible. I was contemplating this while watching crowds go past on a sunny afternoon, at the Lisbon Book Fair. The event takes place in a large park, from the top end of which you get an incredible view over the city, rooftops skittering merrily down towards the river. Writers sign their books in the shadow of canopies. In front of the most fortunate ones, handfuls of readers form themselves into queues.

It was then that I noticed a guy with long hair, a bushy beard and dirty, ragged clothing, waiting in a queue for me to sign a book. I would never have noticed him if he'd been sitting on some street corner, a cardboard box between his feet. But there, in that queue, among young students weighed down by books, kindly grandparents holding up grandchildren (and more books), and solemn-looking gentlemen in suits and ties, the man stood out.

Of course, invisibility depends on our surroundings. I would immediately have noticed Old Tjikko, would have paused for a few moments, curious, to look more closely, if I'd come across it standing in a basilica, for example, rather than in a frozen forest. However, sometimes the extraordinary really does appear extraordinary.

I quickly worked my way through the other readers, curious to hear what this character had to say. Finally, the man sat down beside me. He introduced himself as "Guilherme" and handed me the book.

"I've read all your novels," he told me, in the deep voice he appeared to have stolen from a radio presenter. "But I enjoyed this one so much, I ended up buying it." The others, he'd read in a bookshop. He explained that he spends his mornings reading in a local bookshop with a little café. Guilherme will select a book, find a seat at one of the tables and read. Once he's done, he memorises the page number and returns the book to the shelf. The next morning, he looks for a copy of the same title and picks up where he left off.

I wanted to know where he lived.

"Right here," he replied with an expansive gesture, taking in the entire park. Perhaps the entire city.

"In the street?"

"In the *universe*."

He told me he'd once been a businessman and had made lots of money. He'd had a partner, in whom he trusted blindly. Mutual friends had warned him that this partner was swindling him, but Guilherme didn't believe them: "It's easier to fool people than convince them they've been fooled." He paused so I'd have time to weigh up this statement. Then he added: "Mark Twain. It's his line. There's also that saying: there's no worse blind man than the one who doesn't want to see. It's a good saying, but from being repeated so often it's lost much of its power."

One day, he'd discovered he was bankrupt. On that same day, he discovered that this wasn't such terrible news: "I felt liberated. I had nothing. Therefore, I had nothing to lose. For years upon years, I'd lived in a permanent state of anxiety. I worked sixteen hours a day. I've always enjoyed reading, but had no time. And suddenly, there I was, liberated, with all the time in the world. Why own cars and boats, when what really interests me is the journey? Why own so many books, a huge library, if all I really desire is to read?"

I signed the book and returned it to him: "So why did you buy this one?"

He smiled. "My greatest ambition is to live with fewer and fewer possessions. But I still buy books. One every three months. If nothing else, when you're sleeping on the ground, books make good pillows."

We embraced warmly upon parting. I saw him again, days later, sitting on the ground, on some street corner, a mutt dozing at his feet. He didn't see me. He was reading a book, a big smile on his lips. People walked past him, treading quickly, coming from nowhere, heading nowhere. They walked past him just as, for hundreds of years, other men and women had walked past Old Tjikko – the same distraction, the same confused ignorance – without pausing for a moment, without even suspecting that one of life's small miracles was so near at hand.

An unlikely reader

I see him every year at the Lisbon Book Fair. I went back there a few days ago, on an afternoon filled with light and pollen. Sitting nearby, Augusto Cury was being confronted by an enormous queue. Mine was minimal, made up of a very diverse group of people. I recognised a former Angolan minister, two or three students and a Swedish holidaymaker, very red and sweating beneath the beating sun (I later learned he was actually Danish.) Guilherme, my improbable reader, stood out among this group. He stood out, in fact, among the entire crowd filling the park and browsing books. His long, curly hair had seen neither comb nor water for many months. His dirty, rumpled clothes adhered to his skin. Passers-by glanced at him mistrustfully. I stood up, embraced him and invited him to take a seat. He handed me a copy of my latest novel for me to sign, and afterwards placed a small, black-covered notebook in my hands: "This is one I wrote," he told me. "Now it's yours."

I opened the notebook: poems with fantastic coloured illustrations that leaped out, luminous, against a black background. The poems were handwritten, using various coloured inks.

I am frequently offered books during signing sessions. Young writers in search of a publisher even entrust me with original manuscripts. Unfortunately, I've never been able to get a single one of these texts published. I have no talent when it comes to convincing publishers. On one occasion, in Rio, a girl handed me two dry leaves – real leaves, from an actual tree – each containing a haiku written in white ink:

O gentle rainfall
settle droplets of your thirst
on my outstretched tongue.

The second haiku is my favourite:

In my coat of rain
translucent sheet that suits me
right down to the ground.

It was Christiana Nóvoa. I liked this haiku so much that I checked out her website, the address of which I discovered on the back of the leaf. (I studied agronomy for five years, yet still don't know the term for the back of a dried leaf, written on by hand.) I was delighted with what I found there. Later, she offered me two haikus for my novel *A General Theory of Oblivion*, and we became friends.

Anyone wishing to find Guilherme need only look for him in one of the bookshops of the Chiado, the historic – and increasingly bustling – heart of Lisbon. When he isn't there, reading, he can probably be found on some nearby pavement, sitting in the shade, observing the spectacle of humanity on the move.

My grandmother would have referred to Guilherme as a "vagabond". As a child, I loved that word. It seemed to contain all sorts of old-fashioned resonances, of journeys, adventure, rebelliousness, that set me dreaming. I very much wanted to be a *vagabond*. To wander the world with no commitments. In those days, this mostly meant not having a fixed time for going to bed or waking up. Not having to go to school. Not having to eat my greens. My grandmother tried to bring me back into the real world: "Think of the cold, the discomfort of sleeping on the ground, wrapped up in old newspapers. Think of the hunger, of rainy days."

I didn't pay much attention to her. I dreamed of a life in which nobody told me what to do. I would explore remote cities, travel through deserts and forests, with only a dog for company – a big dog, a mastiff – and some books. I've always had a love of books.

Guilherme is the person I wanted to be when I was a child. A vagabond, yes, but one with a tremendous library. Because, to my mind, a vagabond with a tremendous library was somehow even more of a vagabond. He wandered freely even while reading.

I failed in this project, as in so many others. Yet I did hold out. I'm not the kind of loser who gives up easily. I don't know if it was my grandmother who brought me down to earth, or my back. Because, let's be honest, sleeping on the pavement, upon hard stone, is only poetic when it's someone else's back.

Returning to Guilherme's book, I was quite surprised by a number of his poems – and what more can we ask from poetry than that it should surprise us? I have not, however, been authorised to share these. On the very first page, I came across this solemn warning:

What is written in this notebook may never be divulged. Transgressors will be doomed to wear a tie for the rest of their lives.

I'd sooner death. For my part, I shall remain silent.

A false blonde angel

I am writing this text from the sands of Leblon, bathed in light, an ice-cold coconut within arm's reach. We tend to devalue that which is given to us freely and in abundance. The inhabitants of Northern Europe, immersed in darkness for eight to ten months of the year, look at the sun during the rare moments when it appears with an affection that is seldom displayed by us.

I lived in Berlin for a year. I spent a winter in The Netherlands. In Amsterdam, I was put up at a charming writer's residence in the Old Centre. The apartment was spacious, uncluttered, and had enormous windows facing in all directions. Dutch houses and apartments tend to do without curtains, so as to take full advantage of the scarce natural light. By the end of the first week, I could already recognise most of my neighbours. They would smile at me from their kitchens, their living rooms, their bedrooms, while preparing morning coffees, shaving or changing their clothes. It was harder to recognise them when I bumped into them, now dressed, at the corner café or in the charming bookshop underneath my apartment. All my neighbours would go out to work. Only I remained in the apartment during the day, writing. I made friends with the cat in the apartment opposite mine. It was a huge, black animal that would position itself across from me with the first ray of sunshine, and then circle the apartment, following the fragile light. In the opposite window, sitting in my chair, I did the same. We would sit there, looking at one another, bound by a shared ray of sunlight and the melancholy despair of exiles. That blessed ray of sunshine would last no more than three hours.

The cat's owner was a slim girl with small breasts, a flat bottom and long legs, the blonde hairs of which she rarely shaved. She ate very little: yoghurt with cereal in the morning, a light salad, an apple or a banana at night. After dinner, she would spend an hour or two at the computer, and was always in bed by eleven.

On one occasion, I was invited to sign my books in their Dutch translations, in a nearby town. Beside me, an angel with huge white wings took her seat. She laughed when she noticed my look of astonishment. She showed me the cover of the book she was signing – *The Diary of an Angel*, or something of the sort – and introduced herself: "I'm Bianca. I'm your neighbour, the one with the cat."

I apologised for not recognising her. "It's the wings," I mumbled, still dazed. "I'm not used to seeing you with wings."

As soon as I recovered my breath, I explained how I'd made friends with her cat thanks to the brief ray of sunshine we shared.

She smiled. "His name's Bruno. I found him on the street, in Mexico City, badly mistreated, and adopted him. I think he misses the tropical sunshine. The thing that struck me most about Mexico was the magnificent skies." I was reminded of Ryszard Kapuściński. The Polish journalist had said just the same when I asked him, in relation to his innumerable visits to Africa, what it was that had surprised him most: the light.

At the end of the day, I went home with her. I helped her take off her wings. Then I helped her take off the rest of her clothes. I spotted a fat man in his underpants, in the window of the apartment above mine. The man winked lewdly at me.

"Shouldn't we turn out the light?" I suggested to Bianca.

She affected surprise. "I thought you liked light?"

I could think of no response other than a cheap cliché: "The light from your eyes is enough." It sounded even worse in my basic English. This was the beginning of my decline. My collapse was inglorious. I returned to my apartment, feeling melancholy and defeated. The next morning, there was Bruno the cat, beneath the ray of sunshine. Now, however, he regarded me mockingly.

I sat down to think about the light. It's difficult to be happy in darkness. And yet, how do people in the majority of sunny countries behave? We waste the light. We waste it literally, by not investing in clean energy. We also waste our potential for happiness when we fail to create societies like those of Northern Europe, which are more socially just, with less corruption and poverty, more democracy and transparency. The truth is, just having light is not enough. It also takes a bit of effort.

Thursday, 28 April 2016

Certain mistakes appear able to undermine an entire body of work. I imagine God, looking on from afar, watching the confused procession of humanity. Michelangelo goes by, and God rejoices. Louis Armstrong goes by, and God almost laughs. Josephine Baker goes by, whirling around, her breasts joyfully unconstrained, and God abandons all solemnity and applauds, bursting into unmistakeable African laughter. But then comes a Mussolini, a Trump, a Bolsonaro, and God shudders, horrified: "Are these also works of mine?"

Or maybe God looks upon these cruel and stupid men as a writer looks upon his cruel and stupid characters – not as mistakes, but as human beings in a transitory state of error which, occasionally, is interrupted by death before they manage to set things right.

A man who was no more than a mistake, a definitive and undiluted mistake, would not be human. In all mistaken men there is – there must be – the possibility, even if only very remote, of getting something right. Hitler, who was a mediocre watercolour artist, did paint watercolours nevertheless. Or, rather, somewhere inside him there was a man in search of beauty. Who delighted in the presence of beauty.

I think about this as I read the grim news that reaches me every day from Angola. Regardless of the appalling accumulation of mistakes, I still want to believe that there is a door just waiting to be opened by those who have so often been mistaken. It may be a cliché to say that when a tyrant imprisons a just man, it is the tyrant himself who becomes the prisoner. Yes, it certainly is a cliché. It does, however, contain a solid truth. Clichés are nothing but truths to which we have stopped paying attention.

The tyrant is made a prisoner of his mistakes. In the bunker where he killed himself, Hitler may have looked back on the distant years of his youth and longed for the (failed) painter he could have been. An unsuccessful artist is someone who hits the mark, even when he misses his target. A successful dictator is someone who makes an accomplishment of his own errant ways.

In freeing his prisoners, the dictator would be correcting himself. He would be liberating himself. This first correction would offer a signal of hope. With the first door open, further doors would follow. Freedom is a path that lengthens as you walk it. Freedom is an addiction that becomes rooted inside you.

The future modifies the past. We return, for example, to that humble, twenty-year-old watercolour artist named Adolf Hitler. It is difficult to contemplate him, today, without a sense of horror. However, this horror would never have arisen if he'd spent his entire life as a mediocre watercolour artist.

If the dictator remains capable of liberating himself from himself – setting his prisoners free – it may be that tomorrow we can look upon him not as a definitive mistake, but as a man who erred and corrected himself. Yet, if death intervenes before he can make this correction, then he will always be regarded as a mistake. Eternally a mistake. A mistake from beginning to end.

Thursday, 5 May 2016

In the past few days, an image has leaped onto social media of a woman raising her right fist, in solitary ethical defiance, in the midst of a group of 300 uniformed Swedish neo-Nazis. Tess Asplund, forty-two, says she reacted unthinkingly, moved by the purest form of indignation. The march of the neo-Nazis, members of the Nordic Resistance Movement, took place last Sunday, 1 May. The following day, Tess discovered she had become a celebrity, which frightened her. "It's a circus now. I'm in shock. The Nazis are furious, and I'm left thinking: 'Oh crap, maybe I shouldn't have done that, all I want is peace and quiet.' Those guys are big and crazy. I have mixed feelings, but I'm trying to remain calm."

The first lesson we can draw from this episode is that, sometimes, we think better when we don't think; that is to say, when we act upon impulse. Had she stopped to reflect for a moment, Tess might never have taken that step forward and raised her fist. The second lesson is that a single person can make a difference. Without Tess, there, in that lucid moment, the neo-Nazi march would never have become a news story, would never have been discussed. Now, it is the focus of intense debate, not just in Sweden but across the rest of Europe. The third lesson is the most obvious: anyone who remains silent, consents. We cannot remain silent when democracy and human dignity are at stake. We all want peace and quiet, but there will be no peace or quiet unless we can stand up, courageously, to the advance of racist hatred.

In a democracy, everyone has the right to express their ideas. More than that: people should be encouraged to formulate alternative ideas and defend them publicly. The vibrancy of a democratic society can be measured by its diversity. People who march in the streets dressed up as soldiers, shouting words of hatred, however, are not expressing ideas: they are starting fires within the foundations of democracy. They are waging war on democracy.

Tess's statement, her admission of fear and hesitation, does not diminish her gesture. On the contrary, it magnifies it. Tess is an everyday Afro-Swedish woman, who produced an extraordinary gesture. I hope that, in Sweden, everyday people are able to recognise themselves in her, to see themselves mirrored in her – that woman, standing tall like an exclamation mark in the middle of a dark current of intolerance – and that they can stand tall themselves.

I have visited Sweden on three or four occasions. I retain the impression of a peaceful people, curious about others and educated to respect diversity. Neo-Nazi movements exploit people's worst feelings during a moment of crisis. They flourish amid hatred, like radioactive weeds on the ground at Chernobyl. They expand at the exact rate that democratic values retreat.

In the instant she raised her fist, Tess Asplund transformed into something greater than herself. Standing there alone, she *was* democratic Sweden. When I think of Sweden, it is her face I shall see.

Conviction and skulduggery

One afternoon, in Cape Town, South Africa, a man came up to me brandishing a flick knife. I'm a distracted sort of guy. In fact, I'm such a distracted sort of guy, so ingenuous, so convinced of the kindness of others, that I assumed he wanted to sell me the knife.

"How much is it?" I asked. "It's very nice. How much do you want for it?"

The man began to laugh. A mugger is not supposed to laugh; that's the first rule of the trade. The moment a mugger begins to share a laugh with his victim, he loses his nerve; the mugging is over.

"Where have you sprung up from?" he asked me, still laughing.

I told him I came from Angola and, on a sudden patriotic impulse, raised my right fist and began singing the national anthem at the top of my lungs: *"Ó pátria nunca mais esqueceremos ..."* A cacophony. A spectacle. I sing very badly. The man closed the flick knife, pocketed it and ran off. My girlfriend leaned back against a wall, trembling:

"He didn't want to *sell* you that knife, you big idiot! It was a mugging!"

I leaned back against the same wall beside her, trembling even more noticeably. "Really?! He seemed so friendly."

Behaving like a crazy person can be a good strategy to avoid getting mugged, but it requires considerable sangfroid – and a good dose of creativity, coupled with genuine madness. Anyone who would consider acting crazy to frighten off a mugger is usually a little bit crazy themselves. There are other options: pretend to be a karate champion, Superman, the Incredible Hulk or the Invisible Man. What matters is your conviction. In life, conviction counts for far more than circumstances.

I once knew a parrot that would bark like a dog in order to scare off cats. It didn't merely bark like a dog – it barked with the *conviction* of a dog. When the cats looked at it, they didn't see a parrot barking like a dog. What they saw was a dog barking, even if that dog did bear an uncanny resemblance to a parrot. So they fled.

On the subject of thievery and conviction, but speaking now not of victims but of thieves, I have particular admiration for a famous Angolan scoundrel who managed to get himself appointed to a position in government with a simple phone call. He phoned the prime minister, claiming that the President of the Republic had nominated him for the position in question. For two weeks, this man was Secretary of State for some utterly unimportant government department, with the right to an office and a chauffeur, until the fraud was uncovered. He took refuge in Lisbon, but didn't remain inactive very long. With three more phone calls to Luanda, this time made to the director of the National Diamond Company, introducing himself as the President's brother, he was able to walk away with 2.5 million euros. He was caught a short time later – a result of overconfidence – but managed to avoid prison by striking a deal with the injured parties.

My scoundrel dresses with subtle elegance. He looks you in the eye. He shakes your hand, firmly, honestly, as he addresses you by your first name, or sometimes even by a nickname, as if he's known you since childhood. He does this so naturally, with such sincerity, that when he starts to swindle you, using perfect diction and a warm, gentle voice, you've already been irremediably convinced of his trustworthiness. I think he manages to convince himself. Even when presented with a roster of evidence identifying him as a mythomaniac, a crook and the worst kind of miscreant, it still feels impolite not to trust him.

I know that my scoundrel is at large somewhere, in this vast, chaotic world, because occasionally someone (in São Paulo, in London, in New York) will tell me how they met a very elegant Angolan man – a wealthy businessman, a surgeon, a journalist, a famous economist, named "David", "Rodrigo", "Raul" or some other strong, classic-sounding name – and that this person nearly convinced them to buy shares in a mining company, or to finance some philanthropic organisation.

Imagine that poor bandit in Cape Town waving his knife at my scoundrel. My scoundrel would have been able to convince the man to place the knife in his hands before proceeding to mug the mugger, emboldened by the old saying that "a thief who steals from a thief will receive a hundred years of forgiveness".

At one point, my scoundrel made an appearance at a dinner where, by chance, a genuine economist was present. "He was making all sorts of ridiculous statements," this economist later told me, "but his mistakes were presented with such confidence that, when I tried to correct him, I was the one people began to doubt. His lies appeared truer than my more evident truths."

Conviction is of greater use than talent. Given a talented artist with no conviction and a thoroughly talentless artist full of self-belief, it will be the latter who triumphs.

Sadly, my scoundrel is not alone. There are many others like him out there. Compared to some, such as those who have achieved success in the world of politics, my scoundrel is a mere amateur, a dilettante – in short, a failure! And this knowledge is the thing that scares me most.

Tuesday, 12 September 2006

Quelimane, 1 PM: This morning I interviewed an old huntsman, Senhor Palha, who spent an hour recounting his memories. At one point, he began a sort of contest over who had eaten the most exotic food.

"Ever tried boa?"

"Yes, I tried boa a few years ago, at a hotel in Kinshasa."

"What about elephant trunk?"

"No, I haven't tried that."

"Oh! Elephant trunk's a bit like salami ..."

"I've eaten termites ..."

"Well, I've eaten red locusts. Tried them?"

"No, no. I've never had them."

"What about mermaid? We once caught a mermaid off Ilha do Fogo, not far from here – a small creature, with a fish's tail and a person's face, and ugly whiskers. Ever eaten mermaid?"

"I haven't!"

"It's white meat, a little bit sweet. It wasn't bad. But I think the strangest animal I've eaten was freshwater turtle."

Then the conversation turned to other matters.

Tuesday, 22 June 2010

Fragments from an interview for a literary blog called *Enlightened Ignorance*:

Q: Your novels are transatlantic and miscegenated, from the handling of language to the choice of settings. Is Lusophony an identity, or merely a marketing device?
A: I'm not entirely sure what "Lusophony" means; it seems to me to be one of those elastic concepts that every person interprets in their own way. Naturally, my novels are the result of my own personal journey. That journey has encompassed both choice and accident.
Q: Does spending most of your time living in Portugal not undermine your authority as a critic of the Angolan regime? Is it easier to be critical from afar?
A: That is precisely the thing that characterises totalitarian regimes – it is easier to criticise them from afar. I have never claimed to be an authority, just a citizen who is concerned by the direction in which his country is travelling, and I prefer to remain concerned, but free, and able to voice my concerns.

Monday, 1 June 2015

I enjoy walking along Rua da Esperança in Madragoa, formerly known as Mocambo, then heading up Rua do Poço dos Negros and reaching the Chiado. "Mocambo" may just as well be derived from Quimbundo as from Quicongo or Umbundu, three of Angola's most important languages, as a term meaning *home* or *refuge*. The Bairro do Mocambo was founded by royal decree at the end of the sixteenth century. It primarily housed freed black slaves, who shared the neighbourhood with fishermen's families and many hundreds of nuns from the various convents established in the area.

In recent years, the neighbourhood has undergone a peculiar historical turnaround: the Angolan upper middle classes have begun investing in the debilitated Portuguese economy, buying up companies and newspapers and amassing vast property portfolios. In a parallel development, in some cases supported by the first, Lisbon has witnessed the growing success of musicians, writers and artists from Africa.

Two recent performances confirm and celebrate the triumph of African Lisbon. Last Wednesday, Nástio Mosquito appeared at the Cinema São Jorge. On Friday, it was Kalaf Epalanga's turn to surprise his audience, at the magnificent Centro Cultural de Belém, with a one-off show in which some texts he'd written about Lisbon were mixed with the best Angolan music from the '50s and '60s, in a jazzy, intimate reinterpretation. Kalaf and Nástio are both Angolan. Nástio was recently tipped by the British newspaper *The Guardian* as one of the ten most influential African artists of our times: "A multimedia and performance artist working across music, videos, spoken word and *a capella*, Nástio Mosquito flirts with African stereotypes in western contexts." Kalaf is one of the founders of the most international and decorated of Portuguese bands, Buraka Som Sistema, largely responsible for the global success of kuduro music. Kalaf, a writer and columnist as well, defines himself as a cultural agitator. Buraka

– and Kalaf in particular – have had an enormous influence on Portugal's youth, and can be seen as part of the explanation for a curious new phenomenon: the adoption by this same youth of terms from Angolan Portuguese. In other words, in Portugal it has become cool to speak like an Angolan.

A Portuguese soap opera, *The Only Woman* – which launched recently on one of Portugal's most popular channels, TVI – also bears witness to the cultural turnaround I am referring to. A significant portion of the cast is made up of actors from Africa, or of African descent. However, in contrast to what occurs in most Brazilian soap operas, in *The Only Woman* it is the black characters who are wealthy. The white characters long to gain entry into the opulent world in which the Angolans live.

The top high-end clothing brands along the Avenida da Liberdade have started displaying designs inspired by African patterns – or patterns that the European designers imagine to be 'African' – in an attempt to attract an increasingly important sector of the market. The notion that all Angolans are rich has taken root. In one of his most amusing articles, Kalaf relates how, one night, after finishing a meal at a Lisbon restaurant, he was approached by the owner of the establishment. "May I ask if you are from Angola?" he enquired. When Kalaf confirmed that he was, the man instantly adopted an ingratiating tone and began asking if my friend would be interested in acquiring his restaurant. Kalaf considered telling the man the truth – that he couldn't afford it – but his Angolan pride got the better of him. He asked for some details and promised to go away and think it over. He never went back to that restaurant.

Angolan investment in Portugal has come to the attention of the international press, who talk of a 'revenge of the colonised'. The truth is, it isn't about revenge; it's not even about colonising the coloniser, but rather shared interests and affinity. Wealthy Angolans put their money into Portugal because they know the country well, and feel just as comfortable in Lisbon as they do in Luanda. However, what is more interesting than 'economic conquest' is the cultural exchange that has resulted. We are creating something we might define as 'horizontal Lusophony': a Portuguese language space in which all segments participate freely, as equal partners, without dominated or dominators.

Tuesday, 5 November 2013

Natal, Rio Grande do Norte. This morning I was taken to visit a school. The teacher gestured with her chin towards a girl who must have been around thirteen, sitting in the shade of a bower with some of her classmates and eating the state-provided school dinners. "That girl over there looks after her paralysed father all on her own, as well as four other siblings. The father was a gangster, caught a bullet in the spine. Her mother's in prison because of her links to drug trafficking."
Two boys, both very friendly, came over to hug the teacher. They greeted me, still smiling. When they'd walked away, the teacher confided with a melancholy half-smile: "Those two are caught up in it already. Most of the parents of the students in this region have got links to drug trafficking, and many of the kids end up going down the same path."
She took me to see the library. The school operated out of a sad-looking building by the harbour, which was very much the worse for wear. You could see the river from the first floor. Further in the distance, tall cranes shot up into the sky. The library was the only room with air conditioning. There must have been nearly 500 books arranged on the shelves. Some of their covers were very worn, which I found cheering. Unlike buildings, cars or any other standard consumer goods, the value of books should *increase* with use. I know of no books worth more than the ones in these kinds of schools, read by so many children.
I found José Maria Eça de Queiroz and Camilo Castelo Branco in the "Brazilian Authors" section. They seemed to be in good company: Eça de Queiroz was remembering old arguments with Machado de Assis, while Camilo was listening to Monteiro Lobato. I didn't correct the mistake. The students entered the library and sat down.
"They think that all writers are dead," the teacher told me. "They're very excited to be able to see one who's still alive."

I sat down next to the teacher. Over the last few days, I haven't been feeling great. I've thought to myself that maybe I should look for another profession. The students looked at me incredulously, a little intimidated even, as if listening to a zombie. Little by little, their confidence grew. The questions didn't vary greatly from the ones I've heard from other children in schools in Angola, Congo and Portugal. In all these schools, including the ones in Portuguese neighbourhoods where there is a majority-African population, I've encountered situations of great poverty and violence, but also of great hope.

A skinny boy, wearing glasses, wanted to know how to get started as a writer: "What do I write about?"

It didn't occur to me to say anything other than the obvious: that he should write about the world around him, that convulsive, frightening world. That he should write in order to try and understand it – that this is what writers do. We write to dodge the fear. We write because something is causing us pain. We write out of passion.

"What about money?" asked an asthmatic girl. "Do writers earn a lot of money?"

The others laughed at the question. I laughed, too. No, I replied; if she wanted to earn a lot of money it would be better for her to join a political party. The class's enthusiasm was a little dampened. Not only was I alive – far more alive than the majority of guys my age they knew – but to top it off, I wasn't even rich.

Black people in blackface

I spent last Carnival on the island of São Vicente, in the Cape Verde archipelago. The island's small capital, Mindelo, is famous for its celebrations. Over on the African continent, in Cape Town, there's an early carnival that takes place at the beginning of January. It used to be known as the Coon Carnival, and it brings together the city's sizeable mixed-race community. Luanda and Benguela, in Angola, and Quelimane in Mozambique, were also famous for their exuberant carnivals during the colonial period. Little by little, they are being brought back.

It is possible to map out the territories of Euro–African intermixing and its significance by looking through the lens of Carnival. Mindelo, Luanda, Benguela, Cape Town and Quelimane are all mulatto cities. The different between the first example and the others is that the situation in Mindelo is one of absolute creole hegemony. The entire country is *mestiço*. The other four African cities mentioned above are islands of intermixing in a vast ocean occupied by different Bantu cultures. Over the course of history, the two have not always co-existed peacefully. The creolised urban nuclei tend to ignore the rural world, if not actively hold it in contempt, and the feeling is mutual. In some cases, this has been going on for centuries. (Luanda, for example, was founded in 1576.)

At the Mindelo Carnival, I witnessed a curious example of Africa's estrangement from itself. One of the most popular, dynamic and expressive carnival groups is made up of men and children who paint themselves black, decorate their bodies with necklaces and bangles and go out into the streets wearing loincloths and holding fake spears and axes. They are the *"mandingas"*, a reference to one of the most powerful ethnic groups of West Africa.

In 1940, António Oliveira Salazar's regime held the great Portuguese World Exhibition in Lisbon. For effect, they brought along examples of people from some of the most representative ethnic groups in the African colonies. These people were exhibited in "traditional African villages", like animals in an enormous zoo. On the way back to Guinea–Bissau they must have passed through Mindelo, causing a certain amount of excitement and giving origin to the carnival group of the same name. Today we have this group of blacks and mulattos who paint themselves black: they are Africans dressing up as Africans, representing an archaic and mythical Africa originally intended to shock Europeans.

As it happens, they continue to frighten Europeans in their present interpretation. For the common Western tourist, the *mandingas* are the most original of all the groups at the Mindelo Carnival. I suppose they find them more genuine (more African), while the others are seen as being more 'Brazilianised'. Ironically, Carnival was actually brought to Brazil by Portuguese people and slaves from the islands of Madeira and Cape Verde at the beginning of the eighteenth century.

The tourist seeks difference, and over the course of this search they legitimate whatever appears authentic to them. Too bad if what appears to be authentic is essentially an invented or imagined representation of reality; reality can get stuffed!

Death according to Sacks

On 19 February just past, Oliver Sacks published a text in *The New York Times* which, without being dramatic or pessimistic – far from it, in fact – had the unmistakeable ring of a goodbye. He starts by saying that, at eighty-one years of age, he still feels himself to be a man of robust health, capable of swimming 1,500 m every day. Despite this, he has discovered that he has a tumour in his liver, and has only weeks left to live. He acknowledges that he is scared, but adds that his overwhelming feeling is one of gratitude.

Sacks published *The Man Who Mistook His Wife for a Hat* in 1985. Up until that point he'd already published four other books, one of which, *Awakenings*, was the basis for the film of the same name. But it was *The Man Who Mistook His Wife for a Hat* that brought him global fame. I remember reading it with enthusiasm and astonishment. In the years that followed, I gradually read all the others, always with a similar sense of amazement. The greatness of Sacks's art lies in the way he makes the reader identify with the bizarre clinical cases he describes and explains, enhancing his scientific knowledge with all the techniques (and all the passion) of a great fiction writer. In horror, we realise that the implausible things he is narrating could happen to any one of us: yes, we could be the sympathetic Dr P., the music teacher who stopped recognising people's faces as well as everyday objects, getting some confused with others. He would recognise someone if he heard their voice; he'd recognise a rose, but only if he smelled it. We could be that healthy girl who, from one moment to the next, was no longer able to feel her own body; we could be that Borgesian character who was incapable of retaining recent memories, dazed and immobilised amidst the inexorable flow of time.

Good writers manage to place the reader in someone else's skin. I think that is reading's greatest virtue. In entering the skins of different narrators, in feeling oneself to be a part of other people's lives, readers also begin to understand themselves as being part of the rest of humanity. I have this conviction – a naïve one, a cynic might say – which I will venture to share with all of you, and it is that great readers tend to be less inclined to violence. First, because violence is always a backlash against thinking. Then, because reading, as an exercise in otherness, brings people closer together. I come from a country that endured one of the longest and cruellest civil wars of our time. Warmongers know that in order to triumph they must begin by de-nationalising the enemy. Following this, they go on to question their humanity. First the enemy is a foreigner, then a monster. A monster, and a foreign one at that, can be killed. *Must* be killed.

Good literature works in the opposite direction. It makes us see the humanity inside other people, including those who are foreign to us. Including monsters.

Oliver Sacks's books bring us closer to the victims of cerebral accidents. Different human societies always show enormous difficulty in dealing with mentally disturbed people. In the best examples, they used to transform them into sacred figures, saints or shamans. In the worst, they would burn them alive. To this day, we still tend to isolate them.

Sacks also discusses questions of identity in his books – more specifically, the ways in which certain determined pathologies can become part of a person's identity. In Italy, I met a girl who had got a seahorse tattooed on her right wrist. I wanted to know why she'd done it. She told me that during a big chunk of her adolescence and youth she'd had a tumour in her hippocampus (the genus to which the seahorse belongs, derived from Ancient Greek). That tumour had caused her to have incredible visual hallucinations. As a woman, her time was divided between our world and her own universe – one that was richer, infinitely more extraordinary, but also a little dangerous. "The problem," she told me, "is that a part of me disappeared as well. I got a tattoo of this seahorse done to remind me of who I once was."

Sacks's text has circulated on social networks. Even those who have never read his books feel touched by the dignity with which the writer bids farewell. How can it be that somebody so in love with life, and still, as he puts it, so intensely alive, can give himself up like that, without a hint of bitterness, without a resentful protest, to the gloomy, irrevocable embrace of death? In his serenity, Oliver Sacks gives us one last lesson. Death is necessary. Or perhaps that's a lie, but a necessary one. In any case, it walks alongside us from the moment we are born, and doesn't go away. If we have to leave, then may we leave feeling grateful for life, and at peace with it.

Literature and identities

While looking for new titles in Rio bookshops, I came across one of Gonçalo M. Tavares's most recent books, *Os velhos também querem viver* (*Old People Want to Live Too*). The book came out a few months ago in Portugal, together with another, *Uma menina está perdida no seu século à procura do pai* (*A Girl Is Lost in Her Century Looking for Her Father*). To release two books at once, or only a few weeks apart, is something that would terrify any publisher. "Madness!" they would all insist. "This will harm sales. He shouldn't publish so much. The readers will get bored, and his career will be ruined." Gonçalo just shrugs and publishes the books anyway, each one with a different publisher. The following month he publishes two more, three more, four more – and as he does so, he continues to amass readers and prizes, a little bit everywhere. He is the most awarded and most widely translated Portuguese-language author living today.

I really like Gonçalo. He regards the world with the curiosity, intelligence and ingenuity of a child, or a visitor from some remote galaxy. He sees, and makes us see, things that are already there, out in the open, under the clear light of day, but which we can no longer make out. All of his literature has a great deal to do with the skilful exposition of evidence. Over the last fifteen years, Gonçalo has worked on creating his own unique universe – one that isn't rooted in a specific, concrete geographical setting, but in great universal literature. He is the most extreme case of a trend that has been expressed frequently in Portuguese literature: a surprising denationalisation.

Pedro Rosa Mendes, Afonso Cruz, João Tordo, Francisco José Viegas, Miguel Gullander or Valter Hugo Mãe, to cite some of the younger and more interesting names in Portuguese literature, have all published books in which the action happens beyond the borders of Portugal. In some of them, there aren't even any Portuguese characters. Read, for example, Pedro Rosa Mendes's excellent

Peregrinação de [Pilgrimage of] Enmanuel Jhesus (2010). Set in East Timor, the novel casts a cruel and violent eye over that Southeast Asian country, its history and its inhabitants, displaying a deep, intimate familiarity with Timorese mythology and popular culture. Portugal is almost absent, no more than a bitter memory.

Valter Hugo Mãe's *A Desumanização* (*Dehumanisation*) is set in Iceland, and he, too, makes great use of local imagery.

I have been intrigued for some years now by Portuguese literature's interest in other territories – or its total lack of interest in its own. If we are being optimistic, we could observe a sign of maturity in this trend: Portuguese writers are leaving their country behind, moved by a healthy curiosity for other countries, above all because they are at peace with themselves.

In young countries, as is the case with Angola or Mozambique, literature deals obsessively with questions of identity. Writers use fiction as a way of affirming identity on one hand and, on the other, as a way of better understanding the country and themselves within it. Literature also serves to create or reinforce national myths.

In Portugal, an old, stable country with no identity crisis or serious social divisions, one seems to suffer more from boredom than from unease. As Mart'nália sings: *"Eu hei de ter ao invés de paz inquietaçao / Houvesse paz, não haveria esta canção."* ("Instead of peace, I shall have unease / If we had peace, this song would not be.")

In the United Kingdom and France, questions of identity are once more the order of the day, because of the large numbers of immigrants who have laid down roots and raised families in these two countries over the last few decades. Present-day English literature owes a great deal to these 'new Britons'. You only need to think of V. S. Naipaul, who was born into an Indian family in Trinidad and Tobago and was based in the UK since the beginning of the 1950s, or Zadie Smith, born in London with Jamaican heritage. Cultural unease and the search for identity tend to produce good literature.

Some of the Portuguese writers I have mentioned could argue that they chose to write about other geographies for the simple fact that they know them well. Mendes worked for several years in Dili, the small capital of East Timor, as a news correspondent. Today he lives in Switzerland. Miguel Gullander – whose novel *Através da Chuva* (*Through the Rain*) has as its protagonist a Swiss cryptozoologist who travels to Angola in search of the mythical Giant Sable Antelope – has spent time in South Africa and currently resides in Namibia. The economic crisis has continued to push many thousands of Portuguese people out of Portugal, and it just so happens that some of them are writers.

The relationship of Portuguese writers to Brazil is particularly curious. Francisco José Viegas, Inês Pedrosa and Hugo Gonçalves are among the Portuguese authors who visit Brazil most in their work. Inês is releasing a new book, *Desamparo* (*Abandonment*), which tells the story of a Portuguese woman who left for Brazil as a child and returns to Portugal fifty years later to meet her mother again. In this case, it seems to me that Portuguese writers use Brazil as a kind of mirror in which they hope to see Portugal anew. It's a different situation, then, from what happens with Tavares, Gullander, Mendes or Mãe, in *Dehumanisation*.

If we acknowledge that a country's literature has some role to play in the construction or reinforcement of its identity, what does that country's denationalisation mean? That Portugal is ending? Or, conversely, that it is starting again in an infinitely more ambitious, modern and globalised way?

A toy for creating marvels

I asked Siri, the iPhone virtual assistant, if she believed in God. She replied that while we humans need religion, she needs only silicone. I repeated the question. The insubstantial character abandoned sarcasm and opted instead for poetry: "It's all a mystery to me," she assured me.

I sometimes think about Siri during interviews. A few days ago, for example, a journalist rang me, wanting to know how I would classify the language I write in: "Your novels take place in different Lusophone cities: Luanda, Rio de Janeiro, Lisbon, even Pangim, the capital of Goa [in India]. Which kind of Portuguese, ultimately, is your Portuguese?"

Which kind of Portuguese is my Portuguese?

I thought about replying like Siri: "It's all a mystery to me!" Sadly, I lacked the courage to do so, and mumbled an answer. But I didn't stop thinking about it. There are some things I do know: I know, of course, that my language is not limited by political or geographical frontiers. The Portuguese that interests me is Portuguese in its totality.

A few years ago in Lisbon, at an event to discuss the international Portuguese Language Orthographic Agreement for the umpteenth time, someone stood up at the back of the room and screeched: "The language is ours!" I wasn't surprised. The truth is that in Portugal today there still persists a certain imperial nostalgia, and above all an enormous ignorance regarding the history of the language itself. It's always a good thing to remember that before Portugal colonised Africa, Africans colonised the Iberian Peninsula – for 800 years. Thus the Portuguese language owes a great deal to Arabic. From the sixteenth century onwards, with the Portuguese expansion, the language became enriched by its gradual incorporation of Bantu and Amerindian words and expressions and proverbs from those languages. My language is this collective creation of Brazilians, Angolans, Portuguese, Mozambicans, Cape Verdeans, São Tomeans,

Guineans and Timorese. My language is a happy matron, fertile and generous, who fell in love with Tupi and Yoruba and still today happily yields to Quimbundo, Quicongo and Ronga, letting herself be impregnated by all these languages.

"From my language, you can see the sea," the Portuguese novelist Vergílio Ferreira wrote. "From my language you can hear its murmur, just as from others you can hear the sound of the forest or the silence of the desert. The voice of the sea was the voice of our unease." Ferreira is right. The presence of the sea and this sense of unease are part of the nature of our language.

It is the Brazilians and the Africans who reinvent our language the most. The Brazilians, because they constitute the overwhelming majority of speakers; the Africans, because in Angola or Mozambique the Portuguese language coexists so dynamically with other languages. The new speakers of Portuguese are coming at it from these languages. Every day they bring something from them over to Portuguese. Aside from that, their relationship with Portuguese has a wonderful irreverence about it. Their Portuguese is spoken with no sense of guilt, with its tie undone.

Over the last decade, Portuguese youth have been enthusiastically adopting Angolan Portuguese. Only those who aren't paying attention will be surprised by this trend. Africans dominate popular culture in Portugal today. The two most famous Portuguese *fado* singers have African roots: Mariza is from Mozambique, and Ana Moura has Angolan family. The mightiest and most international Portuguese music group, Buraka Som Sistema – which found fame through its rereading of the *kuduru* music of the Luanda slums – have Angolan members. The most popular singer at the moment is an Angolan, Anselmo Ralph. In the past few years, Anselmo has become a phenomenon among the public, selling thousands of records and filling the biggest music venues in Portugal, such as the Altice Arena with its 20,000-seat capacity. I went along to one of these shows and witnessed Portuguese and Africans – many more Portuguese than Africans – all dancing together. Kizomba schools are multiplying in Lisbon, and to some extent across the whole country.

English, Dutch and German travellers visiting Lisbon in the sixteenth and seventeenth centuries were struck by the number of black people on the city's streets. "Lisbon is an African city," they'd say, disdainfully. That is once more the case, and it's more exuberant than ever.

My language is the result of all this celebration, a toy for creating marvels.

God is sick

"Dropping a bomb," Jorge Luis Borges wrote, "is more of a confirmation than a refutation. It's like giving credence to your adversary, only in the most terrible way."

People who are sure that their beliefs are based in good sense are open to discussion. They put forth arguments. They defend a certain line of thinking to the end. One lashes out only when intelligence collapses. Lashing out is always an expression of defeat, even when it eventually defeats the enemy. It is not any kind of truth, or the purity of an idea, that defeats the enemy in such cases. It's violence.

In fact, the man who delivers the blow often justifies his actions by saying: "I lost my senses."

Timbuktu, a film by the Mauritanian director Abderrahmane Sissako, was recently withdrawn from a cinema in the Paris suburbs following accusations of inciting terrorism. Not only does the film (which received an Oscar nomination in the category of Best Foreign Film) *not* incite terrorism; it does the opposite, apportioning blame for the destruction of Mali's patrimony to the Islamic fascists. Sissako, by the way, is an old friend of Angola. In 1997 he directed a beautiful documentary, *Rostov-Luanda*, which travels the streets of our country from Luanda to the heights of Huila, shedding light on the stories of simple people.

This episode serves simply to illustrate the absurd and nonsensical climate that is threatening to install itself in France and in other European countries after the attacks against the satirical journal *Charlie Hebdo*. If it is the case that, with their bombs and bullets, the Islamic fascists give credence to the Islamophobes, then it is also the case that with their prohibitions and other persecutions of the same order, some European authorities and institutions are giving credence to the Islamic fascists.

The same Borges I have quoted also called our attention to the absurdity of revenge: "The only possible revenge is forgetfulness, oblivion ... forgiving." Many other thinkers, theologians and prophets have said the same before him, using other words.

There are books that incite hatred. There are books that improve us. The Bible, just as much as the Qur'an, can be both things. On one hand, they contain wise lessons, almost always very plainly expressed; on the other, they reflect the cruel spirit of the cruel times in which they were produced. If read in a perverse way, both books can lead (and have led) to intolerance and violence.

Looking back at the last few hundred years, one suspects that nearly all religions have brought more pain than comfort. I don't know whether or not God, at a certain point, was necessary for the progress of humanity. I do know that today God is superfluous. The idea of God does not make us better. Perhaps one of the great battles of our days will be the battle for a future that is free from the idea of God.

In praise of strangeness

I know a woman who loves jellyfish – *águas-vivas*. (In Portuguese they are known not only as *águas-vivas* but also as *medusas* and *alforrecas*, but the first name – meaning "living water" – seems the most beautiful to me.) Despite their beauty, it's hard to find people willing to confess to a love for jellyfish. It's easy to love dogs, cats, rabbits, pandas, dolphins and whales, not to mention monkeys, orangutans and gorillas. These animals are all close to us.

We even share emotions with the majority of them, which is more than we can manage with many of our neighbours and colleagues. This doesn't happen with jellyfish. The existence of jellyfish is something remote and cut off. You can't even stroke them.

Well, you can, but it's not a pleasurable experience. I know whereof I speak. Many years ago, while swimming on a Malaysian beach, I felt a strong lashing sensation on my right arm. I'd already been stung many times in Angola, and on other beaches around the world, but never anything comparable to this. My arm was paralysed. When I came out of the water there was already an enormous, spiral-shaped welt spreading from my shoulder down to my wrist. I was taken to a medical station. One nurse wanted to know if I suffered from any heart problems. As I answered no, he did little more than clean my skin with a cloth soaked in vinegar.

"Now sit down," he told me. "Sit down and prepare yourself, because your heart is about to go crazy." Even so, I was lucky. The most dangerous jellyfish, the Irukandji, is tiny and sometimes leaves no mark. Dozens of people die every year in Australia, Malaysia and Indonesia, victims of Irukandji. Until the 1960s, there was no way of explaining such deaths. Bathers entered the water, felt a terrible pain and were then overcome by convulsions. A myth was created whereby it was the sea itself attacking the bathers.

Loving things close to you is easy. Loving things foreign to us – now, that is unusual. That's why when Luísa told me, "I love jellyfish", with the same ease with which somebody else might say, for example, that they love cats, I rested my acerola juice on the table (we were at a party) and gave her my undivided attention.

"What attracts you to them?"

She talked about the way they dance. She told me she'd love to have an enormous aquarium full of jellyfish in her room. Whenever she felt like relaxing, instead of doing yoga or meditating all she'd need to do was sit down and contemplate the aquarium. I told her that there is a kind of jellyfish capable of rejuvenating itself. It ages to a certain point, then reverses the whole process and reverts to the state of being a juvenile polyp. The cycle repeats itself indefinitely. That doesn't mean they don't die; it just means they don't die of old age. Luísa expressed surprise, though not a great deal.

"That doesn't surprise me. Everything about them is so extraordinary."

There are scientists trying to discover the exact mechanism enabling this process of rejuvenation, working to learn something from jellyfish that could benefit all of humanity. One day, perhaps not too far off, it will be possible to reach eighty looking like someone who is not yet thirty. I think about the scientist who discovered this phenomenon. I imagine him or her being someone who, like Luísa, is capable of loving strangeness. It is an interest in the other, even – or especially – when the other seems totally alien to us that makes us universal, and makes us evolve.

We should be taught at school to love difference. Instead we are taught that the world is divided by borders, and that there are potential enemies on the other side. They tell us not to talk to strangers. Most children don't even know what a stranger is.

"What's a stranger?" I asked the first time I was told not to talk to them. I was disappointed when it was explained to me: "Strangers, my lad, are people we don't know." I thought a stranger should be someone who was possessed of a formidable strangeness: loopy, imponderable people, winged people, something like that.

"Are angels strangers, Mum?"

The thing children want most is to meet strangers: unicorns, mermaids, fairies, vegetarian vampires (such a twenty-first-century thing), Iemanjá or Saci Pererê and other equally marvellous creatures such as jellyfish ... but their parents don't let them. Happily, some of them rebel. The ones who do will end up talking to jellyfish and, eventually, discovering the secret of eternal youth.

Friday, 25 September 2015

Last night's discussion at the Pauliceia Literária festival in São Paulo went very well. And yet I think that at a certain point I was a little too harsh with the moderator, the literary critic Manuel da Costa Pinto, who started and edited *Cult* magazine and has curated the Festa Literária Internacional de Paraty (FLIP). But, to be fair, such moments often enliven these kinds of debates.

At a certain point, while comparing contemporary literary output in Brazil, Portugal, Mozambique and Angola, Costa Pinto noted that in the first two countries, unlike in Africa, literature has become universal. In African countries, meanwhile, writers continue to be shackled to their regional universe. I retorted that he seemed not to be talking as a Brazilian, but as a *paulista*, from São Paulo. Indeed, while in places such as Portugal, São Paulo or Rio de Janeiro we may indeed find writers such as Gonçalo M. Tavares, Afonso Cruz, Bernardo Carvalho or Adriana Lisboa – whose work is more rooted in literature itself than in a specific territory – that is not the case in Bahia, Pernambuco or Ceará.

As I have noted above, young countries are confronted with the construction of their identity on a daily basis, and writers naturally reflect this preoccupation. European countries, with the United Kingdom and France meriting special mention, have been confronting very similar questions over the last few decades, owing to the entry and nationalisation of many people from the old colonies. French and English writers, many of them from African and Asian backgrounds, have begun to deal with these questions once more. Just think of Michel Houellebecq's book *Soumission* (*Submission*).

On the other hand, we must always remember that Africa is an immense and immensely diverse continent. Not all African countries are young. Ethiopia is one of the oldest countries in the world.

Last but not least, I know several African writers who do not write preferentially about the lands they originate from. The most obvious case is the South African writer J. M. Coetzee. I'm also thinking of my friend Sami Tchak, from Togo – an extremely interesting writer who places the action of some of his best-known novels in an imaginary Latin America.

It is a mistake, then, to generalise. African literatures are becoming more and more diverse – or, to put it another way, more mature. There are themes common to the majority of writers from the two continents; there are trends and there are patterns. But above all, there is enormous diversity, and that's a good thing.

On race and justice

You know you're in a country where justice works, and is therefore equal for all, when its citizens don't fear the police. Your average honest citizen in Sweden, Norway, Cape Verde or Namibia doesn't fear the police. The police are there to help. Your average citizen in Angola, Brazil and many American cities, meanwhile, *does* fear the police. In this regard, there's not a great deal of difference between Luanda, Rio de Janeiro and Baltimore.

The main difference between Rio de Janeiro and Baltimore is that Baltimore has just exploded, whereas Rio de Janeiro hasn't (yet). Before Baltimore, there were demonstrations and unrest motivated by racial injustice in Madison; before that, in Ferguson; and before that, in Oakland ... and so on. Police violence is far worse in Rio de Janeiro that in any of the American cities where the demonstrations and disturbances have occurred. The extent of the social abyss, too, is far worse. The link between race and poverty is also much more explicit in Brazil than in the United States – a country that, over the past few decades, has managed to create a middle class of African origin. Black Americans today are well represented among politicians, cultural figures and even entrepreneurs. Meanwhile, in Brazil, they continue to be absent from power and big business. Last but not least, the overwhelming majority of the victims of police violence in Brazil are young men of African origin. In light of what I've just said, some may conclude that there is a high chance that what happened in Baltimore will be repeated in Rio de Janeiro and other Brazilian cities.

But will it, really? I have my doubts. In recent years I've witnessed many young black Brazilians revolting against a society that is incapable of resolving the distortions inherited from the days of slavery. These young people are impatient. And yet the truth is that the vast majority are oblivious to such debates. It seems likely that, over the coming months, Brazil will see yet more social unrest, with demonstrations and eventually violence being perpetrated against the demonstrators. Sadly, though, those demonstrating will not be demanding that these inherited distortions be corrected. The apathy of the majority of the population towards such an important issue is not easy to explain. It goes back a long way, and is probably connected to the whole complex process of racial intermixing, one which ultimately involves the dilution of frontiers; it is a process, then, of de-racialisation.

The exact opposite has occurred in the United States: people in that country have invested greatly in the construction of such borders. Over there, a black person is anyone who possesses a 'single drop of black blood' (whatever that is). In many African countries, especially in rural contexts, there is a tendency to see any individual with some European ascendancy as white. English explorers who visited Angola in the nineteenth century were forever complaining about meeting traders in the jungle whom locals described as 'white', but actually turned out to be either *mestiços* or Portuguese. I think it was Livingstone who, during a speech at the Royal Geographical Society in London, stated that he had been the first white man to visit a certain location in the African interior. An indignant Portuguese explorer stood up and reminded him that one of his compatriots had passed through the same region many years earlier. "I never said that I was the first man," Livingstone explained. "I merely said the first *white* man."

Race does not exist; it is, in large part, a cultural construction. Slavery, however, *did* exist, and its abolition was not accompanied by any reparation of the damage it had done.

Maybe Baltimore will never happen in Rio. Despite this – or perhaps precisely because of it – I feel that it is important to try and open up a debate on this topic in Brazilian society. Something similar to what former US President Barack Obama asked of his fellow Americans when responding to the events in Baltimore: "I think there are police departments that have to do some soul-searching. I think there are some communities that have to do some soul-searching. But I think we as a country have to do some soul-searching."

It's important that we reassess the role of the police forces. But it's crucial that we invest in a politics that makes it possible for Brazilians of African origin (that is, the majority of the population) to ascend in society. We must create mechanisms whereby that majority can be properly represented in every organ of public power. We must, in short, return dignity and full citizenship to millions of Brazilians. The challenge will be to do all of this without creating a climate of racial paranoia – a racialisation of the everyday – like the one that exists in the United States or South Africa.

The nakedness of authors

The Portuguese author Afonso Cruz surprised his Colombian readers by singing, while playing the ukulele, during a session at the Bogotá International Book Fair. Afonso is vocalist with The Soaked Lamb, a band that has released two albums and specialises in revisiting and reinventing old blues songs and classic Mexican folk ballads.

There are some who see Cruz's actions as a sign of the times – the End Times. In recent years, I have been hearing more and more complaints against the commercialisation of literature. The globalisation of the book trade and consolidation of publishing houses – the latter being a negative consequence of the former – tend to make things more difficult for aspiring new writers. Publishers' marketing departments have gained too much power. When I first began publishing, almost thirty years ago, I didn't even know that marketing departments existed. Maybe they didn't. My editor talked to me about book covers, formats and optimal dates for publication. Nowadays, at some of the larger publishers, authors discuss directly with marketing directors which image to put on the front cover, and even the titles of their books. If someone wants a black-and-white photograph on the cover of their book, they should prepare themselves for days of wrangling, as they will have to face the wrath of the entire marketing department. Long titles also usually lead to lengthy battles. I know whereof I speak.

It shouldn't take too long for the infamous 'indirect advertising', so widely used these days in cinema and television, to arrive in the world of literature. I can imagine Rubem Fonseca discussing with some marketing director which brand of cigar Mandrake should smoke. No, on second thought, I'd really rather not.

That said, I have nothing against writers who sing during literary events. In fact, I'm somewhat envious. For the more conservative literary critics, and for academics (always conservative), writers who sing, have themselves photographed bare-chested, date beautiful women or, in general, seem happy with life are not to be taken seriously. They cannot be good writers. In the opinion of such critics, authors who display some other talent beyond writing are nothing more than sad by-products of the marketing department. Academia would like all writers to be bitter, suffering and preferably chaste recluses. Reality explodes this myth. There have always been authors who were exhibitionists, partygoers, carnival revellers, womanisers or simply endowed with many different talents.

José de Almada Negreiros, for example, was all of the above. Born the island of São Tomé in 1893 and descended on his mother's side from a prosperous *mestiço* family, Almada Negreiros made a big impression on Lisbon a century ago with his natural African exuberance and willingness to turn up and provoke. He never hid his passion for dance (he danced in a cabaret), and had himself photographed for posterity in a futuristic suit that he himself designed, and which even today would cause a sensation at any literary festival – or, indeed, fashion show. A century before Almada, Portuguese literature knew another dandy, Almeida Garrett, who at the time was more famous for his elegance and the number of women who fell at his feet than for his prowess as an author.

Mark Twain, Ernest Hemingway, William Faulkner, Tennessee Williams, Ezra Pound ... they all allowed themselves to be photographed stripped to the waist. The Portuguese authors José Luís Peixoto and Valter Hugo Mãe have done the same. Hemingway showed off his broad chest while pretending to box. Peixoto displayed his tattoos. Mãe even posed for the Portuguese edition of *Granta* revealing everything.

Hemingway liked being photographed not only bare-chested, but bare-chested alongside beautiful women. He had many. He lost out to the playwright Arthur Miller, however, who, without ever letting himself be photographed shirtless, married Marilyn Monroe. Both Hemingway and Miller had intense and well-documented love lives, but neither of them came close – even remotely – to Truman Capote. Capote was so frivolous that he even bragged about it. Now read or reread *In Cold Blood*, a work of fictionalised reporting or, as the author preferred, a non-fiction novel, and make up your own mind about the literary futility or inferiority of such an unashamedly frivolous man.

Afonso Cruz sings well. Gonçalo M. Tavares played professional football. Chico Buarque sings well, is good with the ball and even has green eyes (or blue, or whatever they are). However, if we're talking about literature, what counts is the quality of each of these author's books. It so happens that they're good. If their other talents help sell their books, then so much the better.

Thursday, 25 June 2015

On the Internet, reverberations continue following the arrest of the musician and political activist Luaty Beirao and nineteen other young people in Luanda at the weekend. In Portugal, however, silence still reigns. Only *Público* covered the story, suggesting in its editorial that the Angolan regime deserved to be called fascist. The *Jornal de Angola* remains silent, but it can't last much longer. Artur Queiroz must be sharpening his teeth.

The young democrats are still behind bars in Luanda, caught red-handed reading a book about non-violent resistance against oppression and charged, for that reason, with attempting a *coup d'état*.

In recent months, we have witnessed a series of episodes that reveal the hardening of the regime in Angola. On 14 March this year, two citizens, José Marcos Mavungo and Arão Bula Tempo, were arrested in Cabinda for attempting to organise a march against bad government and in defence of human rights. Mavungo is still in detention. On 25 May, Rafael Marques was given a suspended six-month sentence, in an unexpected and underhand manoeuvre that exposed the contradictions of the system.

Let's turn to the coup. It's true that there is a coup underway. But its protagonists are not a small group of pacifist youths with only books and car horns for weapons, but rather the most reactionary, most violent and most blinkered wing of the regime itself. Within the ageing ruling party there still remain some voices of reason. There even exists – I still want to believe this – a strand that argues in favour of democracy. What we can observe, however, is that those voices of reason are silent, or have been silenced. The democratic wing, still extant, seems resigned to its defeat.

The arrest of young democrats, far from taking away their voice, merely amplifies it. The demonstration they were preparing, the "Big Toot" (for which I recorded a short supportive video) would not have had much impact either inside or outside the country. The group's arrest, on the other hand, is having exactly that. Within Angola, a loud chorus of indignation is growing. Abroad, the regime's disrepute is spreading. President José Eduardo dos Santos has never been so unpopular. *The Daily Maverick* newspaper in South Africa openly mocks both the president and his regime:

> So what, exactly, were they up to? Were they distributing weapons ahead of the revolution? Were they drawing straws to see who among them would get to assassinate the president? The reality was even worse. Much worse. These young men, their hearts filled with rage and protest, were reading. They were discussing. They were – keep calm now, it's a lot to take in – *thinking for themselves.*

The regime's conservative wing is scared of the possibility that the economic collapse and a worsening social chasm might bring people onto the streets. First, demonstrators were arrested during demonstrations. Then demonstrators began to be arrested before they reached their demonstrations. Now it's not demonstrators being arrested, but all those who are thinking about demonstrating. Tomorrow we shall be arrested merely because someone reckons we *might* be thinking about demonstrating.

So let's demonstrate today, right now, this very moment, and let's do it noisily, openly and proudly, before the coup consolidates its grip and takes away all our liberties. Let's sound our car horns! Let's argue! Let's make our voices heard! Let's occupy social media, let's occupy streets and squares, let's occupy offices, marketplaces and workshops in peaceful protest, and in the hope that our determination may help to reinforce the ruling Movimento Popular de Libertação de Angola's democratic wing – if it still exists – and enable it to get back on its feet and resist the coup. Because either the MPLA becomes democratic, or it will have no place in the future of a democratic Angola.

Friday, 3 July 2015

The week just ending will perhaps stand in the history of Angola as the beginning of the end of the long reign of José Eduardo dos Santos. On social media, hundreds of Angolans protested against the arrest of the young democrats. Artists and intellectuals who until now have avoided expressing an opinion, or who had always positioned themselves in support of the governing party, have gone public in registering their shock and dismay.

Dos Santos's speech, in which he claimed that the young detainees were preparing a *coup d'état*, and compared this to the tragic events of 27 May 1977*, has strengthened the MPLA's most reactionary wing and made way for a wave of repression and a downward spiral of political violence. It is a step from which there is no going back. Dos Santos will need to prove his 'coup' theory convincingly – something we all know to be impossible. Nobody in Angola believes such nonsense. If the young men are released for lack of evidence, it is the president himself who would be seen as a liar, as well as a dictator. If they are not released, it will mark the beginning of a cycle of protests, arrests, more protests, more arrests and yet more protests.

The political instability instigated by the irrationality of the presidential address comes on top of the deteriorating economic situation and the resulting deepening of social inequalities. We are, therefore, facing a perfect storm.

Together, the young men's arrests and the president's speech mark a real watershed. From now on, silence can no longer be justified. Either you are in favour of the dictatorship, or you are on the side of peace, democracy, stability and social justice.

---

* We don't know how many people died in the furious repression that followed the events of 27 May 1977. Some people speak of fifty thousand dead. What is for sure is that there are practically no families in Luanda who did not lose a loved one in those tragic years.

should use: "The forces of law and order disciplined the demonstrators."

Instead of "the demonstrators were chased by dogs": "The demonstrators took part in a foot race with the generous encouragement of dogs specially trained for the purpose."

Instead of "the authorities have prohibited" or "have not authorised" a certain demonstration: "The authorities have encouraged young people to express their opinions in the comfort of their own homes."

Instead of "protests": "demonstrations of free thinking in keeping with the great democracy that flourishes in this country".

Instead of "political prisoners": "dysfunctional citizens housed at the expense of the government in institutions appropriate to their status".

Instead of saying that people have been "arrested", "detained" or even "brought in": "People have been sheltered." ("Sheltered" is lovely. For example: "Luaty Beirão, sheltered in the bosom of the State for more than a month, calmly awaits the outcome of his trial.")

Instead of "prisons": "reception centres for dysfunctional citizens".

Instead of "police interrogation", "conversation" should suffice.

The fine euphemism "excessive zeal", meaning excessive torture, already has a broad and sonorous historical tradition in our country, and for this reason alone deserves to be revived.

Sunday, 2 August 2015

I wrote a letter to Brazil's President Dilma Rousseff about the arrest of the young democrats, at the request of Mathias de Alencastro, the Brazilian political scientist and journalist. This afternoon I met Mathias at an event at the Zé dos Bois Gallery here in Lisbon, and gave him the letter. He agreed to deliver it to Dilma next week.

Dear Madam President,

On 20 June, fifteen young men were arrested in Luanda and charged with attempting a *coup d'état*. Some of these young men, most notably the musician Luaty Beirão, have achieved a certain prominence over the past three years by organising small demonstrations – most of them thwarted by police – in favour of freedom of expression and greater social justice. The accusation against the young men has not so far been substantiated and does not, in reality, have the slightest credibility.

The young men's arrests have aroused a wave of solidarity in Angola and other countries. Well-known personalities from the cultural sphere – such as the writers Mia Couto and Ondjaki, the singers Chico César, Aline Frazão and Paulo Flores, and Pilar del Río, president of the Saramago Foundation, among many others – have been calling publicly, in videos released on social media, for the young men's release.

Angola and Brazil, as countries, are more than brothers. They emerged together, and have been under each other's influence over the centuries. It is not possible to understand Brazilian popular culture without the influence of Angola, just as the history and urban culture of Angola cannot be understood without taking Brazil into account. Brazil was the first country to recognise Angola's independence, and it is without a doubt one of the countries most beloved by Angolans.

You yourself, Madam President, are a beacon of moral and ethical values for the vast majority of Angolans, including many of those who today occupy positions of power. I am therefore asking you to use your influence to help show the Angolan authorities that the path to democracy – a true democracy such as Brazilians enjoy – cannot include the continual persecution of persons whose only fault is to disagree with the manner in which the party that has governed since independence forty years ago – thirty-six of which have been under the leadership of President José Eduardo dos Santos – has been guiding the country's destiny. What these young men now behind bars are asking for, after all, is *more* democracy, *more* social justice, and economic development that takes into account the interests of the most vulnerable – all of which are causes and values for which you have fought all your life.

I am sure Your Excellency understands better than anyone the torment that these young men are now going through. I know that I can count on your empathy and solidarity.

I take this opportunity to express my own admiration and warm regards for you and your work.

Yours sincerely,
José Eduardo Agualusa

Saturday, 26 September 2015

"You don't need anyone's permission to start a revolution," said Thabo Mbeki at the opening of the second African Youth Conference, which took place in Maputo a few days ago. The theme of the conference was "Democracy and Good Governance", and it included the participation of a delegation of young Angolan revolutionaries. To us, in light of the events of the past few months, Mbeki's ironic observation seems more relevant than ever.

Revolutions do not ask permission. Revolutions happen when there is a very pressing urgency for change, faced with the excesses, incompetence and cruelty of non-democratic regimes.

The hunger strike by eight of the young democrats detained for more than three months without any clear charges has brought to these proceedings a sense of drama that no one in Angola can now ignore. I am worried by the flippancy with which certain people on social media or in the comments section of newspapers online rush to dismiss the young men's sacrifice. I find it difficult not to agree with the young men's goals: to democratise Angola and make it a freer and more just society. I find it difficult to disagree with the method they have been using in their struggle: peaceful demonstration. I accept, however, that there are differing opinions, and that there are Angolans who feel happy with the current state of the country and consider that we live in an advanced democracy. What I find difficult to accept is that some people choose to make fun of the suffering of others.

A hunger strike is not something that is lightly undertaken. It is, at heart, a means of bringing the oppressor face-to-face with their own conscience. Jesus Christ, who, like Gandhi or Martin Luther King, was first and foremost a philosopher of non-violence, expressed this very idea with a lesson that, unfortunately, few people understand: "Love your enemies, do good to those who hate you, bless those who curse you, pray for those who mistreat you. If someone slaps you on one cheek, turn to them the other also."

In turning the other cheek rather than throwing a punch, we are offering the oppressor the possibility of reflection and redemption. Those who opt for non-violent struggle, like Luaty and his companions, are not demanding the oppressor's submission; on the contrary, they are trying to help him. They are reaching out their hand.

The Angolan regime seems unable to see this. Faced with an explosive situation in the streets, it is refusing dialogue and throwing everything into a violent response. This is why we need a revolution: a revolution of spirits, a revolution like the one these young people are bringing about, without brutality, without malice, without aggression. This is, perhaps, the last opportunity the president will have to attempt a peaceful transition to democracy and to give up power, thereby entering the history books with some dignity. Hours and days are going by, and time is not in his favour.

Love letter to Luaty Beirão

As I write this, a friend of mine is dying of hunger in Luanda. Luaty Beirão, aged thirty-three, has been without food since 21 September, in protest against his detention and that of fourteen other young men, for nearly three months, charged with the absurd accusation of attempting a *coup d'état*.

On Thursday 15 September, Luaty managed to write a note and slip it to a friend who was visiting him in jail. In this note he states that he is in full possession of all his mental faculties and declares that he refuses medical assistance in the event of falling into a coma or a state of cognitive disorientation, in accordance with Point Four of the preamble to the World Medical Assembly's Declaration of Malta, save where his provisional release is subsequently granted and his medical condition is such that, following treatment, he would be unlikely to remain in a persistent vegetative state. Luaty further states, as his final wish, that he would like his body to be cremated, and his ashes scattered at sea.

A few days ago, I met with one of Luaty's sisters, Serena Mansini. Fighting back tears, she told me: "My brother isn't a hero. He's an ordinary person, just more determined than most of us." I didn't know what to say to her. I don't think I have ever warmed to heroes.

Later, however, I looked up the definition of "hero" in a dictionary: "An individual who distinguishes themselves by an act of extraordinary courage, bravery, force of character or other notable quality." Therefore, yes, my dear Serena, your brother *is* a hero. Luaty could have chosen a quiet life. He studied electrical engineering at the University of Plymouth, in the UK. When he finished the course, he went to Montpellier, in France, where he completed a second degree, this time in economics and business management. He could have returned to Luanda, where any bank or large corporation would have given him a job – not least because his father, João Beirão, was an important figure in the upper echelons of the Angolan political establishment. Instead, Luaty turned his attention to rap and hip-hop, already with the clear intention of using music as an instrument to awaken conscience.

Before this, he travelled the length of Africa from Morocco to Angola, on foot and hitchhiking, on a journey of discovery both of the continent and of himself. He had little more than 100 euros, four T-shirts, three pairs of shorts and a two-kilogram bag of nuts.

"Everyone I met on the way told me it was too dangerous, and that no one would help me. But I always found help," he told me, adding that when he reached Luanda he still had a kilo of nuts left.

"Luaty is our Che Guevara," I was told by the writer and musician Kalaf Epalanga of Buraka Som Sistema, comparing Luaty's journey to the Argentinian revolutionary's famous motorbike expedition across Latin America at the beginning of the 1950s. It seems to me, however, that Luaty, a pacifist and vegetarian, is more akin to Gandhi than Che. What I most admire in him is his unbreakable determination and his faith in humanity.

"My intention was to set foot in as many African countries as possible, to feed on the experience and to enrich myself spiritually," Luaty told the journalist Rafael Marques, another leading figure in the Angolan democratic movement. "I don't believe in religion, but I believe in the human spirit. I believe that there still exists sufficient kindness to inspire us and to fuel us, for us to become better people. And this, for me, is a manifestation of the divine. Because I am not religious, I don't believe in God – but I do believe in human beings."

The current debate among those who are campaigning for the political prisoners' release is about knowing the point at which we can, or must, put pressure on the young musician to abandon his hunger strike. As I have said, a hunger strike is an extreme form of struggle that aims, first and foremost, to reconnect the aggressor with his own conscience, thereby allowing him the possibility of reflection and redemption. In this case, it's succeeding. In recent days, prominent individuals who have always supported the Angolan regime have been calling for the young men's release. Besides, by putting pressure on Luaty to call an end to his hunger strike, would we not, in some way, be carrying out the regime's own agenda?

Pedro Coquenão – the creator, along with Luaty, of Batida, one of the most interesting projects in contemporary Angolan music – has issued a challenge: "Don't pressure him. Send him love letters instead."

I think it's a beautiful idea. I want Luaty to get better. I want him to be able to return soon to his wife, the photographer Mónica Almeida, and his two-year-old daughter, Luena. But I want this to happen by his own decision, as the final outcome of his own reasoning and determination.

This is my love letter to Luaty Beirão.

The thinker's silence

Gabriel Contino, the Brazilian rapper known as "Gabriel the Thinker", performed recently in Luanda. Various Angolan public figures, among them Luaty Beirão, awaiting trial along with sixteen other young people on charges of attempting a *coup d'état*, wrote him a letter asking him to reconsider. In their estimation, the artist would, albeit indirectly and involuntarily, be supporting the totalitarian regime that has been stifling the country for so many years.

In his reply, Gabriel recalled that his role as artist was not only to thrill and entertain people with his music, but also to inspire them, opening "their minds to new ways of thinking, raising their self-esteem and confidence in the possibilities of change in both individual and collective attitudes, in ways that transform the lives of themselves and others for the better".

Gabriel went on to say that he would prefer not to take sides in situations he knows little about. His first reason strikes me as valid; his second misses the point. Gabriel has made outrage a way of life, and his example has resonated in Angola. Some of the young Angolans currently in jail or awaiting the verdict of their trial under house arrest, including Luaty, are disciples of his. Gabriel recognised his mistake straightaway, adding that the arrests seemed to him "arbitrary and abusive", but that he had no way of getting out of the contract.

I have always had a liking for Gabriel and his artistic project. In September 2002, I agreed to speak at the launch of his first book, *Nocturnal Diary*, a kind of autobiographical exercise. I admire Gabriel for the same reasons that Angolan rappers look to him as a model: his irreverence, his idealism and his generosity.

In their letter to Gabriel, Luaty and his companions wrote that his refusal to perform in Luanda would raise the spirits of the young political prisoners. I believe it would do that, but not much more. I think it highly unlikely that President dos Santos, impressed by the stand taken by Gabriel, would choose to free all the political prisoners and open up the country to democracy.

Cultural boycotts, unfortunately, have little effect. Apartheid did not fall because the big names in music refused to perform in South Africa. It fell because of internal resistance; because, after a certain point, big business leaders in South Africa realised that the regime was hindering them from becoming even richer. Not by chance, the negotiations between the last apartheid government and the African National Congress began under the auspices of a group of South African businessman.

What does bother totalitarian regimes – or democratic regimes in countries such as Israel, with controversial policies – are artists who agree to perform, but then use their performances as platforms in favour of democracy and human rights. Caetano Veloso and Gilberto Gil went to Israel last July, on a tour that provoked enormous controversy. On his return, Caetano published a courageous account of his visit, in which he explained that during his performance he had opted for "total political silence". He added that he had agreed to the tour in order to make contact with groups who oppose current Israeli policies. The tone of the article is very critical of the authorities. By going to Israel, Caetano annoyed almost all those who oppose the country's official policies; by publishing the article, he annoyed those who defend them.

Gabriel the Thinker also maintained a "total political silence" both during and after the show. His performance did not bother anyone. He merely entertained. And after the show – even now, as I write this – he has maintained his ponderous silence.

Luaty wrote a second letter wishing Gabriel good luck with his show. He did, however, give him a warning: "As you take to the stage tonight and speak those words of conscience and all-embracing love that we have all grown to expect from you and by which you have become so well-known, I hope that they will not ring a little emptier in your ears, a little more artificial, a little more sterile, a little more inadequate and disconnected than usual."

Can a thinker choose silence? Yes, but not if he is Gabriel the Thinker.

Wednesday, 14 October 2015

Tonight I took part in a demonstration in Lisbon, in solidarity with the Angolan political prisoners. Sara gave me a lift from my house, and we first went to pick up the Cape Verdean singer Mayra Andrade and the Brazilian singer Maria Gadú. Lots of people had already gathered in front of the European Union's offices on Avenida da Liberdade, and the crowds kept growing as we made our way down to Rossio. Very, very moving. People shouting "Freedom, now!" Many familiar faces. Lots of enthusiasm. A group banging drums.

Thursday, 15 October 2015

Only someone with no heart could fail to be moved by the wave of solidarity with the political prisoners that grows every day, turning itself into something bigger, into an authentic pro-democracy movement, just as Luaty has been dreaming of. The vigil in Lisbon last night displayed exactly this. Many ordinary people, along with many familiar faces from Angola, Portugal, Brazil, Cape Verde – people such as Rafael Marques, Waldemar Bastos, Kalaf Epalanga, Bob da Rage, Mayra Andrade, Maria Gadú, Gregório Duvivier – all showing their solidarity, shouting *Freedom, now!*, and all moving forward, towards the future. It was beautiful to be there, just as it must have been beautiful to be in Luanda, at the peaceful vigils that were nevertheless broken up by the regime's brutality.

Democracy seems to me a historical inevitability. When I was born, more than half a century ago, few countries in the world lived under democracy. In Latin America, Asia and Africa, the overwhelming majority of regimes were authoritarian. Even in old Europe, democracy began at the Pyrenees and ended in West Germany. Today, there are few countries that are not governed democratically, although it is very fragile and rudimentary in some of them. The notion that democracy is inevitable explains why some dictatorships, such as ours, like to dress themselves up as democracies.

The hardening of the regime is happening at a time of economic collapse, precipitated in the short term by the fall in the price of oil, but in fact resulting from a huge number of governmental and strategic errors over the course of decades, in addition to rampant corruption. The large foreign corporations and other political and economic forces that have hitherto supported José Eduardo dos Santos are now looking for someone more adept at managing the disturbances of recent days in a peaceful manner. Dos Santos is now just as inconvenient and harmful to his own party as Jonas Savimbi was to UNITA at the point when he was killed. As has been widely reported,

Savimbi's killing resulted from the direct intervention of soldiers and activists from the movement that he himself commanded. It seems likely that, sooner or later, dos Santos will also fall, defenestrated by his own comrades.

Dos Santos's absence from yesterday's state-of-the-nation address, during the opening ceremony of the National Assembly, strikes me as significant. José Eduardo was replaced at the last minute by his vice president, Manuel Vicente. Even the *Jornal de Angola* was not informed of the substitution, announcing in its headline: PRESIDENT SPEAKS TODAY ON STATE OF THE NATION.

Manuel Vicente harked back to the theme of chaos and disorder in certain African countries, suggesting once again that such "disorder" had been provoked by external forces in the wake of pro-democracy movements. There was not a single word about the political prisoners. And yet the shining light of Luaty's ironic smile was there throughout, in a reaffirmation of hope and salvation.

Freedom, now!

Thursday, 29 October 2015

During a quick trip to Lisbon, the Angolan journalist Rafael Marques agreed to take part in a TV debate on Tuesday's main evening news programme. Also participating was a Portuguese diplomat whose name will not trouble the history books. The debate in question, or at least an edited portion of it (as it was not broadcast in its entirety), was circulated on social media by elements linked to the Angolan regime, as an example of a supposed "thrashing" that the "traitor" Marques received from the Portuguese diplomat whose name will soon be forgotten. I watched the debate. What I witnessed was something rather different. In fact, what I saw left me somewhat taken aback, despite being well acquainted with Portuguese diplomacy's tradition of submissiveness towards the Angolan regime.

The diplomat whose name will not go down in history suggested that the Angolan judicial system works better than the Portuguese one, comparing the case of the jailed young democrats with that of the former Portuguese prime minister, José Sócrates. The enthusiasm with which the diplomat defended the Angolan regime's position was such that he seemed to be there as the representative of that very administration. Anyone listening to the debate who didn't know the nationality and career of the diplomat in question (who, it seems, was once Portugal's minister of foreign affairs), would have been convinced that he was in fact working for the Angolan embassy. The diplomat whose name will soon be forgotten even went so far as to state that, and I quote: "Violations of human rights should be dealt with at the United Nations Human Rights Committee, not in Rossio."

I swear! The man actually said that. I recorded the conversation, and went back into the recording to confirm it. *Violations of human rights should be dealt with at the United Nations Human Rights Committee, not in Rossio.* He carried on speaking, and concluded: "Diplomacy should not be conducted with a sentimental soul."

To me it seems that, quite to the contrary, diplomacy should *always* be conducted with a soul, with all its infinite sentiments. A soulless diplomacy is not even diplomacy – it is pure hypocrisy. Relations based on pure hypocrisy will never withstand the hard test of time.

Much more serious is the idea that citizens do not have the right to protest against violations of human rights wherever they occur. They have both the right and the duty. Among other objectives, such protests serve to awaken from lethargic sleep those politicians and diplomats who, in democratic states, should be fighting for human rights at every suitable opportunity, instead of defending dictators and dictatorships.

In this diplomacy of submission, identical in every respect to a sadomasochistic relationship, Portugal takes a beating, begs forgiveness and then says 'thank you'.

The results of Portugal's soulless diplomacy can now be seen. You need only read the anti-Portuguese editorials in the *Jornal de Angola*. I quote just the first paragraph of the most recent one:

> The anti-Angolan crusade can no longer be ignored. This level of Portuguese interference in strictly Angolan matters has its parallels in only two previous occasions: when Angola declared independence in 1975, and in the run-up to the defeat of Jonas Savimbi's UNITA, prior to 4 April, 2002. On those two occasions, the deep-seated hatred in Portuguese society, always latent and ready to emerge at the slightest opportunity, displayed itself in a way that was very damaging to relations between the two countries.

What I saw, however, was an honest man, Rafael Marques, a man of whom all Angolans can be proud, defending the interests of his country and his people. And I saw a diplomat whose name history will not recall, defending – against the interests of Angola and of Portugal – a dictatorship that is nearing its end.

The convulsive solitude of our days

I took advantage of a brief stop in São Paulo to go see *Vanya and Sonia and Masha and Spike*. The play, as its title indicates, flirts with Chekhov and posits, comedically, intelligent questions about the paradox of isolation and loneliness in a society that pretends to be ever more interconnected.

In one of the high points of the play, Vanya, played by Elias Andreato, has a fit of rage, exploding in a monologue against the arrogance and the blindness of youth that lets itself be alienated by new technologies instead of using them as instruments of liberation. Vanya's wrath looked legitimate, although, truth be told, his particular loneliness is not so much caused by these new times but by the sad times that have always been. You need only recall Chekhov's famous piece of advice: "If you are afraid of loneliness, don't marry."

Vanya lives in a nice country house, in the company of his adoptive sister Sonia (Patrícia Gaspar) who, from the beginning of the play, suggests that maybe it would be a good idea for the two of them to get married – to each other, that is. Sonia does not quote Chekhov; nor does she need to. The idea that two lonelinesses combined more often than not result in an even larger loneliness is implicit. Loneliness amplifies loneliness.

Let us return to Vanya's wrath, and to the motives for it. Yes, we live in a vortex of movements that stumble and stand in the way of each other, and sometimes it becomes hard to tell where we are going. It is true that we are increasingly connected, exchanging information by the minute like ants in an immense colony. For some entomologists, ants are no more than relatively autonomous cells of a larger and more complex organism: the colony. We are becoming ants in this sense, dissolving into a larger organism – humankind.

Such movement should lead to the end of loneliness. Ants don't suffer from loneliness. However, this is not the case. It often happens that we think ourselves alone amid the clamour of the crowds. It is worth remembering, by the way, that ants exchange information by touching each other. Who knows, perhaps we should send fewer text messages and embrace each other more often.

Also, unlike ants and their chemical hugging, which is loaded with important information for the survival of the colony, most of the messages we exchange have no relevance whatsoever.

A compulsion for logorrhoea is not exclusive to technologically advanced societies. All that happens is that the new technologies make that compulsion easier. Brazilian photographer Sérgio Guerra, who is based in Luanda, has been photographing nomadic Herero shepherds in southern Angola for years, and gifted one of them with a mobile phone. The shepherd doesn't speak any Portuguese; nor is my friend fluent in any of the languages of the region. Even so, every afternoon, the shepherd climbs up a hill looking for reception, and calls Sérgio. They talk to each other for a few minutes. That is, they exchange words, but don't communicate.

In the convulsive solitude of our days, we are all this Herero shepherd. We talk too much, and communicate very little. Since I began writing this piece, for example, I have sent around thirty text messages, and many more via Skype and Facebook. I am not sure, however, that any of these messages were actually of any importance.

One time, in Berlin, I looked up from the book I was reading on the U-Bahn because I found the silence a little strange. I noticed that everyone was talking. A group of young people had got on a few stops earlier, and had taken over the carriage. I assumed they were students in a school for deaf people. They were communicating with each other by drawing words with their hands, and they smiled and argued. Watching them moved me, because it was a beautiful thing, people communicating in silent, harmonious uproar. It made me wonder what the world would be like if we all talked like this. From the start, sign language demands more attention from whoever takes part in the conversation. Two or more people talking in sign language are indeed very focused. They can't hear; yet they *listen* to each other.

Vanya misses the time when people used to write letters instead of sending quick-fire text messages. So do I. A letter implies dedication.

A person writing a letter suspends the vertigo of time in order to reflect, to feel, to think of the other person. A love letter really is a love letter. A love text message is to a love letter what Dan Brown is to Chekhov.

I insist I have nothing against the new technologies. I just think that we are making terrible use of them. New technologies, when well used, allow us to gain time. To expand time. Poorly utilised technologies deprive us of it. That is, they deprive us of life.

On untranslatability

Last week I had dinner with my English translator, Daniel Hahn, in Brighton, England. I first met Daniel thirteen years ago, when he was translating *Nação Crioula* (as *Creole*). It was his first translation. I have always found it to be excellent, but he begs to differ. He claims it contains an embarrassing error. The word *saudade* appears on some pages, and Daniel chose to keep it in Portuguese with a footnote. In the note, he explains that it is one of the hardest words to translate. Its meaning, he writes, combines diverse emotions, from everyday nostalgia and melancholy to the sorrow of someone far away from their homeland, or the feelings of one who is losing or has lost certain people or places. "For a translator, to keep a word in the original language, prisoner to a footnote," Daniel added, "is an admission of defeat."

Before dinner that evening, I'd gone to a bookshop to look at the new releases and ended up buying a curious little book, *Lost in Translation*. It is an illustrated compendium of untranslatable words from several world languages. The beautiful-looking book only includes two words from Portuguese: *saudade* and *cafuné*. That book was the reason *Creole* had come up in conversation.

Today Daniel is a respected translator. Luckily for him and for us, he has no shortage of work. There are more and more Brazilian, Portuguese and African authors being published in the British and American markets. "Nothing is translatable. Everything is translatable," Daniel told me during dinner. Nothing is translatable because, on closer inspection, each word contains its own universe. Everything is translatable because there is no feeling, however uncommon, bizarre or singular, that cannot be expressed to some extent in another language. "Today," Daniel assured me, "I'd translate the word *saudade*, depending on the context, as 'nostalgia', 'longing', 'homesickness', etc."

Strangely, I find myself moving in the opposite direction from my translator. For many years I believed that the supposed untranslatability of the word *saudade* was nothing but a poetic myth created by the Portuguese, Brazilians, Cape Verdeans and Angolans, that spoke more about the way we see ourselves or would like others to see us than the word itself. I don't like footnotes. And yet I do like the idea that, now and again, a translator might give up and admit defeat when faced with a language's deepest mysteries. *"Tenho saudades suas"* is not the same as "I miss you". It is, but it's much more than that.

When in doubt, it's best to look to etymology. *Saudade* comes from the Latin *solitas*, meaning solitude or loneliness. *Saudade*, then, is feeling oneself to be alone, far from something or someone, yet still close in the mind or the heart. There is no English word that covers all these different layers of meaning.

The country with the most fervent cult of *saudade* is not Portugal or Brazil, but Cape Verde. To understand this, you need only listen to the fabulous repertoire of Cape Verdean popular music. Six or seven out of every ten songs composed by Cape Verdeans are about *saudade*. The most famous song ever to have come out of Cape Verde must surely be Armando Zeferino Soares's "Sodade", which Cesária Évora helped to popularise, but which has since been reinterpreted by many other voices. The *saudade* cult is not surprising if we remember that more than half of Cape Verdeans live away from the archipelago. *Saudade* is a traveller's word.

In my opinion, *cafuné* – the other Portuguese word that Ella Frances Sanders, the author of *Lost in Translation*, considers to be untranslatable – is more interesting than *saudade*. The word comes from Quimbundo, a language native to the Luanda region of Angola, and refers to the crackling sounds created by the nails of the thumb and index or ring finger as they caress a loved one's hair, in a highly delicate ceremony of pacification and spiritual relaxation. I love *cafuné* so much, and have such respect for this ancient art, that I even wrote a poem, "Recipe for a *Cafuné* According to N'ga Xixiquinha Riá Caxongo", which the Brazilian singer Socorro Lira set to music on one of her albums.

It seems to me that *cafuné* is impossible to translate into other languages without a long footnote, given that it is such a specific ritual, and the word so perfectly conveys this particular intimate, African universe that has been adopted by Brazil.

Placed together, *saudade* and *cafuné* sum up Brazil quite accurately: Portuguese melancholy being soothed and harmonised with ancient African wisdom. Can that be translated? I fear not.

An unintentional anarchist

Last week, there was talk of an American civil rights activist, Rachel Dolezal, who, for years, pretended to be black. I read several articles in the American press, all of them condemning her. Most of her critics attacked her for having lied. Some accused her of having taken advantage of the condition of the black woman, having risen to the top of the National Association for the Advancement of Colored People (NAACP), one of the oldest and most influential civil rights organisations. There were even some who accused Rachel of having appropriated the pain of others. From this perspective, a white person will never be able to understand what it means to be black, even if they put on a disguise and get recognised as such, as they do not share the same history of suffering.

This incident brings discomfort to the majority of Americans regardless of their ethnicity, as it exposes the artificiality and falsehood behind the idea of race and, by doing so, threatens the established social order. I think of Rachel Dolezal as an unintentional anarchist, who, leading by example, managed to shake the system and unleash a curious debate about race and identity.

In an interview after the scandal broke, Dolezal tried to justify her actions by saying that she identifies as black. It sounds to me like an intelligent argument, shifting the focus from race into culture; it just comes too late. However, the truth is that Dolezal has not harmed anyone with her strange and elaborate lie. She rose through the ranks of the NAACP based on her own merit. It appears that she also excelled at university. To argue that she wouldn't have done as well had she presented as a white person would be to say that the institutions in which she distinguished herself have a racial bias in favour of black people and other minorities.

The transracial question – that is, the issue of people who have chosen to transition races, in the same way other people transition genders – is not a new one. In every country subjected to segregation, clear racial stratification or simply racial paranoia, there are records of people who have 'changed race'. During the apartheid years in South Africa, anyone could ask to be racially reclassified, and many did so, mostly for practical reasons – that is, to be able to maintain a relationship, marry and have children with someone from a 'different' race from their own, and to be able to send their children to certain schools, etc. In the United States, there are numerous cases of people of African descent – therefore classified as black – who managed to gain acceptance as white, with different degrees of success. One of the best-known cases is that of the writer Anatole Broyard, who decided, sometime during the 1940s, to pass as white. Broyard died in 1990 as a writer of some acclaim. Only after his death did his 'racial identity' become the subject of discussion. Broyard's friends stood by him, arguing that he was not interested in being seen as a black writer, but simply as a writer. As a black man, Broyard would have been pressured to write about the African–American universe, and he didn't want to do that.

Let us return to Rachel Dolezal's reasons. She says that she identifies as black; that is, she identifies with the culture of African origin present in the United States, and also with the history of African-Americans. Setting aside the web of lies in which Dolezal found herself entangled, what is wrong with that statement? Anyone should have the right to transit between worlds without being subjected to questioning.

A few years ago, in Salvador, I took part in a discussion about literature. At one point in the conversation, my interviewer, a young university professor who specialised in African literatures, wanted to know how I, not being black, could create black characters in my books. I chose the pacifist answer: a writer must be able to change skins. Writing is, in essence, changing one's skin. A writer must be able to put himself, all the time, in other people's skins. I have been a female slave, and I have been a slaver. I have been a torturer. I have been a famous singer. I have even been a gecko. I could have answered that, in strongly creolised societies, which are the ones I know best – the ones in which everybody shares the same mixed culture and families include elements of all 'races' – a question like this one makes no sense. The truth, however, is that the question makes no sense *anywhere*, not even in the United States. Race is a fallacy. In the words of the Angolan writer Luandino Vieira, "skin is merely the wrapping of the soul".

The extinction of unicorns

I like to feel surrounded by books. The presence of books, many books, has a soothing quality, like floating over a peaceful ocean on a sunny afternoon, staring at the sky. I write best at home, in my library. Yesterday I interrupted the novel I am working on to look for a collection of haikus in the poetry section. I couldn't find the book I was looking for, so I started taking everything apart. I noticed, without great surprise – given that such incidents recur whenever I decide to poke around the shelves that, in the back rows, I was finding books I didn't know I had. I don't remember having bought those books. I have no idea how they found their way into my home.

I have believed for a long time that forgotten books at the back of remote shelves tend to summon or originate new books. This is a wonder ignored by science, which does not make it less true. Science recognises wonders that are much more astonishing and infinitely less credible, like so-called quantum entanglement. According to quantum mechanics, two or more objects millions of light years apart can be connected in such a way that, when an action affects the first object, the other objects respond to that same action at the same moment in time. Anyone who believes in hypotheses such as this one has no reason not to believe that forgotten books summon other forgotten books for interaction, or – a possibility that demands a greater effort of credulity – that two or more books might interact with each other, a kind of festive literary orgy, in order to generate completely new and original titles. It might just be that these wonders happen simultaneously: some books arrive by a series of mysterious evocation ceremonies, and other books are concocted right there, on the shelves, after some interaction.

At one point during my search, a thin book fell to my feet: *All Gall Is Divided*, by Emil Mihai Cioran. It was lying face down, open, helpless amid the general chaos. I bent over to pick it up, holding it for the first time with my amazed hands, and I read: "Once we have turned thirty, we should give as much importance to events as an astronomer does to gossip."

I placed E. M. Cioran's book in my pile of 'evoked books' together with a long essay, in French, about Chinese poetry and a biography, in English, of Ryszard Kapuściński, by Artur Domosławski (which, in the meantime, I began reading). All these books were actually published. Their authors are known. Their publishers have more or less asserted their existence. Before they appeared in my library, they must certainly have resided in some other library. Kapuściński's biography, as a matter of fact, had a pencilled note on its third page, from its presumed original owner.

Even more curious are the books that are so unlikely that they could have only been born of the anxious coitus of several unfound titles. For example, I found a Romanian treatise in pogonology (the study of beards), and a poetry book written in a wicked Portuguese dialect. The book of poems contained an indication that it had been printed in 2017. It could have been a typo. It could just be that the whole book is nothing but a painful collection of typos. Or not – perhaps it was really written in a future time, in a future dialect.

I was especially astonished by a particular tome, in Arabic, which looked like a modern reproduction of an ancient essay on the extinction of unicorns. I stored it in between an autographed copy of the first Mozambican edition of *Voices Made Night* by Mia Couto, and a voluminous biography of the great British traveller Richard Francis Burton (this example perfectly illustrates the unruly state my library is in). When I looked for the book again, it was no longer there. I suppose it must have been summoned by another library.

I have recently visited what is probably the largest private library in Portugal. It belongs to the well-known political commentator José Pacheco Pereira. Pacheco Pereira started out by acquiring an enormous house in a village near Lisbon, but quickly understood that he would not be able to store all his books there – more than 100,000 of them. Then he bought the adjoining properties: a school, a winery, a police precinct. Now the library extends through all these spaces. We emerged from a dark corridor and found a patio, and then came across the old police cells, always among books. The library is threatening to devour the entire village. I can imagine the nocturnal furies on those shelves bent under the weight of the books. The crazed titles that were generated there. The ghost of Borges roaming happily down the halls.

The Bar Oficina

It happened during one of those long summer twilights when time, like a cat, stretches out, and light hangs, golden, in the immovable air. It happened on a balcony that leaned out astonishingly over Lisbon. That space had once been a mechanic's workshop. Now it was a bar. There we were, the two of us, me and Richard, drinking and talking. Me refreshing myself with an iced tea; Richard cheering up with a mojito. I talked about books, and Richard talked about himself. Next to us a couple was arguing about Zygmunt Bauman's theories on the effects of social media on relationships, the transitory quality of love affairs and the chronic sense of anguish all of this provokes.

That's when she walked in. My friend grabbed my arm with a trembling hand: "She's the woman of my life," he assured me. "I'm going to marry her."

I stayed silent. She might be the woman of my life, too. She advanced in the backlight as if she wasn't moving at all, or as if she was doing so by stepping on infinity. The flowers on her dress, illuminated by the sweeping sun, seemed to be dancing, loose, over her tanned skin. The woman of our lives sat very close to us, retrieved a mobile phone from her purse and sat there, amused, for a little while, reading and answering text messages. She finally put it away, leaned over towards Richard and asked my friend if he could give her a cigarette.

Richard didn't have any cigarettes – he doesn't even smoke – but he got up at once and went to look for someone who did. He returned, moments later, triumphantly exhibiting two cigarettes and one lighter. He offered one cigarette to the woman, lit it, and then put the second in his mouth.

"You're a smoker now?!" I asked him, surprised.

Richard gave me a punishing look. "So what? I smoke sometimes."

He introduced himself: photographer, born in London, living in

Lisbon for several years now. He was drawn to this city because of its light. That incredible Lisbon light. As for the woman, her name was Esmeralda, and she was a journalist. She worked at a well-known fashion magazine. Richard got excited about her name. He spent ten minutes talking about the properties of gemstones, especially emeralds. He went as far as to invent a Colombian legend about the power of emeralds. He created a story with such talent that even I believed it. The conversation became more interesting. At one point, Esmeralda stood up to greet someone. My friend turned to me in a state of euphoria: "Did you see that?! Perfect match. I'm going to marry her."

That time I agreed with him. It looked like an excellent decision. I would be best man. In the meantime, night descended and the balcony filled with people. More friends arrived. Sometimes I would go back to the conversation between Richard and Esmeralda. He was looking ever more enthusiastic.

"Before," he would say, in a strong British accent, "days would go by like lightning. I was fleeting, like a butterfly. That was before I met you. Now I feel eternal."

The woman laughed a little, distracted: "We met less than two hours ago, Richard!"

"I know," my friend retorted confidently. "My eternity is recent, but sound."

He repeated the sentence in English, and in English, I must say, it was almost convincing. Around midnight Esmeralda got up, claiming she needed to wake up early the next morning. Before leaving, she gave Richard her phone number. They said goodbye with a long hug. An hour had gone past, and I found Richard in the farthest corner of the bar, in animated conversation with a young Angolan model. I sat next to them. My friend introduced us.

"Marta, José; José, Marta." He added: "I think I've found the woman of my life."

"Esmeralda?"

"Who?! No, Marta! Marta and I are a perfect fit."

Marta wanted to know who Esmeralda was. "I think your friend was cheating on me before we'd even met."

Richard protested. He was in love. He really was in love. He'd never felt this way before: "Before I met you, days would go by like lightning. And I was fleeting, precarious, like a butterfly. Now I feel immortal."

"Say that again in English," I advised. "It'll sound a lot better."

Marta shook her head, a disbeliever in all men, and left. I thought of the couple we encountered at the beginning of that same night, discussing Zygmunt Bauman. Bauman was absolutely right. Richard, however, did not pay me the least bit of attention.

"Tomorrow I'll call Esmeralda," he told me. "I think she really is the woman of my life."

The beautiful useless things that save our lives

The Portuguese poet Matilde Campilho was one of this year's sensations at the FLIP festival in Paraty, Brazil. "Poetry doesn't save the world, but it saves the minute," she said, at one point. This sentence was quoted often in Paraty. I found this interesting: either we look at poetry as a pointless exercise, or we demand that poetry save ourselves and the world.

I have never heard anyone ask that kind of question of a grammarian or a geologist: "Has grammar ever saved your life?" Or: "Do you believe you can reach God through geology?"

Matilde tried, elegantly, to remain a poet without looking too crazy. She should have chosen madness. If you're to be a poet, there is no reason to fear madness. If you are to be mad, let it be with poetry.

In truth, I think it's rather more likely that poetry saves lives than grammar. I can already imagine the story of a desperate guy, having lost his fortune, his children or the woman he loves, ready to throw himself out of a tenth-floor window. That's the moment someone shows up who manages to change his mind by reciting some verses by [every reader should feel free to insert here the name of whichever poet would prevent you from jumping]. However, I don't think the same would apply to a child about to drown, for example. In that case, throwing him verses wouldn't be very wise. It's probably best to throw him a float.

Let us then consider madness: yes, I believe that if it's not poetry saving the world, then the world is doomed.

Poetry is an intuition, and in the history of science, intuition plays a fundamental part. English speakers use the word "serendipity" to describe those fortunate discoveries that seem to happen by chance but, in reality, follow the same mysterious laws as poetry. Just as with poetry, serendipity does not just come by chance – it implies a special talent.

The term *serendipity* was coined by the British writer Horace Walpole in 1754, and taken from a traditional Sinhalese story, "The Three Princes of Serendip". The princes in this story make great discoveries by accident. "Serendip" is the ancient name given by Persian merchants to the island now called Sri Lanka, the "Taprobana" to which Camões alludes in *The Lusiads*.

Classic examples of serendipity include the discovery of penicillin by Alexander Fleming, or the development of the theory of gravity by Newton after an apple landed on his head. Scientists inclined to this particular form of epiphany have a tendency to guide themselves by a poetic logic, revealing a special vocation to establish relations between objects that appear distant and disconnected.

I pick a book at random from my poetry shelf: *New Poetic Anthology*, by Vinicius de Moraes. I open it and read: "Think of wounds / as burning roses." I pick out another book: *The Crouching Scribe*, by Mozambican author Rui Knopfli. I read: "Far away the barking of dogs shatters the serene / mirror of the horizon in which trembling casuarinas / line up in the distance." In the first example, Vinicius brings wounds resulting from radiation burns closer to burning roses. In the second, where most people would see only the horizon, Rui saw a mirror shattered by the sudden barking of dogs.

Poetry can save the world, then, by establishing a different type of thought in which intuition is more relevant than linear logic. This way, it seems to me that questioning the uses of poetry is as absurd as questioning the purpose of music, beauty or love. One night, in a village somewhere deep in the bush in Angola, I heard a little boy ask his grandfather: "What are the stars for?" The old man shrugged his shoulders, sighed and said: "The stars have no purpose, they are there just to make pretty."

Years ago, I heard another excellent answer to the question of the uses of poetry, at the Travessa bookshop in Ipanema, during a meeting between Ferreira Gullar and his readers. When asked by a young woman seated on the floor before him, Gullar described how, during his time in exile in Chile, he would have lunch every week with a group of other Latin American expatriates. In this group was an Argentinian economist, the boyfriend of a Brazilian woman, who would sit next to Gullar every time they had lunch and would spend the entire time discussing economics. One day he lost his girlfriend. That day he sat down, as usual, next to Gullar, but this time he did not talk about economics. He only talked about poetry. He talked about poetry for the entire meal. "When the woman leaves," concluded Gullar, "economics serves no purpose. When the woman leaves only poetry can help us."

The death of Cecil

His name was Cecil; he had a brother named Jericho, and he worked involuntarily as a photographic model in a national park, in Zimbabwe. He was struck by an arrow and chased for forty hours before, finally, they shot him dead. Then they cut off his head. Cecil's death provoked widespread outrage on social media. The noise irritated a few commentators because, after all, Cecil was only a lion, and all this vigorous indignation would be better directed against the infinite series of outrages that, day after day, men perpetrate against other men.

I am suspicious of this argument. Firstly, empathy with beings from other species does not deprive us of our humanity. It adds to it. I have enough heart to be angered by the tragic fates of millions of African refugees who try to cross the Mediterranean to reach Europe; by the fates of political prisoners in Zimbabwe, Equatorial Guinea or Angola; by the victims of landmines, those cruel traps engineered not to kill, but to maim – traps that hurt children, women and civilians indiscriminately, and which continue to be made in so many democratic countries – and I still have enough heart and indignation left to protest against Cecil's murder.

The good news, as far as the episode with Cecil is concerned, comes from understanding how far we have evolved in the last half-century. Had there been an Internet and social media in the 1960s, a huge percentage of the pictures from that time would have been of hunters posing happily alongside their dead quarries. Nobody would have been appalled at the death of Cecil.

My father was a hunter. He would wake me up at four in the morning – I must have been eleven or twelve years old – just so I could go hunt with him. I enjoyed the feeling of adventure. The nervousness of the pointers. The morning opening up over the savannah. The tall grass, very green, and the smell of wet earth. However, I hated hunting. I would run in front of the hunters, screaming, trying to scare off the animals. I would fire my gun in the air. I would cry as I hugged the dying gazelles. I would make such a racket, such a drama, that my father, embarrassed, stopped asking me to come hunt with him.

I was a strange boy. Most of my friends would have loved all of that, especially the chance to shoot and kill a real live animal.

Today, I look at the wave of outrage on social media as a personal victory. We, the weird kids, have won. We are now a sound majority. There are fewer and fewer hunters, and they are less and less proud of their feats. I believe that trophy hunting, bullfighting and other cruel and degrading spectacles involving animals will soon disappear. Costa Rica has already forbidden hunting for sport. In Portugal and Spain, the movement against bullfighting is growing; there are many cities that can no longer host such events. In different places all over the world, there is now also a growing movement against animal testing in labs.

Even a few years ago, the most important festivity of Manganeses de la Polvorosa, in Spain, included the throwing of a live goat from the top of a church tower. In Portugal, a video of a cat being burned alive during the São João festivities in Vila Flor caused such a commotion that it led to intervention by the police. The most common argument for defending such 'spectacles' is that of tradition. I've never understood this. An idiotic action does not become more intelligent or more interesting on account of being repeated year after year, generation after generation. It only makes it worse.

Man's relationship with other living beings seems like a good measure for the degree of a society's ethical and moral sophistication. I'm very well aware that a person can be cruel to his peers, yet love little birds. Hitler was a vegetarian and promulgated several laws intended to combat cruelty against animals. Butchers and slaughterhouses disgusted him. I'm sure there are torturers incapable of hurting a fly, and professional assassins who, in their free time, help save the whales. It is also possible to be a bullfighter and a humanist, a hunter and a democrat, a lion tamer and a philanthropist. I am not talking of specific, individual cases. I am talking of civilisations. A society that is moved by the death of a lion is probably better prepared to love and understand its peers. In any case, looking back at the convulsive abyss into which humanity is hurling itself, I have the impression that our moral progress has been running parallel to the acknowledgment of the rights of other living beings, and the slow realisation that we are all connected.

Throughout history, here and there, we have witnessed numerous moments of civilisational ebb and flow; some of them brief and mild, others long and extremely violent. Ultimately, however, we always move forward.

Book of titles

I've spent the last few days devising and discussing titles for a friend's novel. Finding a good title often proves a harder task than writing the novel itself. Sometimes it proves an *impossible* task. We conclude the novel. We're pleased with it, eager to see it published; but the title never comes. We work on the title for days, weeks, first alone, then with the help of our families and friends and then, finally, with the help even of our neighbours, begging our editors for just a little bit more patience. Weeks pass. Still no title, and with the editor in a rage now, with the editor in tears, we give up and hand over any old readable thing as our title. Usually it's the first title on the list.

I once tried publishing a novel without a title, but my editors wouldn't allow it. "A book without a title is like a person without a name," they argued. "People have got to have a name, even if they never recognise themselves in it."

I disagree. There are cultures in which children don't have names. They only receive their names after an initiation ritual that grants them access to the adult world. Up until that moment, they are simply 'So-and-So's son or daughter'. We could do exactly the same thing with books. The first editions would go out to the public as *Untitled* – itself a title, in fact, which so many visual artists give their canvases – and the books would earn their names as they came to deserve them – that is, as they were read. The title would derive from the way in which they were read.

We know the title of a book doesn't work when no readers can remember it: *"I love that book of yours, that one in Rio, what's it called again?"* Sometimes not even the author can remember the title. It happens to me: *"That book of mine about Rio, you know the one, I can't remember the title just now."*

So it's best for us to avoid titles that are too long. And to take care, too, with titles that are poetic or obscure. A title should be capable of attracting the reader without betraying the book. There are, naturally, some long titles, and also some obscure titles, that do work very well. Of the long ones, I particularly like Luis Sepúlveda's *The Old Man Who Read Love Stories*. A title like that is entirely self-sufficient; it can dispense with the fiction. In contrast, Marçal Aquino's *I'd Receive the Worst News from Your Beautiful Lips* – a novel I really like a lot – has an impossible title. Marçal, my friend, please forgive me, but there's just no way. Only an actor with many years' experience, used to memorising long pieces of text, could go into a bookshop and recite that title in its entirety. I've tried to get it to stick, resorting to mnemonics, but I've never managed it. Now I just ask for "that novel, the one with the lips, by Marçal Aquino", and I do usually manage to get the book – along with a complicit smile from the bookseller.

Titles can be a problem when they come to be translated, too. I remember the problems we went through, me and my English translator, to reach a title for the British edition of *O Vendedor de Passados*. A literal translation – *The Seller of Pasts* – wouldn't do, because it didn't sound good according to the translator, and the publishers agreed. We spent two or three days collecting titles and arguing over them. Finally the publishers liked one of them: *The Book of Chameleons*. I, however, was not convinced. The first review the book received was positive, but it agreed with me. The only problem the critic had was with the title: "I don't understand why they didn't keep the original title, *The Seller of Pasts*. After all, there isn't a single chameleon in the book – what there is, is a lizard," he wrote. I've never forgotten that critic's name: Nicholas Lezard. I called my publishers: "Did you read the review? It's an officially authorised opinion, a lizard on the subject of chameleons and lizards."

Months later, I got a call from my German translator, Michael Kegler. He, too, was going round and round with the title. "I think I've found a really good one," he said. *"The Lizard's Smile."*

"It's great!" I agreed. "It's just a shame João Ubaldo's already used it."

"He has? Hold on a minute, let me try to find out if that one has been translated into German." He called me back moments later. "There's no problem – it has been translated into German, but under another name."

"Let me guess: I bet it's *The Seller of Pasts* – am I right?"

Thanks to all the days I spent together with my translators compiling lists of titles, I now have access to a vast collection. That's why my writer friends seek me out. I have become a giver of titles. I've thought about monetising this activity, publishing a *Book of Titles* aimed at writers, editors and translators. It would be a great success. Not a bad title for a book, either.

A dead boy on the beach

In Iceland, the government announced its readiness to receive fifty Syrian refugees. Outraged by the stinginess of the numbers, the writer Bryndís Björgvinsdóttir put out an appeal on Facebook for her compatriots to comment on the subject. In less than twenty-four hours, 10,000 Icelanders were getting ready to open their doors to receive refugees. This impressive wave of solidarity led the government to take another look at its original proposal. It's important to emphasise that Iceland is a small country, with a mere 330,000 inhabitants – half the population of the city of João Pessoa in Brazil.

There are a number of lessons we might take away from this episode: the first has to do with shame and redemption. The huge tragedy that is underway, with waves of refugees from a variety of origins, attempting daily to reach safe ground, has exposed the world to a Europe that is divided, weakened and morally debased. For decades, Europeans had been proud of their supposed moral superiority. It is true that Europe has ceased to be the centre of the world; Europeans acknowledge that. It is true that it has lost its empires and has, day by day, been losing political and cultural influence; yet it remains an ethical reference point.

We see groups of police pursuing and beating up old people, women and children who have managed to flee from a country at war; we see, then, police beating up victims. Then we see bodies floating in the Mediterranean, because nobody wanted to save them. The picture of a three-year-old boy on a Turkish beach was shared the world over, with the caption "Humanity has turned its back". We see all this and we understand, appalled, that the barbarians have taken Europe at last. The barbarians are in power – in Hungary, but also in Portugal. The barbarians govern the UK, France and Italy. The barbarians have won.

The attitude of the Icelandic people restores a little hope in humanity, and at the same time saves face for an ashamed Europe.

With their quick and generous response, the Icelandic people have shown us that outrage, when well directed, can still be moving, can still move real democracies. Democracies – we forget this so often – are made up of the people.

Just a few days ago, Al Jazeera interviewed a thirteen-year-old refugee, Kinan Masalmeh. "Do you have any message for the Europeans?" was one of the questions. The boy didn't hesitate: "We don't want to come to Europe," he said. "We just want them to help stop the war in Syria."

Simple as that. We can have no democracy at home while we support dictatorships abroad. We shall have no peace if there is no peace in our neighbour's house. There will be no development for some people, if there is no development for all people. Hungary can build the highest walls. Israel can build walls. The US can build walls. Walls debase those who build them more than anyone. Besides, they haven't managed to stop thousands of desperate people from getting past them. Despair will always find solutions to overcome the worst obstacles.

What will come after the walls? Ordering firing squads for migrants? Sinking the boats carrying them with cannon fire? Locking up all the surviving refugees, and all those who seek to help them?

It's not enough for us to be appalled at the sight of the dead boy on the beach. *I can't look at those photos*, hundreds of people complain on social media. You can't look?! Well, you should! You should see the dead boy, and you should also see all the vast horror that brought him to that Turkish beach. We are all guilty of his death, whether because of our direct complicity, our support for wars, or our inertia, whenever we look away. That boy will keep dying on that same beach, on other beaches around the world, as long as we don't mobilise together to prevent the devastation in Syria from continuing. As long as we don't all mobilise for democracy to triumph in Angola, Zimbabwe, China. As long as we don't mobilise to impose models of development that are fairer, that respect the environment, that help to pull millions of people all over the world out of terrible poverty.

It is worth recalling Article 14 of the Universal Declaration of Human Rights: "Everyone has the right to seek and to enjoy in other countries asylum from persecution."

The dead boy in that famous photograph that so many people found it hard to face was called Alan Kurdi. He had a five-year-old brother, Galip. His mother was called Rihan. Only his father, Abdullah, survived the disaster. I hope one day he will be able to forgive us.

Monday, 31 August 2015

Two years ago I was with a small group of nomadic shepherds from the south of Angola who had come to Rio de Janeiro to take part in the first Back2Black Festival. The Angolans, from the Herero nation, were in Brazil with the South African artist Esther Mahlangu, a shy, little old woman who wears bright fabrics and adorns herself with bracelets and necklaces of beads. Esther's painting follows the traditions of her people, the Ndebele, who are famous for the geometric patterns with which they decorate their homes, clothes, adornments and everything else that passes through their hands.

 The Hereros and Ndebele might seem close in the eyes of somebody halfway across the world, in that they share certain cultural traditions and the same passion for beadwork. In reality, they are almost as distant – geographically and culturally – as a Yanomami from a Mayan. Esther came to Rio accompanied by a grandson, who serves as her translator from Ndebele into English. The Hereros, a very beautiful woman and two *sobas* (traditional leaders), were accompanied by another translator, also Angolan, who was fluent in Portuguese but unable to communicate in English. When I found the Angolan translator chatting to Esther's grandson, I approached to find out which language they were using. I discovered, to my astonishment, that they were speaking in Afrikaans, the language of the Boers. Afrikaans began to develop in Cape Town from the seventeenth century, with a basis in Dutch, to which the Muslim slaves brought from Indonesia added words from Malay. In the centuries that followed, Afrikaans added many more words originating in African languages. In the 1940s, the Boers created apartheid, and Afrikaans became the official language of the regime.

 I discovered that the Hereros' translator had learned Afrikaans in Namibia, a country bordering Angola that was once a South African colony. I think it's a lovely story: an old instrument of oppression and domination now used as a *lingua franca*, able to unite different peoples – including those oppressed in days gone by.

On a visit to Recife to take part in the first Feira Nordestina do Livro (Fenelivro), as part of a panel to discuss "The Portuguese Language: Bridge or Barrier?", I recalled the above story because the Portuguese language, like Afrikaans, has faced – and still faces – the challenge of transforming itself from an instrument of subjection to an instrument of bringing-closer: a bridge.

In Brazil, Portuguese cohabited for centuries with the indigenous languages – in particular with Nheengatu, or the "general language" (Língua Geral Amazônica), which the Portuguese colonisers were forced to learn if they wanted to prosper in that society. In 1758, the Marquis of Pombal forbade the use of Nheengatu, which gradually lost speakers – though it continued to be used more widely than Portuguese in certain regions, such as in Amazonas and in Pará, almost up until the end of the nineteenth century. Quimbundo, the language of the Luanda area, managed to hold out until the first decades of the twentieth century on a par with Portuguese. The nineteenth century even saw a newspaper printed in Quimbundo. Publishing a Quimbundo newspaper in Angola would be inconceivable today. It wouldn't have the readers.

The sad truth is that the Portuguese language crushed the indigenous languages of Brazil, and it is doing the same in Angola. Sadder still, this process of annihilation was heightened after independence in both countries, led by their own political elites.

Many people believed that the end of apartheid would be followed by a decline in Afrikaans. This didn't happen – quite the contrary. After being tossed out of power, Afrikaans went back to fulfilling its role as a bridge, which is the vocation of any language, at the same time as it has been re-Africanised. Today it is no longer just the language of the Boers and the mixed-races. There are more and more urbanised blacks for whom it is their mother tongue. This has been happening naturally, without violence, and without harming the country's remaining African languages. South Africa, as a matter of fact, is an excellent example of how to build a multilingual state, which could be useful to Angola and Brazil. Yes – to Brazil, too: all is not yet lost. In São Gabriel da Cachoeira, in Amazonas, Nheengatu,

Tucano and Baniwa have the status of official languages alongside Portuguese. In Tacuru, in the state of Mato Grosso do Sul, Guarani is also an official language. These are still isolated examples, however. By rescuing indigenous languages, we are also rescuing our own. What I hope for the Portuguese language, ultimately, is that it might serve as a tool of pacification and of bringing-closer – not of extermination.

The awareness of evil

On some mornings, as I read the papers, I am distressed by the hard evidence that humanity is irremediably evil, and that the world is on the verge of a great catastrophe. The following day, however, the opposite seems to be true: the world might, perhaps, be restarting after all. Perhaps we're just at the confused border of a new time, dazed by the light of the future, finding some difficulty in freeing ourselves from the brutality with which, for millennia, we have dealt with one another and with the nature that surrounds us.

On one hand, you have the images of a Hungarian journalist as she kicks children and trips a refugee who is carrying his child in his arms. On the other is the news that there is a vaccine on the way for malaria, an illness that continues to kill millions of people every year. Malaria has been one of the main obstacles to development in many tropical countries, especially on the African continent. If we manage to prevent malaria, some of these countries would be able to make up for a delay of decades in a matter of a few years.

On one hand, I come to learn that flowers are losing their scents, owing to the greenhouse effect and atmospheric pollution, and that this misfortune will make the already difficult existence of bees more difficult still, while the lives of plants – and our own lives – depend on the work they do. On the other, I read that the pace of deforestation of the world has halved in the last quarter-century. The tragedy is not over yet, but it looks like the beginning of the end.

One day they tell me that El Niño will be stronger than ever before, and that the next few months might be the hottest on record. (It's worth remembering, while we're on the subject, that the concentration of carbon dioxide in the atmosphere reached a record high in March of this year.) On the next day I read that Russian and Spanish scientists are on their way towards managing to halt or reverse the aging process; that other scientists mean to clone a mammoth, and that others still are going to carry out the first head transplant on a man suffering from a rare muscle-wasting disease.

Maybe I should only read the papers every other day – only the even days. "Nothing reveals the common man so much as his refusal to be disillusioned," wrote Cioran, and I read this and feel myself the very commonest of all common men. I realise, however, that the commonness of optimism, which Cioran is intending to ironise, is itself unexpectedly optimistic. Above all, we should keep in mind another aphorism by this same Cioran, a Romanian philosopher who flirted with Nazism and who was a deeply cynical, melancholic man: "Pessimism combines an ineffectual goodness and a dissatisfied evil."

This being the case, I would rather remain optimistic and believe that the attitude of that Hungarian journalist has more to do with the past of humanity than its future. She and the Islamic fascists and others of their ilk are all a kind of moral archaism – they are in the world to remind everybody that there was a time when the majority of people were brutish, stupid and evil; when slavery was legal and institutionalised; when systematic torture was a part of judicial systems; when burning people alive in public was considered an edifying spectacle, recommended for children … and so many other depravities and vast cruelties.

There is no more cruelty, evil or horror in our time than there was fifty years ago. What there is, is more *visibility* of the horror. Let us imagine that journalist is kicking children – not Syrian refugees in Hungary in 2015, but Jewish kids in Hungary in 1935. Maybe some of her colleagues would have noticed what had happened. But they didn't. No great global movement of outrage would have exploded. One fellow journalist or another might have criticised her. However, faced with the vast general silence, they too would have gone quiet. The woman would kick young Jewish kids again. The people around her would start thinking this was normal behaviour, this business of kicking Jewish kids, and so, bit by bit, evil would settle in, just as it did indeed settle in, everyday and common.

The great difference between a developing country such as Angola and a developed country such as Norway is that in the former, the horror is on the surface and the beauty is hidden away, while in the latter the beauty is on the surface and the horror lies hidden. The novelty, the happy novelty, is that these days it is becoming ever harder to keep that horror out of sight, wherever it may be. No, there isn't more evil today. There aren't more criminals. Corruption has not got worse. What has increased is the reporting of it. What has increased is an awareness of evil – and that's good.

Monday, 21 September 2015

António Zambujo has turned forty. To celebrate the event, he brought together a group of friends on a patio in Lisbon. When I arrived, the Tejo river, off in the distance, still retained the last blaze of the day. It was like a fire draining out into the darkness of the sea.

I first encountered Zambujo in São Paulo. It was Marília Gabriela who mentioned him to me: "Have you heard of a Portuguese fado singer called António Zambujo?" she asked. I said I hadn't, adding: "There isn't one. If there was, I'd know about him." Then she gave me an album, *Outro Sentido*, from 2007, and I was amazed. I didn't know there was anybody in Portugal making music like that. I tried to justify my ignorance: "You told me he was a singer from Portugal, but this António guy is from the Alentejo."

Just the same way Brazilians like telling jokes about the Portuguese, the Portuguese like telling jokes about the Alentejans. The Alentejans are the Portuguese's Portuguese. I love the Alentejo. I'm very fond of Alentejans. If I'd been born in Portugal, I'd have liked it to have been in Évora. The broad Alentejan plains are, in a way, rather like the African savannahs. The Alentejo is the only place where Portugal feels big.

For centuries, the south of Portugal received black slaves. In 1761, the year the Marquis of Pombal decided to end slavery in Portugal, there were still at least 5,000 working on the Alentejan plains. There are still signs of this presence in the occasional place name and even in certain family names, of Bantu origin.

What is quite obvious is the Arab influence, including on music. Fado, actually, is so close to certain Arab traditions that there are people who combine the two, and it's as if that's how it's always been. Listen, for example, to young Ricardo Ribeiro, singing in Arabic and Portuguese, happily accompanied by the lute of the Lebanese Rabih Abou-Khalil. Then listen to the Tunisian singer Amina Alaoui on *Arco-iris*, one of the most beautiful fado albums I know.

I was thinking about all this at Zambujo's birthday, while a group of Alentejans at a nearby table were starting to sing. That stunning patio could have been in Tangiers. It could have been in Marrakech, or Casablanca. That very afternoon I had seen a report on the tragedy of the Syrian refugees. A shrill-voiced young woman, interviewed in the street, spoke out against the possibility of Portugal taking in any of these refugees or any other "Arabs" – people, she said, without any ties of blood or culture to Portugal. I listened, appalled. I just cannot reconcile myself to ignorance.

I remembered an episode Mário Soares told me about. One day, in a meeting that the then-Portuguese president was having with Yasser Arafat to discuss the unending Arab–Israeli conflict, the other man drew his attention to the Arab heritage of the Iberian Peninsula: "You Portuguese people have got to support us. You're Arabs yourselves, after all."

"It's true," Soares acknowledged, and then added: "But we're also Jews."

The Portuguese are, indeed, that ancient mixture of Arabs, Jews and blacks. The Brazilians are the even wilder mixture of Portuguese, Africans, Indians, Lebanese, Japanese, etc. A Portuguese person who hates "Arabs" is a Portuguese person who hates himself. A Portuguese or Brazilian neo-Nazi is the weirdest, most ludicrous, most repulsive of oxymorons. And yet – miracle of miracles! – they do exist. The comments on social media, or in online newspapers, are a modern version of the old cabinets of curiosities or halls of wonders, rooms in which, in the sixteenth and seventeenth centuries, moneyed gentlemen accumulated collections of spectacles, mysteries and impossibilities such as taxidermied mermaids, unicorn horns or crocodile tears. In the comments sections, the wonders, deformities and monstrosities are not physical, but ideological and moral. There, with a strange kind of pride, these people show off their worst moral deformities, their troubling narrowness of spirit, their most monstrous ideas. There you'll find the over-excited preppy-girl of Rio defending the idea that the beaches in the city's Zona Sul neighbourhoods should be off-limits to blacks and poor people, or the Lisbon worker who wants to destroy the city's mosque. There's everything.

In Dresden, Germany, a group of Colombian neo-Nazis were beaten up by German neo-Nazis when they tried to join a protest against the arrival of Syrian refugees. One of them complained bitterly: "It's no longer enough that in Colombia we get called the 'brown-skinned Nazis'. We're purebred, we are, we've just got a bit darker because of the climate." (This story was reproduced in countless newspapers all over the world. It was later shown to be false. It is false; yet it remains very true.)

The intelligence of life

Gün Semin, aged seventy-one, is a Turkish psychologist who studied in Germany and the UK, worked in The Netherlands and currently lives in Lisbon, where he runs a research centre that deals with, among other subjects, the transmission of feelings through sweat. Apparently, the sweat of happy people infects anyone who breathes it in. Likewise for sadness, rage, fear ... all these feelings can be transmitted to other people, with no need for words or gestures, simply through subtle (and sometimes malodorous) chemical processes. Semin talks about this in a recent interview with a Portuguese newspaper, explaining in some detail all the workings of the research he is leading.

None of this is new. What is new is that these forms of communication might be more important than we imagine. The interview with Semin was published at more or less the same time as NASA revealed, at a packed press conference, a series of photographs and other pieces of evidence that demonstrate not only the presence of water on Mars, but also that it occurs in a liquid state, trickling, in the summer months, down the high mountains of the red planet. As one might have expected, the NASA scientists were then immediately faced with the tired old question of the existence of life on Mars. Yes, they said, the existence of water in liquid form means it is likely that life exists. Next question: with the existence of life, could there be *intelligent* life?

I've always thought this the wrong question. In the first place, we would have to discuss what we're talking about when we refer to "intelligent" life. Picture a golden trumpet tree, an avocado tree, a baobab, to mention just three species of tree I love very much. All of them strike me as types of incredibly intelligent lifeforms. They nourish themselves on water, light and air. They feed without killing. They have developed clever and generous mechanisms for dissemination – fruit – without any need to move around. In addition, they are capable of communicating via complex chemical processes, similar to those being studied by Gün Semin – not only with one another, but even with other forms of life such as bees. "Intelligent life" seems redundant to me. *All* life is intelligent. Intelligence is one of the properties of life.

On the other hand, if we can barely understand how we ourselves communicate with one another, and if we are unable to communicate with the different lifeforms that surround us and alongside which we have always lived – if we can't talk to an avocado tree, for example – then how the hell are we going to chat with a Martian?

Communication does not end with words. From the moment we become capable of deciphering other kinds of transmission of information, such as the kind studied by Semin, we might then be more able to initiate those dialogues I have referred to. We have known for centuries about experiments in communication with different species, in particular those closest to us, and which we consider "intelligent", that is, which have an intelligence that resembles our own, such as primates or dolphins. However, even these experiments, up until a few years ago, have entailed forcing other species to use our own forms of communication. Koko, the famous gorilla, has the use of more than a thousand signs in American Sign Language to communicate with her keepers. The images of Koko crying, when she learned the news of the death of Robin Williams – who had been a friend of hers – touched the world.

As a child, I learned that 'man is the only animal that uses tools'. Even back then, however, countless examples of animals that used tools were known. I also learned that 'man is the only animal that builds complex artefacts'. Later, we started to understand the wondrous complexity and intelligence of beehives and termite hills. 'Man is the only animal with self-awareness,' it was said, but recent experiments demonstrate that this is not so. As our knowledge of other species progresses, we come to understand that what we considered exclusive to our 'intelligence' is, after all, common to many other life forms.

We will first need to abandon our basic arrogance before we can finally be able to begin a conversation with life – not with 'intelligent life' but with 'the intelligence of life'. Maybe then we shall discover that the Martians have been here among us for a long time. We just weren't looking at them. Because all this time, even when our eyes were turned towards the stars, we have been looking only at ourselves.

Saturday, 3 October 2015

I got off the plane at Heathrow Airport, in London – the first stop on a journey that was to take me to a pretty little coastal town, Aldeburgh, to participate in the most Brazilian of Britain's literary festivals: FlipSide. There was a friendly driver waiting for me: Sam, a tall man with a thick, black beard and a blue turban. Over the course of the three hours we spent together on the drive, he told me his life story. His father had arrived in the UK from the Punjab, India, in the early 1950s. In his first few months, he tried to make a living as a fortune teller, going door to door – but neither his exotic turban, nor his sharp countenance, nor his amazing fakir's thinness convinced people, and instead of unlikely futures he decided to sell fabrics – and prospered. He had six children, the oldest of whom, Sam, had six in turn.

"Is your wife English?" I asked.

Sam was startled by the question. Oh no, he hastened to answer, he'd gone to fetch her from India. He hadn't even known her. "It was an arranged marriage, the way all marriages should be."

"Your kids' marriages, too?"

"Of course, theirs too."

Sam is Sikh. Sikh men wear turbans, and never cut their hair. Sikhism arose in the fifteenth century, in the Punjab, seeking to reconcile Islam and Hinduism.

Sam speaks three languages in addition to English. His children speak English and Punjabi; his grandchildren, only English. Sam is disgusted when he sees Indian movies in which couples kiss on the mouth – a man and a woman, you understand. He doesn't watch Western movies so as not to have to see excesses of that kind. In his opinion, TV shouldn't show people's intimate lives.

Sam was born in London and lives in London, but in several respects his life is in no way unlike the lives of his many cousins who have never left the village in Punjab from which his family originates. As I hear him talk, I wonder what his life would have been like had his father immigrated not to London, but to Rio de Janeiro. Sam's father would have made a success out of fortune-telling. Sam wouldn't wear a turban. He would have married for love, to a Salgueiro samba dancer; he'd be a Botafogo fan, he'd eat oxtail stew, he wouldn't spurn Umbanda ... and on some nights, after a lot of beer, perhaps he'd tell his friends about his father's country, this place called "the Punjab", about how his old granddad, who had visited when he was still a boy, had become enraged at the sight of a perfect ass swaying sensuously from side to side on TV.

If there's one thing that separates the Anglo-Saxon societies from the Afro-Latin ones, it is the philosophy of welcome and relationship to the Other. In Anglo-Saxon societies, the idea predominates that immigrant communities have the right to maintain and preserve their original cultures. Afro-Latin societies, meanwhile, devour the Other – they make them theirs.

In recent years, with Islamic terrorism and new waves of refugees and immigrants, mostly in Europe and the US, debate over the respective merits and demerits of these two philosophies has returned. To Anglo-Saxons, assimilation always implies a violence. It's true, it often does. A foreigner who arrives in Rio de Janeiro, in Luanda, in Havana, will only have a future from the moment they abandon the ballast of the past. On the other hand, these devouring Afro-Latin societies tend to assimilate those they devour – that is, they too are transformed and enriched, which is what explains the extraordinary vitality of creole cultures.

France has often been held up as an example of the failure of societies that prefer integration to the Anglo-Saxon model of separate development. I'm not arguing in favour of the French model, which, in truth, seems to me to be a sort of halfway house (a halfway that is bewildered and hesitant) between the British model and the assimilating voracity of Afro-Latin creole societies. I think the French model is a failure precisely because it is not daring enough.

On one of the panels at FlipSide, the Brazilian writer and actress Fernanda Torres, talking about the racial situation in Brazil, couldn't find a word in English for *mestiçagem*, the mixing of races. I don't think the word exists, because even the *concept* doesn't exist. Fernanda argued in defence of *mestiçagem*, as an integrating and pacifying model. Obviously, as she herself pointed out, *mestiçagem* doesn't mean the absence of racism. I don't know a single creole society – not even the Cape Verdeans – that doesn't suffer from inequalities, and where you can't find signs of racism. But one might say of it what Churchill said about democracy: it's the worst model, apart from all the others.

Starting again

I lived in Berlin for a year, thanks to a creative-writing bursary. Behind the apartment that was allocated to us was a huge garden with a big pond. Some months earlier, in Goa, India, I had bought some little tin boats. You light a candle inside them, and through some rudimentary mechanism the boats would be set in motion, producing a convincing motor-like noise. I paid the equivalent of two euros, at most, for each one. I used to take my son to play at the pond. Or maybe it was my son who took me; in the event it makes no difference. What's for sure is that those toys were a big hit with the German kids, much more so than the remote-control luxury speedboats some of them boasted. The great advantage of our boats was in not being controllable. Where they ended up going depended on a simple gust of wind. It could be half an hour before they returned to the bank, or they might be shipwrecked in the middle of the pond – which did, as it happens, befall every one of them eventually – and because of this, because we never knew what was going to happen, it was so exciting launching them out onto the water.

An adventure suggests something unforeseen, without a schedule, with a certain risk, including physical risk – but without adventure, where's the pleasure in life?

When I compare my own childhood to my children's, I am always surprised to realise how much theirs has gained in safety, but lost in excitement. Between the ages of seven and fifteen, I cracked my head open something like four times, I cut through my Achilles tendon when I smashed a glass door with a poorly judged karate kick, and I suspect I did, on occasion, even place my very life at risk, scaling buildings under construction or sliding down beaten-earth slopes on go-karts. I would be horrified if I saw my children repeating the many lunacies I perpetrated myself – but I regret almost none of them. (Well, OK, I do regret that moment when the Karate Kid took me over just as I was standing in front of a glass door. There was really no call for that.)

With the passing years, most people trade risk for comfort. They settle – and so they grow old. To grow old is to give up on adventure. People whose curiosity remains awake over the years, who continue to take risks and surprise themselves, these people are forever young.

"Any creative process is an act of courage," Picasso said, and it was right that he should have said it, as, on many occasions, he had the nerve to abandon a successful path to venture out onto others previously unexplored. When he was already very advanced in years and younger than ever, he said, looking back: "When I was fifteen, I knew how to draw like Raphael, but it has taken me my whole life to learn to draw like a child."

I think about Picasso while I read the new novel by the Mozambican writer Mia Couto, *Women of the Ashes* – the first volume of a trilogy titled *Sands of the Emperor*. There are several examples like Picasso in the visual arts. In popular music, too. You only have to look at Caetano Veloso, who every now and then reinvents himself, and after so many years is still able to surprise even his most faithful listeners.

In literature, however, it is rare to come across authors who dare to change an already consolidated style, which is so hard to come by, for different propositions. Mia Couto has done this. He started to move away from the style that brought him acclaim, built on a lexical inventiveness that is lyrical, dreamlike and intensely playful – almost baroque – from the novel *Before the World Was Born*. I believe that with this trilogy, he is completing this process of moving away. One factor that contributes to this is that these historical novels, set in the final years of the nineteenth century and the first years of the twentieth, require a more purified language.

Woman of the Ashes is structured around the mythical figure of the last emperor of Gaza province in Mozambique, Ngungunyane, who was captured by Portuguese troops in 1895, displayed in the streets of Lisbon like a circus oddity and finally exiled to the Azores, where he died in 1906. Ngungunyane proceeded into exile in the company of seven of his wives, in addition to three other senior dignitaries of the defeated empire. The four men remade their lives in the Azores. Three of the African men married Azorean women and left descendants on those islands. And so, in a way, they too reinvented themselves, and in doing so they emerged triumphant from the long humiliation to which Portuguese colonialism had subjected them. The Portuguese descendants of Ngungunyane's princes proudly boast their African names and dark complexion to this day. They are not descendants of defeated men, but of warriors who crossed the seas and in a distant land fought against all kinds of prejudices – and won.

On drugs and literature

Between 15 and 25 October, the Óbidos International Literature Festival (Folio) brought together more than 200 writers, musicians, illustrators and other creators in the small Portuguese town. I chaired a discussion between Mia Couto and the Brazilian neuroscientist Sidarta Ribeiro, director of the Brain Institute at the Federal University of Rio Grande do Norte. At a certain point in the conversation I wanted to know what Sidarta thought of the use of psychotropic substances by writers: "Might there be some drugs that could help a writer to write better?"

Sidarta does think so. In his opinion, marijuana, taken in moderation, can be useful for a writer by encouraging a slackening of reason and thereby facilitating unlikely associations between words and ideas and the creation of metaphors. However, Sidarta added, it is always good to spend some time going back over the text the following day, when all the effects of the substance have passed.

"Sidarta" is a good name for somebody who, in recent years, has stood out in the struggle for the legalisation of marijuana in Brazil. According to the legend, Siddhartha Gautama, the first incarnation of the Buddha, fed himself exclusively on hemp seeds, one a day, for the six years he spent preparing himself to attain nirvana.

Humans have always used psychotropic substances, whether in magical and religious ceremonies or for recreational purposes. And not just humans, as it happens: there are countless records of animals seeking out certain herbs, roots or mushrooms with psychotropic properties. They seem to enjoy consuming them a great deal.

It is impossible to talk about drugs and literary creation without recalling the French poet Charles Baudelaire, who in 1860 published *Les Paradis artificiels* (*Artificial Paradises*), a book that brings together two essays on the use of opium and hashish. Baudelaire used to get together with other writers and artists at the Hôtel Pimodan, in Paris, with the aim of consuming hashish during sessions in which they dressed up in Moorish clothing. The group, which included names such as Théophile Gautier and Alexandre Dumas, came to be known to history as the *Club des Hashischins*.

Reading *Artificial Paradises* doesn't really make you very eager to experience opium or hashish. On one hand, Baudelaire was suspicious of abstainers ("A man who drinks only water has a secret to hide from his fellow men"), but on the other, he was afraid of the long-term effect of the drugs that he had experienced himself: "Those who resort to a poison for thinking, very soon will be unable to think without that poison."

Baudelaire describes how Balzac showed up at one of the group's meetings. When he was offered hashish he sniffed at it curiously, but ended up turning the offer down: "The idea of not controlling his own thinking," Baudelaire concluded, "was one he found intensely shocking."

The use of drugs was also discussed at another panel at Folio, which involved the Brazilian João Paulo Cuenca and two of the very newest stars of Portuguese literature: Bruno Vieira Amaral and Valério Romão. Cuenca admitted having consumed various kinds of drugs, alcohol most of all. To write, however, he needs to be entirely sober.

As for Mia and me, meanwhile, we are dreadful abstainers (we are hiding a lot of secrets). We don't drink alcohol, we don't smoke and we rarely have coffee. I only need one little shot of coffee to be tormented by a whole heap of effects usually associated with illicit drugs. Once I had two cups in a row and spent a good fifteen minutes levitating five centimetres in the air. I'd dissolve into the air completely if I had three, I'm sure of it.

Mia says he usually writes immediately before going to sleep, on that diffuse border separating reality and dreams. As for me, I often wake in the middle of a dream and then rewrite it in my head. Many of my short stories were born out of this process. Some of the best passages of my novels, too.

Sidarta recalls that the active elements of marijuana, and of other psychotropic substances, exist naturally in our organisms. That is why our brains respond to their presence: it has mechanisms available for connecting to them. Perhaps some people, like me and Mia, owing to some chemical deficiency or efficiency, already produce these substances in more than reasonable quantities. Let's just say we fell into the cauldron of magic potion when we were still in our mothers' bellies. We live our whole lives stoned.

The boy who walked through walls

Rubi used to walk through walls. For four years, between first and fourth grade, he always sat in front of me. He was a very thin boy with glazed eyes and a wispy voice, who preferred reading on his own during break-time rather than joining in the games. One afternoon, Chantal announced that she had seen him step straight from the classroom into the corridor, through the wall. Chantal was blonde and French – the only blonde and the only French girl at the school. This gave her a strange kind of credibility. And besides, I think we were all in love with her.

After Chantal it was Aristóteles. Aristóteles was the nephew of the school's owner, a lady of Greek origin who was incredibly courageous and got involved in the nationalist movement. In 1992, when the civil war restarted, she was shot in the face and arm and nearly died. I went to see her in hospital. I was expecting to find the large, powerful woman who for years, long after I had left Huambo, chased me in my dreams waving a big cane. Instead, I found a tired, timid, softly spoken old woman. Aristóteles, who had the same reputation for honesty as his aunt, swore blind that he had seen Rubi slip through the playground wall while running after a football.

When I returned to Huambo more than twenty years later, the city had shrunk. My neighbourhood had shrunk. Only the trees retained their original proportions. The school playground, which had previously been huge, now seemed like a small backyard almost entirely consumed by a mango tree, as large and dense as a forest. I ran into Rubi at a party, at the home of mutual friends.

"People used to say that you walked through walls!" I remarked, towards the end of the party, when the beer had run out. Rubi looked at me very solemnly. His eyes were still the same – glazed and featureless, like a Sunday afternoon under a hot sun. But it was only his eyes that were the same. He had grown taller, put on weight.

He spoke with a drawl. "Is that what they said? Well, they said *you* could see in the dark, like a cat. Back then we all had superpowers." He was silent for a moment, waving his empty glass in front of my eyes. "I still do it, but not very often."

"Do what?"

"What you said. Walk through walls."

"How? What's the trick?"

"Back then I didn't think about them, the walls. I just ignored them. The moon only exists because we look at it."

Einstein said something similar, but in the form of a question and by way of derision, because he found it difficult to believe in some of the more bizarre theories of quantum mechanics. Perhaps my friend was interested in quantum mechanics.

"You probably don't remember, I used to read a lot," Rubi continued. "It's reading that helped me to walk through walls. But then my dad died and I had to start working in the family bakery, very young, and I never went back to reading. I began to see walls everywhere. I had to walk to find doors, but not all these walls had doors. One day I woke up and couldn't move."

"Why was that?"

"Just because. I couldn't move. They took me to hospital, but the doctors couldn't find anything wrong with me. They said it was psychosomatic. At first I slept, dreamed – and in my dreams I would walk and run. But after a while walls began sprouting up in my dreams as well, and even in my dreams I couldn't move."

"What happened then?"

"My sister began to read to me, and bit by bit I went back to normal."

Nowadays, Rubi runs a chain of bakeries. He also breeds parakeets. He divides his time between bread rolls and parakeets. He told me he lived alone in a huge house across the street. It was only when he stood up that I realised he had drunk too much. I helped him home and opened the front door for him. My old classmate gazed at me wearily. He jabbed his right forefinger into my navel.

"As time goes on, people find there are walls even in there," he said. "No one manages to walk through those. But there are others that are only there when we look at them; it's us who make them.

Those are the ones I can still walk through."

I met him again a week later, at another party, but this time he was sober, well-dressed and smartly groomed. He greeted me with a certain aloofness. When I asked him, half-jokingly, if he had walked through any walls that day, he pretended not to hear me. Perhaps he really hadn't heard. Years afterwards, someone told me that Rubi often makes stuff up when he's drinking, and that later, when he's sober, he can't remember a thing. That must be it.

A river's lament

"I've known rivers / I've known rivers ancient as the world and older than the flow of human blood in human veins," wrote Langston Hughes in one of his most famous poems, "The Negro Speaks of Rivers". The following line contains the key to the poem: "My soul has grown deep like the rivers."

The history of humanity runs parallel to that of rivers. Almost all the great rivers have produced great cities along their banks. "Whoever offends a river, offends God," says an African proverb. When a river dies, everything within it dies, as does all the land it flows through. I'm surprised that the Rio Doce tragedy has not provoked more emotion and outrage, both inside and outside Brazil. For me it was very shocking, like the worst of terrorist attacks.

It was an accident, they say. An accident is when the brakes fail and one car hits another. An accident is when someone slips on a banana skin and falls flat on their back. Huge environmental disasters, such as those that occurred at Chernobyl, Fukushima, Bhopal and Minamata, are not accidents. They are the almost-inevitable result of mistakes in government policy, private-sector greed – or both.

I was struck by the statement of a woman from the Krenak indigenous people. "The river already knew it was dying," she said. "When all the muck came downstream, the river rose up crying, making a din. And my mother crying with it."

If the river knew its destiny, whoever killed it must also have known, decades in advance.

The good news is that rivers are much more resistant than people. History shows that where there is political will and the means to enact it, it is possible to resuscitate biologically dead rivers. We should remember what happened with the Thames. In the sixteenth century, the Thames was already so polluted as it flowed through London that the city's inhabitants avoided drinking its water. In the mid-nineteenth century, after two large cholera epidemics, a network of sewers was built that dumped the city's excrement several kilometres downstream. At the time, the river gained the sobriquet "The Great Stink". In the 1950s, when not a single fish was left in the Thames, the first sewage treatment plants were built. Two decades later, the reappearance of salmon caused a big stir, and confirmed that life could return to the river. Today there are not only salmon and more than a hundred other species of fish and crustaceans, but also seals. From time to time, even dolphins venture to visit the British capital. In 2006, a stranded whale more than five metres long died during an attempt to rescue it, after it had swum upriver as far as Battersea Bridge in southwest London.

The photographer and environmentalist Sebastião Salgado says that it will take three decades to restore the Rio Doce, in an operation that would cost, or will cost – let's say *will* cost – close to 100 billion *reais*. These are enormous numbers; but even so, this sum may fall short. Salgado believes that the companies implicated in the death of the river will pay, without quibbling, the costs of its rehabilitation. It is certain, however, that they will not pay for the devasted lives of the riverside communities, and the cultures and traditions that will be lost. The costs of this whole immense tragedy can still barely be estimated.

Replying to a journalist's question, Salgado refused to assign responsibility to one particular company, saying instead that we must all question our way of life. He's right, but not completely right. We need to investigate, hold to account, judge and then convict. We *also* need to start questioning our way of life. If our way of life leads to rivers dying, then it isn't a way of life. It's a way of death.

When I was a boy, I had a river. My river was small and tame, and so humble that it didn't even have a name. But, like Alberto Caeiro's, it was freer and bigger than any river in the world. It was so big that even today it flows through me and nourishes me with the mystery of its shifting sands, the tall maize field where we played hide-and-seek, the raucous rumble of frogs, the singing of birds and all the dreams we built along its banks. I think that for a child, having a river is as important as having a dog. Rivers are ribbons of water that tie us to the land of our childhood. Rivers, as the poetry of Langston Hughes suggests, deepen our soul.

Books burn well

Next January, a new edition of *Mein Kampf* by Adolf Hitler will be published in Germany. It will be the first official new edition in German since the end of the Second World War. The book had never been reissued because German law prohibits the publication of Nazi propaganda. Moreover, the book's copyright belongs to the Bavarian government.

The new edition, with notes and commentaries, comes to almost 1,500 pages more than the original, and is the work of the Institute of Contemporary History in Munich. The intention is not to give a voice to Hitler, but rather to refute his theories. Nevertheless, the book's publication has provoked heated debate.

Dieter Graumann, Vice President of the World Jewish Congress, argued that "*Mein Kampf* was and continues to be a work of irrational hatred, purely anti-Semitic, which should be banned forever." The Zentralrat der Juden in Deutschland (Central Council of Jews in Germany) thinks the opposite, and supports the new, annotated edition. The book sold 9,473 copies when it was launched in 1925. Editions multiplied after Hitler took power. Six million copies were sold in 1940 alone. The new edition is not expected to be a success in terms of sales. The book is already available in many European countries, including Portugal, with sales figures that are insignificant; it's a matter of interest principally to historians and researchers.

The controversy over the re-publication of Hitler's book is interesting insofar as it brings us to a wider debate about the good or evil of books, and the right to ban or burn them. The only people who fear a book, on the basis that it could contaminate anyone who reads it, are those who are not secure in their own judgment. Books are always a place for discussion. It is not books that breed Nazis; a lack of dialogue, a lack of reading, a lack of books themselves, are what breed Nazis.

In all countries, there are books that cause discomfort. The ones that discomfort the most are good books, from great authors, but with bad ideas. Some of these ideas did not seem so wrong when those books were written. They were, in many cases, the prevailing ideas of their day. Such is the case of Monteiro Lobato and his manifest paternalism, if not outright racism, towards those of African descent. However, Lobato's ideas can seem progressive when compared with some of the things written by Fernando Pessoa. Read, for example, this snippet from his *Introduction to the Study of the National Problem (or Empire)*:

> Brazil is a typical case. It confirms [...] that territories which are subject to climatic excesses, such as intense heat and excessive humidity, are not prone to creating indigenous races that are susceptible to civilisation. [...] Slavery is logical and legitimate; a Zulu or Landim warrior represents nothing of any use to this world. Civilising him, whether by religion or otherwise, is to attempt to give him something he cannot possess. The legitimate thing is to compel him, since he is not fully human, to serve the needs of civilisation.

Shocked? José Maria Eça de Queiroz, who, along with Fernando Pessoa, is one of my favourite authors, wrote racist texts – many of them directed against Brazil and Brazilians. He didn't, however, agree with Pessoa on the particular issue of climate:

> On the same soil and in the same air, there can be two cities of Athens, one glorious, the other tawdry. And yet in the tropics, those deadly incubators of indolence, vice and servitude, there flourishes an abundance of energy, virtue and civic-mindedness. [...] There is no other way to explain the heroism, nobility and social discipline of the Zulus, who occupy some of the most torrid regions of Africa.

In other words, Pessoa's problem was that he didn't read Eça de Queiroz enough. As for Hitler, judging by his library it would seem he read quite a bit, but only to confirm his own prejudices. He despised fiction, and great literature in general (with the exception of Goethe), concentrating on encyclopaedias, anti-Semitic texts and books about the occult.

The problem always lies in too little reading, not in reading itself.

We can and must continue to read Eça de Queiroz and Fernando Pessoa. We can and must read Monteiro Lobato to our children, even if it is necessary, at times, to add some comment, to explain and to put into context. Most importantly of all, we need new voices that share Lobato's virtues, but not his outdated thinking. The thing is, for these new talents to emerge, they too must first read Lobato, not to mention Eça de Queiroz and Pessoa.

Black power (or the power to be black)

The swearing-in of the new Portuguese government led by the socialist António Costa provoked an unexpected and interesting debate about race, identity and belonging in one of Europe's oldest and most ethnically cohesive countries. António Costa, the new prime minister, is the son of Orlando Costa, a Mozambican poet and novelist of Indian origins, and Maria Antónia Palla, a Portuguese journalist who has distinguished herself in the struggle for women's rights, including abortion. António Costa has appointed Francisca Van Dunem, a black Angolan woman, as Minister of Justice, and Carlos Miguel, the son of a Romany small trader, as Secretary of State for Local Authorities.

The Portuguese newspapers have spent the last few days combing through Van Dunem's background. They all emphasise her competence and integrity as a lawyer; prior to her ministerial appointment, she served as Lisbon's Deputy Prosecutor General. Van Dunem, born in Luanda sixty years ago, is descended from one of the oldest and most powerful urban families in Angola. There is scarcely a single important incident in the history of Angola since the seventeenth century that has not involved one of her forebears. The Van Dunems, like so many other black and *mestiço* families in Luanda, made their fortune selling slaves to Brazil. As well as commerce, they also stood out in the military and political spheres. With the establishment of the Portuguese Republic in 1910, the old black families of Luanda were gradually excluded from circles of power and influence. Many fell into poverty. The Salazar regime nonetheless attempted a rapprochement with these families, appointing some of their members to important positions in public administration and the diplomatic service. In the 1950s, there were several black members of the National Assembly in Lisbon, including at least two Van Dunems.

Not a single Portuguese newspaper managed to remember that

the country has already had an African prime minister, albeit for only three days. That was in 1926. Martinho Nobre de Melo was born on the Cape Verdean island of Santo Antão in 1891, and in his youth he even espoused the African cause. Later on, he became Portuguese ambassador in Rio de Janeiro.

There are now several countries in Europe with black and *mestiço* ministers. France is, I believe, the European country with the most politicians of African origin. As long ago as 1887, the Afro-Cuban Severiano de Heredia was appointed Minister of Labour. The current justice minister, Christiane Taubira, was born in Guyana and is also of African origin. The UK, Italy and even 'blond' Sweden all have black parliamentarians and ministers.

Before achieving political power, Europeans of African descent had already conquered the world of culture. Popular music in France, Britain or Portugal would not exist without African contributions to it. Literature has followed. What happened in the UK with the likes of Zadie Smith and Bernardine Evaristo (who identifies as the descendant of Brazilian former slaves who returned to present-day Nigeria) is now happening in Portugal. As it happens, the most recent revelations in Portuguese literature, Djaimilia Pereira de Almeida and Bruno Vieira Amaral, are both of Angolan origin. Pereira de Almeida, daughter of an Angolan mother and a Portuguese father, was born in Luanda in 1982 and grew up in Lisbon. Her first novel, published in English as *That Hair*, had a subtitle that said almost everything: *The Tragicomedy of Curly Hair that Cuts Across the Story of Portugal and Angola*. The novel, which has received effusive praise, steers between an essayist's style and an autobiographical tone, telling the story of a young girl who gradually discovers her own black identity. *First Things*, the debut novel by Amaral – son of an Angolan father and a Portuguese mother – takes place in an imaginary neighbourhood on the outskirts of Lisbon where blacks and whites live side by side. *First Things* has won the most important literary prizes in Portugal, including the Saramago Prize for young writers.

Compared to Portugal, the black population of which is only 10 percent, Brazil still seems very (and I mean *very*) backward when it comes to the complete integration of its Afro-descendants, who are the majority. In order to deracialise society so that the skin colour of a minister or president is not news, it must first become part of everyday life.

Integration implies sharing power. It also implies sharing resources in such a way that people have the same opportunities to access education and culture. What black power wants is simply the power to be black.

Beware of the clown

People hear "Donald Trump" and can't believe it. Trump, with that plastic hair – very blond, very fluffy and very false, reminiscent of a fat, ageing Barbie – is the proof, if proof were needed, that wealth does not mean sophistication. The man is crude and simplistic. Next to him, Barack Obama seems a wise and highly polished prince. Boorishness, however, can be more effective than intelligence, charm and good manners. So with Trump. Every time he utters some nonsense, "the Donald" rises in the opinion polls.

Right in the middle of announcing his candidacy for the presidency, Trump attacked the Hispanic community, saying:

> When Mexico sends its people, they're not sending their best. They're not sending you. They're not sending you. They're sending people that have lots of problems, and they're bringing those problems with us. They're bringing drugs. They're bringing crime. They're rapists. And some, I assume, are good people. But I speak to border guards and they tell us what we're getting. And it only makes common sense. It only makes common sense.

The Hispanic community, which makes up a significant slice of the electorate, did not like it, but Trump nevertheless rose in the opinion polls.

A few hours after the infamous speech, he explained how, if elected, he would solve the problem of Islamic State:

> I say that you can defeat ISIS by taking their wealth. Take back the oil. Once you go over and take back that oil, they have nothing. You bomb the hell out of them, and then you encircle it, and then you go in. And you let Mobil go in, and you let our great oil companies go in.

More recently, Trump objected to Syrian refugees entering the United States, saying that President Obama must be completely crazy for disagreeing. The most recent notable 'trumpeting' relates to this. Trump now supports restricting entry not only to Syrian refugees, but to any person of Islamic faith.

When Trump announced his interest in running for President, the other Republican Party candidates tried to ignore him in the same way you would ignore an annoying fly during a ceremonial dinner. "He's a clown!" they said. This all changed the moment the polls began to show him as the favourite.

A rich clown is still a clown. A clown with power, lots of power, is no longer a clown – he's a catastrophe. Conservative folk, who usually vote Republican, like Trump because they see themselves in the directness and simplicity of his opinions, and they even laugh with him.

There was one episode in Hitler's life which, although little known, was perhaps a determining factor in his political rise. In 1918, Corporal Adolf Hitler of the 16th Bavarian Reserve Infantry Regiment was admitted to a psychiatric ward, suffering from hysterical blindness. The illness, which affected many soldiers, was viewed by psychiatrists of the time as a sign of weakness and cowardice. Hitler was treated by Dr Edmund Forster. Soon after Hitler was appointed Chancellor in 1933, Forster provided the writer Ernst Weiss with some documents relating to Hitler's treatment. These documents enabled Weiss to write the novel *Ich, der Augenzeuge* (*The Eyewitness*), published in 1963. In the novel, a psychiatrist cures the hysterical blindness of a soldier identified only by the initials "A. H.", using hypnosis and auto-suggestion. The psychiatrist convinces A. H. that while his blindness is real, resulting from a mustard gas attack, he is a special person with incredible willpower and a great destiny ahead of him. The psychiatrist turns out the light in the room and then says to the soldier: "Maybe you, like Jesus Christ, have the power to perform miracles. A normal person would remain blind forever. But perhaps you, with your exceptional gifts of willpower, will succeed in seeing again. For you, anything is possible." The doctor then lights a candle and, little by little, A. H. becomes aware of its glow. His sight returns, and from this moment on he becomes a man who is capable of anything.

The incident teaches us that we must not disregard grotesque figures with absurd and extremist opinions. Like Trump, Hitler had ridiculous hair (just to be on the safe side, it's a good idea not to trust any politician with ridiculous hair), and used the same type of populist discourse. He came to power because he *believed* he would. I suspect that Trump himself was not convinced that he might one day be President of the United States. My biggest fear is that he may have begun to believe it now.

The light of our language

The fire that struck the Museum of the Portuguese Language in São Paulo did not cause major damage – save the loss, always irreparable, of a human life – for the simple reason that what it houses is fireproof. The Portuguese language is an intangible heritage. There is no fire that can destroy it, except that of ignorance.

Inaugurated in March 2006, the Museum of the Portuguese Language, or Estação da Luz da Nossa Língua, was an immediate success. Said success can be explained by the quality of the main displays and the temporary exhibitions put on since the opening; the principal reason, however, has to do simply with that fact it is so necessary. The museum is a triumph because we need it. The only surprise is that it did not emerge sooner. The astonishing thing is that there is not, in every country and territory that speaks our language, or in every Brazilian state, a similar endeavour.

Understanding how the language we speak was shaped and maintained, discovering the many variants of Portuguese, helps us to understand world history better and – I believe – can make us a bit more open to others. The racist and xenophobic views that are returning and beginning to spread, like a vile disease, in certain sections of Brazilian and Portuguese society are, in large part, an expression of ignorance of the history of the language that birthed us.

I believe there exists today a greater mutual awareness of the different variants of Portuguese, not least because new technologies often break down borders. All the same, a lot of ignorance still persists. One time, a few years back, travelling through the Pernambuco countryside, I stopped at a small bar to ask for directions. The man I addressed did not understand my accent. I repeated the same question over and over, without any success. I tried again, but this time in my best Pernambuco accent. The guy's face lit up: "Man, if you speak Portuguese, why were you talking foreign to me?"

Another time, in Rio, a taxi driver, puzzled by my accent, wanted to know where I came from. "Angola?! What state is that in?" When I explained to him that Angola is a country on the west coast of Africa, he began to compliment the quality of my Portuguese. I told him that in Angola we also speak Portuguese: "Seriously?!" he replied. "I thought it was only Brazil that spoke Portuguese."

If we create languages, languages create us, too. It is not the same thing to grow up speaking Portuguese, Tupi or Swahili. One of my nephews, Samuel, was born and grew up in Luxembourg, son of a Luxembourger father. He learned to speak Portuguese with his mother, and Luxembourgish and German with his father. As his parents speak to each other in French, he has been fluent in that language as well from an early age. Whenever he switches from Portuguese to German, and then to French or Luxembourgish, there is something about Samuel – a subtle aspect of his personality – that seems to change as well. It is as if there coexist within him several people, each one expressing themselves in a different language.

In Cape Verde, bilingualism is commonplace. It fascinates me the way educated Cape Verdeans switch language mid-conversation, depending on the topic and their interlocutor. When moving from Creole to Portuguese, a slight personality shift takes place in them, too. A Cape Verdean, when speaking Portuguese, becomes a touch more formal. It is no coincidence that the vast majority of Cape Verde's rich music uses Creole, while Portuguese reigns, almost in isolation, in literature.

One of the as-yet little-studied consequences of the rise of social media concerns the return of written communication, and the greater attention paid to the languages used in said communication. A good command of language is an ever-more valued requirement when choosing friends and partners. "I sleep with any man who knows how to use vowel contractions properly," the satirical paper *Sensacionalista* joked some time ago, giving voice to a supposed reader: "My name is P. and I'm 39. I would like to be married, have at least two children and a quiet life. But I was born with a vice: lust for men who know how to use the tongue. The Portuguese tongue. Ever since I was a girl, at school, I shunned handsome friends and sidled up to pimply classmates who could correctly conjugate irregular verbs."

I hope to see the Museum of the Portuguese Language reopen

soon. I hope the tragedy that has befallen it, rather than diminishing it, can serve to draw attention to its importance, and that it will rise, just like the language itself, mightier and more diverse than ever. P., 39, would appreciate that. As would I.

The boys of Porto Mosquito

Benfica, the Portuguese club I (vaguely) support, shared a short video over Christmas about a Benfica Foundation programme in a small part of the Cape Verdean archipelago called Porto Mosquito. Ex-footballer Nuno Gomes went to Porto Mosquito to hand out a dozen pairs of boots to children in the community. In an early scene we watch the boys playing football, barefoot, on a bare pitch. Then we see their joy when they receive the boots, put them on and start playing. Meanwhile, another group of boys arrive, feet naked on the dusty ground. Every one of the first boys then takes off one of their boots, offering it to one of the second group. In the final scene, Nuno Gomes asks one of the boys: 'Why do you play with one shoe off?' The boy looks at him, amused. 'No, mate, we play with one shoe on.'

The video reminded me of an old anecdote. Many years ago, during the civil war in Angola, I visited a prosthetics factory located in a small town, Viana, a few kilometres from Luanda. In one of the rooms I found a strange object, which would not look out of place in a modern art exhibition. It was a leg, or something like the shape of a leg, random materials held together with wire and iron bands, in a rather crude and bizarre assembly. "This was a prosthesis," a doctor enlightened me. Months earlier, a farmer had entered the factory on foot, but limping somewhat. He had lost a leg in colonial times. He had been given a prosthetic one and returned to the remote village where he lived. Then came independence and the civil war. Decades passed. The man had broken the prosthesis several times, and, with no one to turn to, had patched it up himself with whatever he had to hand. The prosthesis had grown heavy and misshapen, eventually becoming this thing before me.

"He came looking for a new prosthesis," the doctor told me. "He said he couldn't dance anymore with that one."

I never learned that farmer's name, never saw him, but I think of him every New Year's Eve as I observe the tradition of eating twelve raisins, one for every month to come, making twelve wishes. While I have never quite understood the relationship between grapes and wishes, I try to take the challenge seriously. Supposing that these twelve wishes really were granted to me, what could I ask for? For an initial and fleeting moment, my list looks like the shopping list of someone who just won the lottery; soon afterwards, however, I think about that farmer who just wanted a new prosthesis so he could dance again, and the list becomes unsettlingly similar to a Miss Universe acceptance speech: health for all, justice, world peace.

Perhaps we should pay more attention to the wisdom of the Misses. The philosophical work of reference for this professional class (let's call it that), the work that all the Misses quote when asked what they are reading, namely *The Little Prince* by Antoine de Saint-Exupéry, says it all: "What is essential is invisible to the eye." A friend, more *au fait* with the Misses than I, assures me that Saint-Exupéry is old news. Now the Misses read Paulo Coelho and Dan Brown; more recently, E. L. James. If this is true (I must check), we are dealing with a huge backwards step as a civilisation.

My grandmother, who was never a Miss, nor read Saint-Exupéry, said that the best lessons are the simplest. One time, after a debate with literature students in Stockholm, I found myself in the middle of another discussion, much more alive and interesting, about the virtues and defects of Nordic social democracy. Irritated by the (utterly justified) outrage of one of the students who had visited several Portuguese-speaking countries and come away shocked by the social injustice in Angola and Brazil, I mocked the very high taxes to which everybody in Sweden is subjected. I thought – stupidly – that by criticising taxes, I would have the students on my side. On the contrary. They looked at me, scandalised, as I would look at a racist skinhead. One of them explained to me that the new centre-right government had, just weeks earlier, proposed lowering taxes, and that this had been greeted with widespread abhorrence. "I'd rather go without half my salary," one of the students assured me, "as long as it meant, in Sweden, that everybody had the right to good health and education systems."

So, for this year, I am going to recite, in unison with the Misses: *health for all, justice, world peace.*

Non-places, non-people

I don't like airports – those "non-places", as the anthropologist Marc Augé called them – but I recognise that they are conducive to extraordinary encounters and, in that sense, quite useful to desperate writers. I met William at Johannesburg's airport. At that time, a few years ago now, the Oliver Tambo Airport had an excellent bookshop. I was taking advantage of the connecting time between two flights to have a date with some beautiful ornithological volumes (in South Africa, birdwatching is almost a religion), when a smart individual with a well-trimmed grey beard and hair tied in a ponytail, like a tango dancer, approached me:

"Excuse me, are you South African?"

He wanted some recommendations of new South African literature. I told him no, I wasn't South African, but I could point him in the direction of some good novels by young authors – not least because I was returning from a meeting in Cape Town that had brought together a considerable number of new-generation African writers. The man's face lit up. He asked if I wanted to get a coffee. He told me I could call him "William", or "David", although he did not identify with either name. Curious, I accepted the invitation.

For some people, a writer is a sort of confessor. More than a few times I have had someone tug my arm at a party or some public event, while whispering in my ear: "You need to hear my story." I never know if they tell me these stories in the hope of becoming fictional characters, or if, on the contrary, they *are* fictional characters, looking for someone to help them cross the border into the real world.

William was born "David" in a small Australian town and studied architecture in London, where he married and settled down. He never identified with his given name. Worse, he did not identify with the life he led: "It wasn't a bad life. It just wasn't mine. I woke up next to the woman I married, and it was like waking up next to two strangers."

David travelled a lot. He bought a yellow suitcase so it would not be confused with the majority of other suitcases on the airport luggage belts. One morning, after arriving in Barcelona, he picked up the yellow suitcase and got ready to leave. He had already gone beyond border control when he realised he had grabbed the wrong case. This one had a label on it with a name that was not his: *William K.* Now David hesitated. He was going to head back when he saw, among the people waiting for passengers, a tall man dressed all in black, holding a sign: WILLIAM K.

David took six steps forward and said to him: "That's me – William K." The man bowed slightly, took the case from his hand and led him to a metallic-blue Mercedes. He left him, half an hour later, by a brick-coloured mansion in the Raval neighbourhood. David, or William, interrupted his story to order another coffee. He savoured it before continuing: "All identities are forged. All men are an invention. It's just that some live that farce with more conviction than others."

"Perhaps," I agreed. "What happened next?"

"Oh! I began another life."

"What life?"

"An interesting life. I still don't feel this is my true life, though, but I'm closer."

I looked at him mischievously: "In the next airport, there could always be another suitcase, another life." William (or David) did not seem to pick up on my humour.

"Or we could swap bags right now," he said. "I'll have your life and you mine."

"I'm happy with my life."

"A shame. You'll never know the fate you have scorned ..." He rose and, for a horrifying moment, I hesitated. Oh, the curiosity! How many times had curiosity led me to foolish deeds?

"Wait!" I said, as William (or David) turned triumphantly. "Changed your mind?"

I shook my head, stood up and offered him my hand, certain I would never see him again. "Goodbye, William. Good luck! All the best with your lives ..."

He smiled and shook his head in mild derision. "You'll never know ..."

It is true, I shall never know. Some empty and lonely afternoons, if I happen to be taken by a bout of tedium, I remember William and his proposal. It passes quickly. I do not need more lives. I need more *time*. I would like to find, in some random airport, a suitcase full of time. To open it and find a thousand new days. Now that would be good.

Saturday, 16 January 2016

I am in The Hague, in The Netherlands. I came here to take part in a literary festival the theme of which, "Hello Darkness!" promised an original programme. And so it was. Over the course of numerous discussions and readings, the writers present were challenged to explore the darkness in their lives and work. Many, such as the Syrian poet Adonis, the Egyptian novelist Alaa Al Aswany and the Chinese novelist Jung Chang, came from countries under dictatorial regimes. Others had gone through long civil wars. Several claimed to write as an attempt to understand evil. Goodness is like pure water: it has no great mystery.

Wicked characters fascinate me. I try to find something in them that redeems them, a glimmer of humanity. I am also interested in understanding how someone chooses one side or the other: people whose destiny pushed them, from a young age, towards the darkness, but who manage, laughing, to lift themselves over to the bright side of life; or people who, conversely, were born with their path unobstructed, yet chose corruption and evil.

In a war, combatants and non-combatants alike are allowed to be bad. Evil is encouraged. Fellow citizens become monsters. Something similar happens in totalitarian regimes. In countries that are democratic but have serious social imbalances, like Brazil, the situation can be little better. Sick societies push people to the dark side.

When I am in Lisbon, I like to run by the river. In winter this is a little more complicated, because the weather is not always favourable. So I joined a gym with views of the water of the Tejo. I run on a treadmill, but my eyes remain on the river, following it as far as the bridge, come rain or shine. A few days ago, a friend, Luís Pedro Nunes, introduced me to one of the trainers. "The guy has an extraordinary story," he told me. And he really does.

Sérgio was born on a farm in the Alagoas countryside. Abandoned by his mother at birth, he was taken in by another couple and raised in a nearby town. At twelve years old, he fell out with his adoptive father and set off by himself for São Paulo, hitchhiking. He ended up living in the streets with other boys, stealing food to survive. One day, when he was fourteen, he bumped into a beggar. It occurred to him with an abrupt feeling of horror that he himself could become, a few years down the line, that dirty, foul-smelling man. That same day he began working as a delivery boy for a market seller. Later, he got a job at a jiu-jitsu academy. He cleaned the facilities and trained. He slept there. He became a Mixed Martial Arts world champion. After a two-year spell with the Foreign Legion in France, he settled in Portugal. He recalls living out on the cold Lisbon streets for forty-five days. He was used to that, so it was not too difficult for him. Today he is one of the most in-demand personal trainers in the city. People like him because he is always laughing and joking, and what could be an hour of physical torture ends up becoming something fun.

There are people who are good through pure laziness. Others are bad for the same reason. Real goodness and real evil demand effort. Sérgio is a good example of someone life conspired against, from a young age, with hostility, and who seemed condemned to remain forever on its shadier side. However, he chose to fight the darkness and won. "Have you read *Captains of the Sands*?" he asked me. Yes, I replied, I have read Jorge Amado from end to end. I learned from Amado that which he, in turn, must have learned from Orisha philosophy: that we are all made from a bit of light and an equal amount of shadow.

I met an old guerrilla fighter who lived for almost twenty years in the forests of Angola, fighting an insane and particularly cruel war, who today grows and sells "porcelain roses". The porcelain rose (*Etlingera elatior*) is a plant native to Asia, which was introduced to Angola with great success in colonial times. It sprouts a large, beautiful and delicate flower, which truly seems to be moulded from porcelain. I visited the former guerrilla fighter in Benguela, an old city by the coast where he now lives. I asked him, as I always ask anyone who fought a war, how he manages to sleep at night, with so much death and pain behind him. "Killing was easy," he told me.

"It was what was expected of us. What's much harder is thinking about those deaths now. What saves me these days is the beauty of the roses."

I am not sure that beauty does save us. But it helps.

Thursday, 21 January 2016

In the beginning, the so-called deadly sins were not seven, but eight, and Melancholy was among them. At the end of the sixth century, Pope Gregory I cut the Eight Deadly Sins down to Seven, and Melancholy was pardoned. The elders of the Catholic Church considered that persistent, stubborn melancholy – what today we would call a state of chronic depression – offended the Lord God, as melancholic individuals lost all joy, isolated themselves and were disagreeable to others. Eventually they would commit suicide, and in doing so shun the daily miracle of life. In short: they would disrespect the work of God. Not everyone agreed. Other theologians argued that melancholy could not be a sin, as it did not consist of a concrete action but rather a frame of mind. It is as if someone were born with a deformity that prevented them from marvelling and rejoicing at the splendour of the world. Blaming them for that would be the same as blaming the lame for not running quickly. The debate lasted centuries.

I understand the Church leaders who defended the first thesis. Sadness as a lifestyle always seemed to me to be a grave sin. Pessimism, that bastard son of melancholy, is often a kind of haughty badge that some thinkers pin to their lapels to seem intelligent. Pessimism is, in truth, an ease of spirit, a luxury of happy people, as I wrote somewhere. It is hard to be an optimist. It is a matter of urgency that we should be optimists.

For us Angolans, there is not even – this is true – any *alternative* to optimism. We wake up, we read the papers and we laugh at what would make a Swede or Dutchman cry. We laugh because, despite the news, we are alive. We are still alive. We laugh because we breathe. We laugh because we hear, in the next room, the giggles of our children. We laugh because we know how to dance. We laugh because we *can* dance. We laugh because hope fuels laughter. We laugh because laughter is subversive. We laugh because laughter is revolutionary. To laugh is to resist.

"Laughter," wrote Eça de Queirós, "is the oldest and still the most devastating form of criticism. If a laugh goes around an institution seven times, the institution falls down."

"A good laugh," said Nabokov, "is the best pesticide."

This evening I had dinner in Chiado with a group of friends: Kalaf, Ângelo Torres, Orlando Sérgio and Victor Hugo Mendes (who has left Huambo and is back in Lisbon). The conversation centred around a completely mad interview that Fernando Alvim, the former visual artist now reinvented as an art dealer for the Angolan upper classes, gave yesterday morning on the radio station Luanda Antena Comercial, in which he insulted almost everybody. It was a sort of machine-gun fire of insults. He attacked Pepetela, suggesting his criticisms of the regime were those of a mentally handicapped person; he attacked Jacques dos Santos, calling him racist; he attacked Aline Frazão and Rede Angola, etc.

We spoke, too, of the imprisonment of journalists. Of the unprecedented illnesses spreading like weeds among the mountains of litter on Luanda's streets, of yet another corrupt man accusing of treason and of "speaking ill of Angola" all those who dare to raise their voices to call out injustice, incompetence and unfairness and, in doing so, opting for the old tactic of conflating the country with those who have hijacked it.

The news is not good, but our souls are greater than the despair. So we laugh. We laugh at those who want us silent. We laugh at those who abandoned their art and sold out, and who would like us all to be for sale. We laugh at those who want us paralysed with fear. Laughter is the weapon with which we face down wickedness and stupidity. Melancholy is a capitulation. Melancholy is a blindness that prevents us from seeing the obvious. The obvious is the life thriving around us. The obvious consists of the possibilities that persist, even when everything around us seems impossible. Resisting is almost an addiction.

From magical to autophagic realism

Few questions irritate a Latin American writer travelling in Europe as much as those that try to evaluate their potential belonging or link to so-called "magical realism". African writers also rarely escape the question. Recently, sharing a table with Luiz Ruffato in Frankfurt, the issue came up. Ruffato quipped that the majority of Brazilians do not feel Latin American. He pointed out that Brazilian writers did not even form part of the famous boom in Latin American literature, driven, in the late 1960s, by the success of *One Hundred Years of Solitude* by Gabriel García Márquez – the work that, while not the movement's foundtional text, most successfully popularised it. "Brazilian writers," claimed Ruffato, "aren't even usually included in anthologies of Latin American authors."

Latin American writers are weary of the fact that people want to limit them to one literary movement, always the same, especially as most of them do not identify with it. "I'm an urban writer," they usually reply, in a vague suggestion that magical realism is not only rather archaic in literary terms, but socially, too. Magical realism might be to literature what country duos are to popular music. Among Brazilian writers there are many who, doubtless, would sooner be mistaken for European than Latin American. They are not bothered if someone suggests a certain closeness between their work and that of Umberto Eco or Saramago. (Saramago, incidentally, did wander the paths of magical realism.) They are annoyed, however, if someone suggests they have been contaminated by reading García Márquez. Not Jorge Luis Borges; having Borges as an influence is acceptable. But Borges, as we know, was a European writer born in the least African country in the Americas, who chose to die and remain in Switzerland.

The truth is that Jorge Amado and, therefore, Brazil, were a few years ahead of the rest of Latin America in the literary use of the fantastical integrated naturally with the everyday. Miguel Ángel Asturias published *Men of Maize* in 1949. The novel, which mixes the supernatural, dreamlike world of the Mayas and the reality of Guatemalan farmers, is widely considered to have founded the genre. The extraordinary *Pedro Páramo* by Juan Rulfo, which so influenced García Márquez, is from 1955. Yet *Sea of Death*, by Amado, published for the first time in 1936, draws on Brazil's African mythology to build characters and justify certain actions. Yemanjá is a character in the book.

The path opened by Amado – Orisha mythology, such an incredibly rich universe – has only rarely been revisited by other Brazilian writers. In that conversation of ours in Frankfurt, Ruffato made some strong statements. He called attention to the fact that Brazilian literature today is being produced mainly by people from the middle and upper classes, who rarely attempt to leave their small, sheltered, urban world. Ruffato bemoans the fact that these writers do not bring into literature the lives of workers and the least fortunate in Brazilian society. I am particularly troubled by the absence of important characters of African heritage and their world. I do not believe, however, that the explanation for these absences lies in the social origins of the writers.

The lack of interest in African mythology in Brazil is perhaps – paradoxically – related to the huge national and international success of Jorge Amado. The writer from Bahia suffers to this day from the famous prejudice of success: *an author with millions of readers cannot be good*. Real quality is to be found in the little-known author, loved by few, and preferably a recluse someplace at the end of the world. On the other hand, there does persist in Brazil a small racist mentality, which, above all in literature, continues to privilege those who are European or North American, disdaining Africa and Latin America.

It is even harder to explain the absence of characters of African heritage in modern Brazilian fiction. The few authors to break the rule – off the top of my head, I am thinking of Ana Maria Gonçalves, Paulo Lins and Nei Lopes – are themselves black or mixed-race. With this in mind, Ruffato's complaint about the predominance of middle-class and upper-class writers, and their lack of interest in the life of the majority of the population, seems to make more sense, also explaining the sad absence of colour on the pages of contemporary Brazilian literature. Between this autophagic realism and Afro-Latin magical realism, sincerely, I prefer the latter.

Tuesday, 9 February 2016

I have been responding to a kind of serialised interview with Cara Benson, a friend of Daniel Hahn's, which is to be published on an American literary blog called *Bookslut*. Every week she sends two or three questions.

CB: Can you give us any examples of ways in which reality frequently overtakes fiction in Angola?

JEA: Newspapers in Angola, and particularly the *Jornal de Angola*, which is one of Luanda's only two daily papers and which belongs to the government, do with some frequency include stories that involve fantastical situations and even, occasionally, beings from popular mythology such as kiandas, which are aquatic divinities. I remember one news story about two children who had disappeared at the mouth of the River Quanza. A fisherman dived underwater and found the children alive, at the bottom of the river, imprisoned by an old man with a long white beard. The children were recovered. The old man was locked in a house, with guards on the door, but the following morning he was no longer there. That would have been a kianda.

I also saw a TV news report about a man who'd had a spell put on him by his wife after he cheated on her. The man woke up with a small wound in his chest out of which flowed not blood, but water. The man was interviewed on television, wrapped in a soaking wet blanket. Though I guess he must have transformed into a river by now. I suspect Angola must be a country with vast rivers, given the frequency with which men betray their wives. And given the power of those wives.

CB: Do you feel close to Ludo [the main character of Agualusa's novel *A General Theory of Oblivion*]? Like her, you sit in silence while you write, catching snippets of dialogue, watching people walk past the window . . .

JEA: Yes, it's true. There are a lot of similarities between the small miracle that is writing a novel and Ludo's silent, albeit attentive, existence. In the first place, writers are witnesses. They observe. A writer works on an island surrounded by voices on all sides. Ludo wrote on the walls, and, as she didn't have much space and she also needed to save on charcoal, what she wrote was dry and pared down to the bone. This exercise of paring down is something that concerns me as a writer, too. I spend more time cutting than writing.

Private drama, public comedy

If you want to really get to know somebody, divorce them. Wars cause a person's soul to develop the most unexpected deformities. Divorce does the same, but without the excuse of 'orders from above'. Men and women who are normally lovely, generous, polite and model citizens turn from one moment to the next into wild animals, frothing at the mouth, ready to destroy, with two or three sharp phrases, the reputation of the person who – months earlier – they had sworn to love until the end. My grandmother warned me many times: "Don't get married, son, but if, by some misfortune, it does happen, then never get separated. There's only one mistake worse than marriage – divorce."

There is no more fearsome foe than an ex-wife or ex-husband. The rise of social media has opened new possibilities for the abandoned party's ancient desire for revenge. I always remember, with a certain terror, the day I helped a friend pack his bags and leave his family home. That same afternoon, his ex-wife posted on Facebook: "You can rest easy, Frank, I'll never tell anyone about that little secret of yours." Six thousand 'likes' by the end of the day. Three hundred comments: *Go on, tell us, is it really that small?*

I am at a stage in my life where I attend more funerals than weddings. I think funerals are more honest. There is, for sure, the awkward part when everyone lies, inventing qualities the departed did not so much as value. Worse: pretending to have forgotten the three or four defects that redeemed them as a human being. In general, however, the tears are sincere and the pain very real. Funerals are dire ceremonies, but purifying. Looking death in the eye makes any person a bit humbler. It helps us, furthermore, to put into context the tiny dramas of our daily lives and better appreciate the good times. Ultimately, funerals are permanent events. I have never been twice to the funeral of the same friend. Weddings, on the other hand, have an increasing tendency to become displays of vanity, where almost everything is false, starting with the declarations of eternal love. While the couple kiss, lawyers prepare the divorce papers. (Lawyers, of course, love weddings. By a lawyer's logic, the grander the wedding, the more prosperous the divorce.)

From a certain point in litigation onwards, the couple can no longer exchange two sentences without one of them taking ill and being hospitalised, and so they begin to communicate through the intermediaries of their respective lawyers. Terrible idea. It is like asking a pyromaniac – or, rather, two pyromaniacs – to help control a fire, like asking a shark for help when you are tired of swimming. The process drags on. The accusations rise in tone. Worse than washing your dirty laundry in public is washing the public along with your dirty laundry.

My best friend married the wife of his – until then – best friend. Many people find this strange. To me it seems, of all the evils, a lesser one. If we must lose the love of our life, let it be to our best friend. Our best friend knows our secrets, mistakes and defects, and has already forgiven them. What is really bad is losing your wife to an enemy. In the first scenario, when, eventually, our best friend separates from the ex-love of our life, we can meet up and cry together, or laugh together, or both.

There are many films about divorce, and almost all of them are comedies. Two that immediately spring to mind are *The Break-Up*, with Jennifer Anniston and Vince Vaughan, and *Intolerable Cruelty*, with George Clooney and Catherine Zeta-Jones. Dramas about divorce are far less popular. I think this is because what, to us, seems like an intolerable ordeal when we are the ones going through it – and while we are going through it – looks like a comedy to those on the outside; varying in stupidity, incongruence, boredom and extravagance, but always a comedy.

It is much harder to make good comedies about funerals. At a push, ration four weddings for every funeral, and then, yes, it could work.

Moral of the story: in divorce, try to look at the whole process from the outside. Remember what Charlie Chaplin said: "Life is a tragedy when seen in close-up, but a comedy in long shot."

Monday, 15 February 2016

I've come to Maputo, the capital of Mozambique, to give a creative writing workshop. The participants, who are mostly very young, seem to have similar concerns to other writers and aspiring writers I've worked with in Brazil, Angola and Portugal. I ask them to tell me why they want to write. I take down notes: *for the pleasure of writing*; *because writing helps me to understand the world and to understand myself*; or *because writing works as a kind of therapy*.

Over the years, many well established writers have offered similar responses to this same question: "I am a person who likes to write, who has perhaps been able to express some of his preoccupations, his intimate concerns, by projecting these onto paper, practising a kind of poor man's psychoanalysis, without a couch, without anything," wrote Carlos Drummond de Andrade.

Fernando Pessoa said practically the same, but in a different way: "I write to save my soul." For his part, José Saramago began writing because he "didn't want to die". He then progressed to writing in order "to understand".

"I am under the impression that we write for one of two reasons: either because we experience an excess [...] or because we experience a lack," wrote João Cabral de Melo Neto, adding: "I feel I lack something. Therefore, writing is a way to complete myself."

There are also those who write in order to be loved (García Márquez), or because they don't have green eyes (Lúcio Cardoso).

A few of my young, aspiring writers, here in Maputo, provided answers that you don't often hear (anymore). A number of them said they wrote to "give a voice to others". Two young women claimed they wrote because they believed writing could change society. I tried to get a better understanding of each of them. One, close to tears, told me she'd begun writing a blog, under a pseudonym, to expose the difficulties faced by Mozambican women in their day-to-day lives. She used the pseudonym so her husband wouldn't find out: "Men here in Mozambique won't tolerate a woman who reads, much less one who writes or publishes a book. My husband would beat me if he knew." The other woman agreed. She had an almost identical story. The pair have a point of reference in Paulina Chiziane, the first woman to publish a novel in Mozambique. Today Paulina, who has had books translated into numerous languages, still faces an enormous amount of resistance inside her own country, and even from within the literary scene.

In countries such as Mozambique, literature is characterised by a sense of emergency. While it is necessary everywhere, it becomes even more necessary in regions plagued by all kinds of social problems, which are still emerging from violent conflicts and in the midst of a process of consolidating identities.

In contrast to Angola, a country with some kind of urban tradition, Mozambique is essentially rural. Apart from the Island of Mozambique or the small city of Quelimane, which is steeped in history, with a long and complex tradition of miscegenation, all other Mozambican cities are recent. The majority of families that today inhabit the principal Mozambican urban centres arrived from the countryside, and are still adapting to life on asphalt. Many of the conflicts and social problems – including the challenging situation for women, victims of an exacerbated machismo – have their origins in this difficult process of adaptation. Literature can operate as a mechanism for reconciliation between these worlds. The young women who enrol in my literary workshop publish their texts on blogs and social networks in order to denounce their treatment and spark debate, in the hope of starting a revolution in people's attitudes.

"Here, we writers are often stopped in the street by people asking us to tell their story. All of them have wonderful stories," says Mia Couto, adding that the only way this generosity can possibly be repaid is to respond to their requests.

Mozambique, meanwhile, currently finds itself in the midst of a process of self-invention. As in other countries, as always happens in these situations, literature has been called upon to take part in this process. It is no coincidence that two of the pre-eminent names in Mozambican fiction, Mia Couto and Ungulani Ba Ka Khosa, are, each after their own fashion, working on novels that draw upon and recreate one of the most controversial and monumental figures in proto-nationalist mythology: Ngungunyane, the last emperor of Gaza.

In contrast to the praise of emptiness and the turn towards nihilism and tired self-contemplation – characteristic of some Western literary trends – Africans are proposing a return to the essential, with the essential being the fight for human dignity, listening to others and knowing how to make their voices heard.

Something maybe like a forgiveness

I'm writing this piece in Maputo. I've come to Mozambique, at the invitation of the Fernando Couto Foundation, to give a short creative writing workshop. I also took part in a discussion with Mia Couto during which we talked about our books, and, in a more general way, about creative writing. Listening to my students at the literary workshop, and then to many other Mozambicans during informal debates, my thoughts turned once again to a subject that has long troubled me. What is the best way of overcoming the collective wounds resulting from a civil war – to remember, or to forget?

For years, I defended the South African solution – that is to say, the implementation of a truth and reconciliation commission. This commission's objective was to bring victims of apartheid and their tormentors face to face, as a way of examining and recording the crimes of the past, and, most importantly, of achieving genuine reconciliation. The perpetrators would confess to their crimes, obtaining forgiveness. The victims would be granted the spiritual peace that can only be attained through forgiving.

Mia always argued in favour of the opposite: for him, to talk would be to awaken old ghosts. Silence seemed to him to be the best balm for healing the wounds. Many of the guerrillas and soldiers responsible for the terrible atrocities now distance themselves from these acts, alleging that it wasn't they, but rather the demons inside them, who were involved in the atrocities in question. It is rhetoric we hear in other regions where genocides have taken place, such as Rwanda.

In recent months, the spectre of war has once again hovered over Mozambique. In the north of the country, shots have been exchanged between RENAMO guerrillas and government forces, with casualties on both sides. This situation has led the defenders of silence, such as Mia, to partially review their position. The truth, however, is that in South Africa there have also been signs of unrest. Anyone visiting the country even briefly will have understood that reconciliation has not been accomplished. The deep divisions caused by the apartheid regime persist to this day, splitting communities along cultural lines as well as skin colour. It is never easy to forgive. Or to be forgiven.

I don't look kindly upon the evangelical churches that have been gaining ground in Brazil, and, from there, Angola, Mozambique and many other countries. However, it seems impossible not to recognise the fundamental role these churches play in the rehabilitation of criminals. Evangelical preachers are prepared to go down to Hell, into the prisons, in order to convert tormented souls. These pastors – like the guerrillas I mentioned – believe that people are forced into violence by powerful demons. Once these demons have been exorcised, anyone can start a new life, free from guilt or sin.

In all likelihood, what is required is dialogue and, at the same time, a cultivation of, if not forgetting, then at least a kind of compromise with erasure. Or, to quote Fernando Pessoa:

> Will there not be, after all,
> for the things that are,
> not death, but alternately
> another sort of end
> or a higher reason –
> something maybe
> like a forgiveness?[**]

[**] Based on the translation by Steffen Dix in Portuguese Modernisms: Multiple Perspectives in Literature and the Visual Arts.

That precise instant of glory

On two or three occasions, I've heard the Portuguese writer Gonçalo M. Tavares tell the story of a time when, while writing, in a deep, trancelike state, he failed to notice he'd left a tap running in the bathroom, from which water was gushing out, taking over the whole apartment. Only once the water had risen to his ankles did he emerge from his fiction and awaken to reality – and reality was sopping wet.

It's a good story. I might not have believed it had it come from the mouth of another writer. But, knowing Gonçalo, and, in particular, knowing the kinds of books he's been producing, I'm not so surprised. At forty-five years old, Gonçalo is the most widely translated Portuguese-language writer, as well as the recipient of the greatest number of international prizes. Almost every one of Gonçalo's books appears to have been written by a very old child. He observes the simplest things – leads *us* to observe the simplest things – as if each of them was extraordinary. Or rather, he leads us to understand that each of them *is* extraordinary. It isn't surprising to learn that these texts were written, if not in a quasi-mystical trancelike state, then at least in a state of creative rapture during which the author absents himself from the physical world (a physical world that is subject to flooding).

In a famous letter to Adolfo Casais Monteiro, dated 13 January 1935, Fernando Pessoa wrote of how he came up with, or how he embodied, Alberto Caeiro:

> I remember one day playing a trick on Sá-Carneiro, inventing a bucolic poet, of the complex variety, and introducing him, I don't remember how, into some kind of reality. I spent a few days developing the poet, but achieved nothing. On the day I had finally given up – it was 8 March, 1914 – I went over to a tall dresser, and, taking some paper, began to write, still standing, as I do whenever I get the chance. I wrote thirty-something poems on the trot, in a kind of ecstasy, the nature of

which I could not possibly define. That day was the triumph of my life, and I shall never have another like it. I began with the title, *The Keeper of Sheep*. What followed was the arrival of someone inside me, whom I named Alberto Caeiro from the start. Forgive me the absurdity of this sentence: my master appeared inside me. That was my immediate sensation.

The Portuguese author António Lobo Antunes doesn't like Pessoa ("Fernando Pessoa bores me to death," he stated recently), but he shares with the poet the notion that writing implies a kind of elevation. Repeatedly, in countless interviews, he has insisted upon the thesis that good books, the best moments of a book, occur unexpectedly, almost independent of their author's will: "I don't write what I want, I write what the voices dictate, what the book itself wishes to be. [...] In a bad book, the person writes what they want to write. In a good book, the person writes what the book wishes to be written."

In line with this thesis, Lobo Antunes has even gone as far as to argue that books should be published without their authors' names. He added, laughing: "I find it very strange that I get paid for them, because I'm not certain they belong to me."

There are those who become irritated listening to Lobo Antunes. António Guerreiro, one of Portugal's most formidable critics, has suggested the writer's comments are nothing more than an extension of his own fiction:

> It's this theological conception of literary creation – the writer, possessed by a demon, becomes an intermediary between men and gods – which António Lobo Antunes has long been asserting in his interviews. And he asserts this not only about himself, but about writers in general, these creatures that "appear to be in contact with some higher power". We would be foolish, or at least ingenuous, to take his words seriously rather than interpret them as a great parody.

I disagree. I don't even regard Lobo Antunes's statements as a sign of arrogance. On the contrary, I see them as a show of humility. Clearly,

he is aware that his books come from someplace inside him. What Lobo Antunes, Pessoa and Tavares are telling us is that they write best when they forget that they are writing. When they allow themselves to be caught up in their passion for the written word. This, applied here to literature, can also apply to any other human activity. Who, at some moment in their lives, in some precise and unrivalled instant of glory, has not experienced a similar emotion?

When passion takes control of us, we are greater than ourselves. We are, in some apt and mysterious way, all of humanity.

Lynchings

I was not yet twelve years old when I witnessed a lynching.

I saw a boy fleeing on a bicycle. A man started chasing him on foot, and suddenly there were five, ten, an impassioned rabble, running, yelling, flinging stones. I remember being entirely, wholeheartedly, agonisingly, on the side of the fleeing boy. There was nothing I could do to help him. Moments before, I'd been reading in the sunshine, out on the balcony. Now the boy was pedalling for his life, down below, between a red dirt road and a vast wasteland covered in wild grass.

Ever since then, I've always been on the side of the person who, all alone, finds themselves pursued by a mob. I care little about what may have been done by the running boy; the man raising his hand to fend off a blow; the woman who, weeping, faces the insults of a gang of predators.

The emergence of social media signalled the arrival of a new platform for lynch mobs. I am well aware that this comparison will always seem excessive. Words, no matter how sharp, no matter how hard or heavy, do not crack heads. Words, no matter how poisonous, cannot kill. On the other hand, this new stage has the power to bring many thousands of people together within minutes, all yelling at the top of their lungs. The stupidity of virtual crowds is every bit as concrete as that of real crowds.

Practically every week some public figure suffers persecution on social media. Last week it was the turn of Brazilian actress Glória Pires, and, in Portugal, of a young writer and political commentator – for whom I do not harbour the least bit of sympathy – named Henrique Raposo. Pires was attacked for the narrative economy, shall we say, of her commentary on the broadcast of the 2016 Oscars. The actress managed to turn the situation around with intelligence and a good sense of humour, creating a line of T-shirts emblazoned with some of the conspicuously brief statements at the heart of the controversy: I'M TERRIBLE AT PREDICTIONS; I COULDN'T SAY; GREAT, LOVED IT.

Raposo is being persecuted for having published a book, *Alentejo, Promised Land*, which offers a very negative and highly reductive view of this region of Portugal. Internet users have called for the burning of the book; others, for the death of its author.

Raposo has become infamous for the insensitivity of his statements, many of which are xenophobic and racist. In one interview he gave recently to promote the book, he suggested that, in the Alentejo, suicide was seen as something trivial, as was rape: "Old women from the Alentejo don't even possess the word 'rape' to describe the many abuses they have suffered." The book launch on the eighth of this month, at a well-known Lisbon bookshop, will take place with police protection.

I disagree with nearly all of what Raposo thinks and writes. In fact, I believe he writes without thinking. It is one thing, however, to disagree with what he writes, and to publish this opposition, and quite another to try to prevent him from writing, and burn his books.

Some years ago, during an interview in Luanda, I stated that I couldn't understand why the government insisted on promoting the poetry of Agostinho Neto, the first president of Angola, which to me had always seemed very mediocre. João Pinto, a well-known jurist, political commentator and a deputy of the ruling party, wrote an article calling for my arrest. He went further, arguing for the return of the death penalty and for me to face a firing squad. According to him, I'd not only offended a former President and national hero, but also a divinity, given that Neto had been a *quilamba* – in other words, an interpreter of mermaids.

Over the following weeks, many more hateful texts were published. My phone number was targeted for death threats. I was told people were burning my books. At the time, this was all very frightening. Today, I can look back and laugh. I recall how difficult it was to explain to European journalists that I stood accused of having offended an interpreter of mermaids. Naturally, I ended up turning this episode into literature. In Europe and North America, they read this and call it magical realism.

The burners of books are afraid not of the ideas books promote, but of their own inability to offer a response to them. Those who join in with virtual mobs to threaten or belittle someone are almost as dangerous as those who run through the streets, chucking stones – and even more cowardly.

I close my eyes and once again see the boy on the bicycle. A stone struck his head and he collapsed. The mob swarmed over him. On that day, I lost my innocence.

Mad not to dream

Utopias and dystopias are powerful exercises of the imagination that help us to understand the errors of our current political models, and to project and build better ones.

We're living in tumultuous times. Uncertain times. After Barack Obama, a model of elegance and intelligence whether or not you agree with his ideas, nobody believed the US could go back to someone (or something) as terrible, for example, as George W. Bush – and that's when Donald Trump arrived. To begin with, it seemed like nothing more than a minor error in the system, an amusing spectacle before the serious action, like circus clowns preceding the trapeze artists. Now it is starting to look like what it always was: a nightmare.

In Brazil – a country whose process of democratisation I followed enthusiastically, and which I later watched grow, prosper and overcome inflation and unemployment (before the current crisis) – there are those who today head out onto the streets clamouring for a return to dictatorship. Looking on from outside, it's hard to understand. Looking on from inside, it's even harder.

Giving up on democracy because you have a few corrupt politicians is like cutting off your head to ease a migraine. Dictatorships tend to be far more corrupt than democracies. The difference between a dictatorship and a democracy, in terms of corruption, is that in a democracy, the corrupt cannot always sleep for fear the police may enter their homes in the middle of the night; under a dictatorship, it is the honest who cannot sleep for fear the police may enter their homes in the middle of the night. A democracy is only as advanced as its capacity to fight corruption – in particular, corruption in the world of politics. I'd go as far as to say that the more advanced a democracy, the less wealthy its politicians will be. I like The Netherlands because the prime minister rides to work on a bicycle. I love Cape Verde because, among so many other good reasons, the government is based in Praia (Portuguese for "beach"), and also because, on entering any given neighbourhood bar, you can never be sure whether the guy sitting next to you strumming the *cavaquinho* is a humble baker or the President of the Republic.

There are no good dictatorships, just as there are no good illnesses. There are advanced and vigorous democracies, and democracies in crisis; fragile democracies; democracies in need of a new beginning. What you certainly won't find is a democracy that can be advantageously replaced by one dictatorship or another. No democracy is so bad that it manages to be worse than the best dictatorship.

When times of uncertainty and turbulence are analysed, at a distance of centuries, they are often shown to have signalled important historical advancements. The people who awoke in Paris on the morning of 14 July 1789 could not have imagined that the confrontations taking place that day, which culminated in the storming of the Bastille, would give rise not only to fundamental political changes, but – more importantly – to positive changes in attitude, particularly the enshrining of the idea that all men are born equal and remain free and equal in rights. For many in France, those were days of utter terror, which witnessed a world's end. But today, looking back, what we see is the beginning of a new world.

Times such as the ones in which we are living are prone to engendering monsters. However, they are also capable of generating huge and powerful dreams. Now more than ever, it is urgent that we revisit old utopias and project new ones. Thomas More's book was an inspiration for, among others, Pierre-Joseph Proudhon, one of the fathers of anarchism. Even those who have never heard of Proudhon are surely aware of his most famous proclamation, "Property is theft"; and many repeat it without fully understanding it. Some of Proudhon's antiauthoritarian ideas are even more relevant – and less 'utopian' – today than they were when he first conceived them.

Communism is dead, and capitalism threatens to kill us all. Corruption in the political classes, the refugee crises, global warming … all are problems resulting from the very nature of the capitalist system. It is imperative that we look for other paths. It is not madness to dream. Today, it would be madness *not* to dream. However, we must do so with the certainty that those paths, those dreams, can only be discovered using peaceful and democratic means. Democracy, that primordial utopia, cannot be called into question. Its defence falls to all of us.

The zombie's bite

Last Thursday morning, Kalaf Epalanga phoned me from Zaventem Airport, Brussels, to tell me that a terrorist attack had just taken place. Kalaf had landed in the Belgian capital, arriving from Geneva, to catch a flight to Lisbon. While looking for his boarding gate, he had heard the explosions.

"Why?!" he asked, close to tears. "Why do they do this?"

I tried to calm him down. I'm not the ideal person to reassure someone who has just survived an attack at an airport. Airports unnerve me. I was afraid of airports even before they became preferred targets for terrorist attacks. What frightens me even more than terrorists (because, evidently, I have never confronted one) is the whole system of security that surrounds airports, supposedly to prevent tragedies like the one that had just taken place at Zaventem.

After my friend hung up, I sat down to think. What is in the heart of a man-bomb? I don't suppose the man-bomb ever asks himself the opposite question: *What is in the heart of the innocents?*

This, perhaps, is the principal difference between an ordinary citizen and a citizen who decides to turn himself into a man-bomb – the man-bomb is incapable of empathy. Every one of us can imagine ourselves in the place of another, which is why we are left shocked and horrified when we see images such as those that came in from Belgium, of the perplexed, bloodied victims, the air still heavy with dust from the explosions.

Amid the devastating chaos that reigns in Syria, in the smoking ruins of its cities, laboratories – more or less clandestine, more or less improvised – have sprung up to produce a drug called "Captagon", synthesised from caffeine and amphetamines. Captagon, a commercial brand of the drug fenethylline hydrochloride, was first produced in the 1960s as a way of treating sleep disorders and bouts of depression. It has, however, become the drug of choice for jihadis and man-bombs. Captagon diminishes fear responses, inducing a sense of euphoria; most importantly of all, it seems capable of shutting down any feelings of empathy.

None of this should surprise us. The history of war walks hand in hand with the history of drugs. For every war, a different drug.

A man-bomb is a bit like a zombie, one of the living dead, who bites in order to infect healthy people. Man-bombs blow themselves up with the sole objective of transforming ordinary citizens into fanatics just like themselves, but rooting for the other side. What Islamic terrorism intends is for the West to react with identical fury, first against Daesh, then against any eventual suspects and, finally, against all peace-loving European Muslims – the vast majority of European Muslims – in order to justify all-out religious war.

Left dazed by the media outcry, it's easy to convince ourselves that the recent terrorist attacks in the United Kingdom, France and now in Belgium are a new kind of threat, something Europeans have never faced before. Nothing could be further from the truth. The 1970s and '80s were, by far, the years that witnessed the greatest number of people killed on European soil as victims of terrorism. Far-left separatist groups such as ETA in Spain, the IRA in the United Kingdom and the Red Brigades in Italy were responsible, during those two decades, for dozens of terrible attacks. The majority of these groups have now disappeared – largely due to a lack of popular support rather than the result of police pressure.

I have met former militants of the Red Army Faction / Baader-Meinhof Group and other now-defunct terrorist organisations. They struck me as normal people. Yet whenever someone tried to question them about their past, they would shrug and shut down. I never heard any of them defend their past actions. I presume, though I could be committing the sin of placing excessive faith in humanity, that the majority are still struggling to understand what happened to them, like zombies who have returned to a human state.

A few days ago, I read an interview with the Cameroonian philosopher Achille Mbembe published in the Portuguese newspaper *Jornal de Notícias*. According to Mbembe, we are living through a period of civilisational regression, with outbreaks of intolerance cropping up everywhere: "The more means we possess for the discovery of other people, the more we aspire not to know them.

Never in the history of humanity have we had so much opportunity to discover other cultures, societies and histories, and yet, indifference is increasingly the norm. This is the paradox we are witnessing and which we must resolve."

I would prefer not to have to agree with Mbembe. But it's difficult.

Trained not to smile

Each of us has their own particular paranoia. Mine is border police. I've been through half a dozen unpleasant experiences with them. During the time when the Angolan regime was emerging as a dictatorship (of the proletariat), the border police were assiduously trained not to smile. Training an Angolan not to smile is a tall order. Angolans, just like Brazilians, like to smile. They smile elegantly and proficiently.

Interrogations would take place inside stuffy little rooms. The border agent would open up the passport, leaf through it and then fix the traveller with a long, intensely penetrating metallic stare. It wasn't exactly an interrogation, because they hardly spoke. The best ones didn't speak at all. Their silences pushed travellers towards the most perilous verbosity:

"Is there something wrong with my passport?"

Silence.

"Have I done something I shouldn't have?"

Silence.

No enemy of the revolution could withstand even five minutes of such devastating silence. I, who had nothing to confess, would invent crimes against state security: "I read a lot," I would say, "including books by bourgeois authors ..." But the police never believed me, and let me go. I would leave the airport feeling exhausted and humiliated.

A few days ago, upon entering the United States at the invitation of my North American publisher to take part in a series of literary discussions, I went through a very similar experience – but without the silences. When the blonde border security officer turned his sombre face toward me, I shuddered:

"What is your occupation?"

"I'm a writer."

His small blue eyes flashed, mistrustfully: "What kind of books do you write?"

I recalled the Portuguese writer Agustina Bessa-Luís, who was once asked this same question. "The Dostoyevsky kind," replied Agustina. I wasn't quite so bold: "Good books."

The officer ignored my attempt at light-heartedness. "About what?"

A terrifying question. I hesitated for a couple of moments: "About memory and forgetting. About questions of identity …"

"And God?"

"What about God?"

"Are you a Muslim?"

"No."

"You're not a Muslim? Are you sure? Have you been to Syria? Iraq? Afghanistan?"

I thought this officer must have been trained by agents of the former GDR. It was as if no smile had ever lit his face. It was as if they'd removed all twelve, or forty, or seventy-three (the exact number varies depending on the source) of the muscles responsible for forming smiles.

In January, during the literary festival in The Hague, I met Alaa Al Aswany, a large, affable man – a dentist by trade – who had been one of the faces of the Arab Spring. We exchanged grievances about the difficulties we faced when travelling through Europe these days because of our respective Arab appearances (his more genuine than mine). He told me how, one afternoon, upon disembarking in Paris following a long literary peregrination, he'd found himself facing an unfriendly passport control officer.

"What have you come to France to do?" asked the officer.

Alaa, tired of having to respond to the same question a thousand times, experienced a moment of madness: "I've come to buy cows!"

"Cows?! But on your passport it says you're a dentist!"

"So? Do you suppose a dentist can't take an interest in cows? You have magnificent cows in this country. I'm going to buy my cows and then take them back to Cairo with me. Is that allowed?!" The officer shook his head, stunned, and returned the passport.

I experienced a similar moment of madness when, after twenty minutes of incoherent questioning, the blonde officer asked me to provide him with a summary of the book I'd be presenting in New York.

"It's about the great artistry of a man who blows himself to smithereens," I said.

No, I didn't say that. I told him the truth, or something resembling the truth, and was allowed in.

Towards an ethics of spitting

I absolutely love Eça de Queiroz, and *The Maias* in particular. My favourite pages are those involving Dâmaso Salcede, a petty scoundrel and bootlicker who, at a certain point, publishes a pathetic article criticising Carlos da Maia. João da Ega, Carlos's best friend and an alter ego of Eça de Queiroz himself, goes to Dâmaso's house and demands that he either retract or take part in a duel. Poor Dâmaso refuses both options. Ega explains to him that, in this case, Carlos da Maia will have to resort to extreme measures: "If he met him henceforth, wherever it might be, in the street or in the theatre, he would spit in his face." Jean Wyllys's historic act (I think we are justified in calling it historic) of spitting at Jair Bolsonaro seems to me to be far more legitimate than Carlos da Maia's spitting at Dâmaso Salcede. The latter involved a lady's dignity, the former the dignity of an entire country. Bolsonaro's declarations, which have had (and continue to have) great repercussions in the international press, do immense harm to Brazil's image abroad. Anyone who says such things is not on the left or the right: they're behind! Far, far behind, in a time and a society in which torture was viewed as a refined form of entertainment for gentlemen. The best thing to do, then, would be to send Mr Bolsonaro back to that remote age. Because obvious technical difficulties make that impossible, he should instead be sent to those territories still occupied by Daesh, the closest thing we currently have to the Middle Ages. Bolsonaro will surely fit in well there, in those harsh deserts, living among torturers and rapists, among men who hate women and stone homosexuals to death.

I imagine that Bolsonaro sees himself as a true Brazilian nationalist. But, at least to my still somewhat naïve foreigner's eyes, Bolsonaro represents the opposite: he is the Anti-Brazil. Bolsonaro has as much to do with Brazil (which I love) as a polar bear with a savannah. To my ears, *"Bolsonaro brasileiro"* sounds like an unpleasant oxymoron.

Notwithstanding the heavy atmosphere of terse aggression that has established itself in Brazil over the last few months, Brazilians continue to be seen abroad as an affectionate, celebratory, tolerant and generous people. On many journeys have I witnessed the value of a Brazilian passport. One need only say "I'm Brazilian", and the smiles break out. Sometimes I myself pretend to be Brazilian in order to receive better treatment in remote countries.

To spit in someone's face is a universal expression of disdain. For some anthropologists it signifies symbolic regurgitation, in the vein of *I've eaten you and now I'm spitting you out, for you are completely indigestible*; for others, it represents the threat of contamination.

Illustrious spitters of our time include Brad Pitt, Naomi Campbell and Justin Bieber (he has spat in the face of a DJ, at fans from a hotel balcony, at a woman in a gym, and so on). Football players, known for spitting on the turf, also occasionally project their athletic fluids onto the faces of adversaries or referees (Falcão, Diego Costa, Neto). It's harder to imagine similar situations taking place during chess games, perhaps because chess players aren't in the habit of spitting on the board. Even Bobby Fischer, renowned for his explosive temper, never used his spittle in public except to land it on a document from US authorities that prohibited him entering Yugoslavia.

All the incidents of spitting listed above clearly constitute cases of simple bad manners. They have nothing to do with the aristocratic and noble spitting of a Carlos da Maia. Quite the opposite: Jean Wyllys may have managed to rehabilitate spitting as an honourable act. One could question its elegance or the hygiene of it but not, I believe, its righteousness. Maybe it would be best if Wyllys were to stick to metaphorical spitting ("I spit on your soul!"); if the Bahian deputy were to go around spitting on every scoundrel who came along, he'd end up dying of dehydration.

On the other hand, sometimes the villainy is of such magnitude, and so shameless, that we might even consider hiring professional spitters. In a similar way to wailers, who are paid to cry at funerals, these professional spitters would go around official ceremonies spitting in the terrified faces of corrupt politicians and noted scoundrels. It might actually achieve something.

In case of emergency, use poetry

I attended a concert by Caetano Veloso and Gilberto Gil at Lisbon's Coliseu dos Recreios, during which the two friends celebrated fifty years of an extraordinary shared career. The stunningly beautiful, historic venue was completely packed. I imagine many of the Portuguese in the audience had never been to Brazil. But I am absolutely certain they recognised themselves in many of those songs.

If there exists such a thing as a Brazilian identity, then there is no doubt that the songs of Gil and Caetano, along with those of Chico Buarque, Djavan, Milton Nascimento, Martinho da Vila and so many others were – are – a big part of it. More interesting and less discussed is the fact that this extraordinarily rich cultural heritage has continued to form identities *outside* Brazil. The Portuguese people who were there to hear Gil and Caetano were looking for a certain idea of Brazil, for sure, but they were also there in search of a part of themselves.

Brazil came to me through poetry. I was born in Huambo, Angola, a young city built 2,000 metres above sea level, in a very green region with a gentle climate. When I was born, Huambo was almost a European city surrounded on all sides by Africa. My mother taught Portuguese and French. She loved theatre. At one point she founded a student theatre group, which made its debut with a performance of João Cabral de Melo Neto's *Life and Death of Severino*, with music by Chico Buarque. At the time I must have been eleven or twelve years old. I saw the play several times. I suspect I became a writer because of de Melo Neto and Buarque. I don't know. What I do know, without a shadow of a doubt, is that this was the point at which I began to be interested in Brazil and, in a certain way, to discover that I was Brazilian. I read Carlos Drummond de Andrade, Jorge de Lima and Manuel Bandeira. Later on, when I discovered Ferreira Guilar and Manoel de Barros, my early talent for being Brazilian was confirmed.

Over the past few months I have witnessed, to my horror, the muddled emergence of a Brazil I never knew existed, a Brazil that doesn't fit inside the Brazil that, through poetry, had been slowly building up inside me, and building me into the person that I am. I am well aware that Sérgio Buarque de Holanda's concept of the Brazilian as "a cordial man" is nothing more than a myth, and always was. Yet it still feels significant that so many Brazilians have chosen to see themselves reflected in it, just as it is significant that a high percentage of Portuguese people insist on thinking of *saudade* as something that defines their nature. They may be falsehoods, but they are beautiful falsehoods.

The whole world believed the myth of the cordial Brazilian man. Brazil pretended to believe, and after much pretending it really did end up believing it a little, too. That aside, we tend to be what others think we are.

The myth of the cordial Brazilian came undone in the streets. It came undone this past 17 April, in that ridiculous, oppressive and depressing spectacle that took place over a painful eternity in the Chamber of Deputies, watched live by half the world. Some European newspapers spoke of Carnival. It had nothing to do with Carnival. A masked dance, perhaps, but a funeral dance, a grotesque farce, nothing that would recall the vibrant creative intelligence and powerful redemptive spirit of Carnival.

Which Brazil do we have now? Which face does Brazil reveal in the mirror now? Which face does it show to the world?

It's not just Brazilians who are watching each other in a perplexed, fearful state. A similar feeling has paralysed the foreigners who love Brazil; the ones, for example, who flocked last Thursday to the Coliseu dos Recreios. We also feel a little like orphans. We listened to Gil and Caetano in the same desperate way that someone might seek to reconstruct the face of a loved one from an image that has been torn into a thousand pieces.

On 17 April, after half an hour of listening to the "illustrious deputies", I turned off the television and went to my library to find some of the foundational titles of Brazilian poetry. In order to forget my lamentable namesake, Eduardo Cunha, I spent part of the night rereading Carlos Drummond de Andrade and Vinicius de Moraes. Call me naïve, but I believe in the magical properties of poetry. When I read Adélia Prado, it is as if praying:

> I establish lineages, whole kingdoms
> (pain is not bitterness).
> My sadness has no pedigree,
> but my longing for joy –
> its root goes back a thousand generations.

As I read, I know that somewhere, over there, where dreams are made, a new day will have begun to dawn. And on that new day, the light of which we can barely make out now, Brazil has already begun to reconcile itself with Brazil, and is once again conquering the world with its joy and its songs.

Amen.

The magicians' reawakening

When I first met the American philosopher David Abram, I was left with the impression that I knew him – not from real life, which we (erroneously) tend to think of as being less imaginative than literature, but from the pages of some novel read many years ago. Perhaps in an obscure Bruce Chatwin text; perhaps in one of Roberto Bolaño's ironic stories; perhaps, who knows, in one of the novels Juan Pablo Villalobos has written to send up magical realism.

Born in the suburbs of New York, Abram earned a living for many years as an itinerant magician, wandering from city to city, showing up in bars and small venues. Years later, while travelling through Nepal, Indonesia and Sri Lanka, his magic tricks helped him approach traditional shamans. These genuine mages were fascinated by their phoney colleague and his trivial, rudimentary illusions – a fascination similar to what a real cat must feel towards a toy feline, able to meow and jump but incapable of everything else that makes a cat a cat: congenital elegance, a vague disdain for humans and their frantic, hurried lives, aristocratic indolence and a playful passion for cardboard boxes.

Abram doesn't care about being called a "philosopher". He prefers to be seen as a cultural ecologist. "My work is centred in the relationship between human cultures and the living landscapes that surround people and sustain them. I search for the link between people and other animals, plants, earthly elements; between the many living landscapes that sustain us and of which we are a part," he explained in an interview with the online newspaper *Observador*:

> As a cultural ecologist, what fascinates me is perception, the ecology of the sensory experience. Our feelings, our eyes, our ears, our skin, can be viewed as a glue attaching us to the nervous systems of the ecosystem that surrounds us. I'm

fascinated by the ecology of perception, and also more and more by the ecology of language, because language profoundly influences the way we see and experience the world.

Abram quickly understood that Indonesian or African shamans are far more than simple healers. In reality, they act, or seek to act, as mediators between the world of men and the immense living world around us.

Shamans take on the role of border crossers, in particular that final border that separates, or appears to separate, humans from all other living things, be they animals or plants. In the United States and Europe, more and more people are interested in the ritual consumption of ayahuasca and other similar experiences as a way of re-establishing dialogue with a supposed 'vegetable intelligence'. I'm not interested in discussing here whether or not that dialogue is authentic or just a mental illusion, a magic trick. What interests me is interrogating this desire felt by a growing number of people.

The idea of a border between the human and the vegetable or animal world does not even exist in non-urban cultures in Latin America or Asia, or in the majority of African countries. Travelling through the jungle in Angola or Mozambique, I've heard innumerable reports of people who take on the form of animals such as lions or hippopotamuses by night. David Abram's comments might seem revolutionary to European ears, but they sound trivial or obvious to those of an African peasant. In the 1950s, the Angolan poet Mario António evoked elderly women draped in cloth, guardians of ancient knowledge:

> Ladies who perceive the intimate
> obscure unity of the mystery and the design.
> Alert to the accident that is life.
> (There are evil gusts in the wind! Evil cries
> in the river, in the night, in the woods!)

The environmental movement has flagged over the past few decades as the traditional parties, especially those on the left and far left, have taken on its principal ideas. It's of no little interest that the renovation of this movement – represented by figures such as David Abram – is based in the retrieval of an idea that only a few years ago Western philosophy had categorised as being archaic.

Before there was blue

A few days ago, I found a book in my library, the existence of which I had been completely unaware. It happens a lot. I'm looking for a specific title and can't find it, though I know where it should be. Then, in its place, I discover a different one. In this case it was a thick volume written in French: *Couleurs: pigments et teintures dans les mains des peoples* by Anne Varichon – an essay about colours and their meaning throughout history.

At a certain point in the book, Varichon recalls that for the ancient Greeks the sea was green, brown or wine-coloured. There was no word that designated 'sky blue'. Nor was the sky even blue. Poets described it as pink at dawn; burning at dusk; milky on melancholy winter mornings. Theophrastus, who wrote about almost everything and also authored a study on colours, dyes and inks, never made any references to the colour blue. There is no mention of this colour in the Old Testament. In Western painting the sea only began to be portrayed as blue in the fifteenth century. Until then, it was represented by different shades of green. The Maoris, according to Varichon, classified the sky in terms of the clouds passing through it. A cloudless sky was not a blue sky. It was 'a nice day'.

The word *blue* eventually appeared in several languages, and it was then that the sea and sky took on this colour. From this historical detail we might conclude that it is names that give existence to things. Indeed, such an idea goes hand in hand with what the Bible states: "In the beginning was the Word and the Word was with God and the Word was God."

It's worth remembering that when poetry first emerged it was linked, in the form of songs and evocations, to magic rituals. Once again, we have the word at the origin of the world.

The idea is pleasing to me. I imagine a secret society of powerful demiurges. Behold, they reach a magnificent vale, proclaim the secret word, and the sky turns a luminous, unmistakeable blue.

They murmur another word, and the first rainbow appears; they speak again in an imperious guffaw of light, and the first orchid sprouts, attached to the wizened trunk of an orange tree. I see them over the long, drawn-out centuries, losing themselves in crowds as they continue on their fantastical mission. They say *pizza* and the first margherita comes out of the oven. They say *tie* and instantly a sad bureaucrat in a sad office in a sad suburb lifts his sweaty hands to his neck in order to loosen the knot of his useless item of clothing.

Perhaps here and there my imaginary demiurges have stumbled upon a word that is a little more complicated, and has caused a prolonged error to emerge from nothingness. For example, the platypus – *ornitorrinco* in Portuguese. May the platypus forgive me, but I assume it is the work of a stammering, nervous or inexperienced demiurge.

The Head Demiurge sees the platypus and calls over the Amateur Demiurge:

"What's this one, then?" he asks, pointing at the horrifying travesty.

"B – b – boss, it's a ... a ..."

Poof! The first platypusologist in history appears. The man looks perplexedly at the two demiurges. Then, even more afraid, he looks at the platypus. It looks back at him, equally terrified, and they both run off to occupy their respective positions in the grand scheme of things.

Nature is stingy with blue. There are very few blue fruits, very few blue foods. Nature has bountiful substances from which it is possible to extract yellow, black and red pigments, but the ones from which blue inks can be extracted are far rarer. The West imported blue from the East: Afghan painters around the turn of the fifth century would have been the first to grind the rare lapis lazuli stone in order to obtain a pigment that was an intense and luminous blue, to which the Venetian painters gave the name *ultramarine*. For centuries it was considered the most beautiful colour – and the most expensive.

Lapis lazuli is made up of several minerals. *Lapis* means "stone" in Latin. *Lazuli* came to Latin from Arabic, which in turn came from Persian, and in turn from Sanskrit. The Portuguese word *azul* comes, of course, from "lazuli". In most other European languages the word for blue appears to originate from old German *blenda*, which designated a brightly coloured mineral: *bleu* (French), *blau* (German), *blu* (Albanian), *blue* (English), etc. In each case we are talking about relatively new words, which seems to support Varichon's curious hypothesis. True or not, it's a beautiful theory. I keep thinking about the colours still hiding among us, just waiting for the right word so they can open up or explode.

Sunday, 15 May 2016

Today we travelled to London for the Booker Prize ceremony. A driver was waiting for us as we left the airport. The parallel programming included a series of readings at the British Library – one of the world's best. I enjoyed hearing the Korean writer Han Kang, whose novel *The Vegetarian*, is nominated. I'm sure she's going to win.

Monday, 16 May 2016

I went with Yara Monteiro to hire a suit for the ceremony. It was very entertaining. If I'd come alone, it would have been torture. Hell always depends on the company. Heaven, too. As Sartre put it, "Hell is other people." But so is Heaven.

I had lunch alone in a Chinese restaurant. Then I stopped by a bookshop, where I met my translator Daniel Hahn along with a member of the jury and a young Indian writer. Han Kang was there, too. I invited her to participate in this year's Folio, the literary festival in Óbidos. She told me she'd need to check her diary, but seemed interested. It would be good to have her there.

We got dressed and left. It was the second time in my life I've worn a bowtie: the first was when I got married. I've only worn a tie on one occasion, in order to get a photo done for my Angolan ID card. Back then it was obligatory for men to wear a tie. Photography studios all had a tie that they'd lend to clients. Many thousands of Angolans have posed for the future wearing the same tie.

I didn't feel as bad in the suit as I'd imagined I would. I almost felt comfortable. My agent Nicole Witt came to meet us at the hotel. The driver got the address wrong, and took us somewhere else. We had to call an Uber.

I found the ceremony very formal. The Austrian writer Robert Seethaler, who is also an actor and is a tall, good-looking man, could not hide his boredom. We chatted to him for a while. I felt ill during dinner, and Yara had to accompany me to the bathroom. I vomited. Nerves, I presume. Minutes before they announced the name of the winner – Han Kang – I received a message from my older sister Rosa, and another from Francisco José Viegas, sending me their commiserations. ("I hate vegetarians," Francisco commented.) Han's translator sat down in a chair on stage, crying. I was also moved. We return to the hotel, alone and happy.

The writer who beat me

The writer who beat me (that's how the papers put it) is forty-five years old, but looks no older than thirty. When she was introduced to us at the British Library event, Han offered me a small, frightened hand. In a disastrous move, I brought my face towards hers to kiss her. She took two miniscule steps back, then ceded and smiled – a polite smile that made me feel enormous and a little rustic. Onstage she read an excerpt from *The Vegetarian* in Korean.

I closed my eyes as I listened to her read. Han's voice was like the sound of water gliding along moss and pebbles. Though I didn't understand a word, just as I don't understand the language of water gliding along moss and pebbles, I was able to sense a delicate but sombre flow of feelings in her voice. In the conversation that followed, with the BBC journalist Razia Iqbal, Han confessed that she felt bemused to be there, talking about a book she wrote more than ten years earlier. She explained that the novel hadn't achieved great success when it was released in Korea.

"Why?" Razia wanted to know.

"Maybe because it was too bizarre. Too bizarre for a country like mine."

Razia agreed. *The Vegetarian* is a strange novel, she said, but moving and highly courageous. Then she asked the inevitable question, nearly always the most uncomfortable for a writer: "Where did this book come from?"

Han sighed softly. She explained that the novel had started as a story about a woman who turns into a tree. "Magical realism," she added. I smiled. I find it vaguely ironic how so-called magical realism, loathed by present-day Latin American writers, has been reborn in Asia and continues to spread there. Just think of Haruki Murakami. On the other hand, I recalled Mia Couto, who, in many of his books, has a collection of characters who transform into trees – or are born from trees.

Yet *The Vegetarian* goes way beyond this simple plot. Divided into three parts, if not three autonomous novellas, it is a reflection (violent at times) on the role of women in a conservative and closed society that doesn't allow much room for difference. That's why Razia talked about courage. As soon as Han left the stage I was sure the book would win the prize. (The announcement took place that same night.) Later on, I stopped by a bookshop and bought a copy. The English translator, Deborah Smith, is just twenty-eight years old. She's a pretty young woman, almost as shy as Han Kang. She decided to study Korean because she felt the language was at once remote and relevant. *The Vegetarian* was the first novel she translated.

A few hours later, in the great hall of the Victoria and Albert Museum, Deborah Smith and Han went up to the stage to receive the Man Booker International Prize. While the public stood and applauded – the men (myself included) dressed in austere black suits and bowties and the women showing off their scintillating maxi dresses – Deborah sat down in a chair and cried.

The English aren't much inclined towards crying in public; the Koreans far less, I imagine. As for me, I had to make a tremendous effort not to cry with her. I imagined the same ceremony happening in any Angolan, Brazilian or Portuguese city. I'm certain the whole crowd would have wept. Finally, Deborah calmed down, went up to the microphone and said that, contrary to what one might think, the translators selected for the final round of the prize had not spent the last few days thinking about how best to assassinate the other forerunners. "We're a family," she stated.

She's right. I witnessed the sincere joy shown by Daniel, my own translator, the moment the chair of the judges announced the winner. I thought about Deborah's words several days later when a journalist asked me if I wasn't a little disappointed. I just said no. I was unable to explain the him that we writers, just like translators, are also a big family of sorts. Just as important: we are all readers. A prize, especially one such as the Booker International, is also there so that one can get to know new authors. When I discover a book I like, a writer I identify with, what I feel is an immense happiness, like gaining a friend who will accompany me for the rest of my life. Like growing wings, but without the terror of falling.

Wednesday, 6 July 2016

Barbershops have always been subversive places, free-thought zones where gentlemen meet to debate all manner of topics, especially questions of a political nature. In my first novel *A Conjura* (*The Conjuring*), Jerónimo Caninguili's barbershop Fraternity is a true club for ideas, the centre of a conspiracy that seeks to bring down the colonial power at the end of the nineteenth century. Totalitarian regimes continue to fear free debate, only nowadays they are more afraid of bookshops than of barbershops. At least that's what I've concluded from the recent news that the private school in Vila Alice that contained the Kiazele bookshop, and where thirteen of the seventeen activists imprisoned for preparing acts of rebellion and associating with wrongdoers were arrested, has now been turned into a barbershop.

Not to split hairs (and I don't intend any barbershop puns by that), were I in the place of the gentlemen in power I would have turned the school into a funeral home instead. I feel that the chances of a funeral home giving shelter to young plotters or ideological wrongdoers, at least to living ones, are far lower.

Cafés, however … cafés certainly *are* dangerous places. Cafés have a long, proud tradition as places where subversive spirits can rest, if not actually be born. There is an obvious connection between terraces and thinking, between coffee and revolution. It's worth remembering that the mother of all revolutions, the French Revolution, began at the Café de Foy one afternoon when Camille Desmoulins, a pistol in one hand and a sword in the other, jumped onto one of the tables and shouted: "Citizens, to arms!" Two days later Parisians stormed the Bastille.

It's no coincidence that at the time many cafés were practically public libraries, their shelves loaded with bags of perfumed black seed and rammed with books. I suggest that our wise government not only destroy all the bookshops (luckily there aren't many left), but all the bars and cafés too, substituting these places that breed potential terrorists with the funeral homes I mentioned above. They'll also need to close all the pastry shops, restaurants and nightclubs. Everything. Everything. Close everything. Build funeral homes, for we sorely need them!

Last Wednesday a group of young people linked to the ruling party made their way to the Tombo Tower in Lisbon to show their opposition to the launch of Carlos Pacheco's voluminous biography, *Agostinho Neto, o Perfil de Um Ditador* (*Agostinho Neto, Sketch of A Dictator*). In a bourgeois democracy, young people attending book launches in this way would be worthy of applause. In a country like ours with such a, let's say, singular democracy, to me it has a whiff of destabilisation about it. In the first place, Pacheco is himself a dangerous agent of subversion. I read Luandino Carvalho's article about him in *Jornal de Angola*. "Carlos Pacheco," the artist writes, "tortures historical facts, tramples on the truth, slaughters integrity and strangles not only intellectual independence but, above all, our very Angolanness."

For example, Pacheco sees Neto as a dictator. Now then, Carvalho argues, how can he be a dictator if he was only in power for four years? "No one can become a dictator in just four years." Brilliant argument. As we all know, Adolf Hitler was a sweetheart for the first four years of the eleven he was in power. If only he'd died after those four years, today he'd be remembered as a democrat. Onwards.

What I am trying to do is to alert those in charge of state security to how irresponsible it is to send young militants to attend a literary discussion, unless it is with the healthy aim of burning down the premises and stoning the writer to death. What is this nonsense about presenting arguments, even bad ones? You run the risk of them being won over by opinions different to their own – subverted. This, at the end of the day, is the immense power of books: they can cause us to change our opinions. But why, in a country like ours, where we already have the Supreme Opinion of the President of the Republic, should there be any others?

Burn the books! Close the libraries! Build funeral homes!

The flooded airplane

It was in Hong Kong. I was getting ready for a nearly thirteen-hour flight to London after a tiring week of speaking events and readings. When I consulted a doctor friend of mine a few days earlier, complaining of a series of mysterious ailments, she quickly concluded: "All that's wrong with you is sleep."

In those days I was travelling excessively, accumulating air miles, sleeplessness and a completely messed-up body clock. I would wake, confused, in an unfamiliar bed in some strange bedroom at 2.00 AM. To my brain, however, it was already 11.00 AM, so I would get up and try to write. The doctor prescribed me sleeping tablets. I have never smoked, don't drink alcohol or coffee and only rarely take medication. I thanked her and put the pills away, deciding to forget all about them.

As I boarded the plane, however, I thought about the thirteen hours I was about to spend contorting myself in my seat. So I took out one of the pills and swallowed it. Half an hour later, with all the passengers seated, the pilot announced that we would have to wait a few more minutes on the tarmac due to a technical problem. By this point my head was already dropping, seized by an uncontrollable drowsiness. Half asleep, I noticed three or four female flight attendants making their way down the aisle carrying blankets. Slowly, as if performing an elegant and mysterious ritual, they bent down and covered the aisle with blankets, and yet more blankets. I rubbed my eyes. This could not be happening. Perhaps it was a hallucination caused by the medication. Yes, it must be a hallucination. The other passengers, for the most part Chinese businessmen, watched the spectacle without showing the slightest reaction. I called one of the cabin crew over and asked her what was going on. "There's been a flood," she replied. I repeated my question incredulously, and she gave me the same polite response. She added that they were bringing a machine to remove the water. The plane would not be able to take off until then. I closed my eyes and immediately fell asleep.

I dreamed that I was on a transatlantic liner. The ship had hit some rocks in the middle of a storm, and was beginning to sink. Freezing water was gushing up from the deck. I opened my eyes, and there in front of me were the flight attendants gathering up the sodden blankets. I glanced out the window and saw the myriad lights of Hong Kong. I wondered about asking my neighbour whether we were on a plane or a ship. I looked at him in search of moral support. The man returned my gaze without even a hint of a smile. To my horror, I realised that we were inside a ship in the midst of a shipwreck, and that I would not be able to get out of my seat and reach the lifeboats. My legs were not responding. I had barely enough strength to move my hand. I leaned my head against the window and closed my eyes again.

I woke up in London. The plane had come to stop on the tarmac, and the passengers were beginning to retrieve their luggage from the overhead compartments.

I find myself thinking about that incident as, years later, on another plane, I prepare myself for a panel discussion at the sixth Rubem Braga Biennial in Cachoeiro do Itapemirim, where I will speak about reality and fiction. It is a recurring theme at literary festivals. Even when it isn't on the programme, there will always be someone, at some point, wanting to know where reality ends and fiction begins.

In Lisbon, there is a statue of Eça de Queiroz which shows him holding, with pleasure if not a certain lasciviousness, a naked or nearly naked woman. It is a reference to the subtitle of *The Relic*, one of his most famous novels: "Over the sturdy nakedness of truth, the diaphanous cloak of fantasy." Unlike Eça, I don't know whether or not the woman exists beneath the cloak.

Let's return to that morning I stepped off the plane in London, dazed and stumbling over my own feet. In my mind was the image of flight attendants spreading blankets along the aisle of the plane, blurred together with that of a ship foundering in a storm. The shipwreck had not happened; I had imagined it. Yet the overwhelming fear I had felt as, in my dream, the hull splintered and the sea rushed in, had been very real indeed.

Something similar happens when we read a book. We think about the impossible love between two young people from warring families; about the man who, maddened by the blinding sunlight, kills an Arab on an Algerian beach; or about the tale of an aging Cuban fisherman battling an enormous marlin on the high seas. All these plots and characters are fictitious. Nevertheless, they genuinely move us. Feelings are always real. More than that: we are real insofar as we feel. We attain reality by crying real tears at the death of imaginary characters. The brain secretes fiction, and the heart, reality. Or, to put it another way, everything is real provided it is felt.

Paradise and other hells

Jorge Luis Borges died in Geneva, Switzerland, on 14 June 1986. So it's been thirty years. Marking the event has provided an occasion for trotting out old clichés such as "the writer died, but his work is eternal". Nonsense, of course. Eternity is not what it was; in fact, I don't even think it has a future. The sad truth is that books also die. They die even before they physically decompose: they die when they stop being read. As a general rule, this happens a few decades after the death of their respective authors. Even within the Portuguese-speaking world, one need only think of Fernando Namora (d. 1989) or José Mauro de Vasconcelos (d. 1984), whose books, immensely successful while they were alive, are now almost forgotten.

Happily, Borges continues to have readers across the world. Sales, however, have fallen. There are few young people – by which I mean young, avid readers – who know Borges's work. I think Julio Cortázar, just to cite another Argentinian writer, is more popular than Borges among young people today in Portuguese-speaking countries. I can understand why. Cortázar has an explicitly playful side to him, like a little boy on holiday, whereas Borges, despite bequeathing us greatly entertaining pages, can seem formal and tiresome to an unwary young reader. You have to enter Borges's work through the front door of *Ficciones* (*Fictions*), and only then start discovering the other collections of stories, essays and poetry. (Borges's poetry is not obligatory.)

Borges liked to define himself as a conservative man. Above all, he liked to look like one. Nevertheless, the moment he began to think, an anarchist blossomed within him. It is undoubtedly true that politically, he supported extreme right-wing causes and individuals. It is said that the Swedish Academy refused to give Borges the Nobel Prize for literature following his unfortunate visit to Chile in 1976, during which he praised the dictator Augusto Pinochet. Throughout his life he also came out with a series of racist statements, for which he never showed any remorse. At the same time, however, he developed a remarkable philosophy that had nothing conservative about it. Regarding God, for example, he assembled a phenomenal collection of blasphemies scattered through his stories and observations. I quote from memory: "Believing in just one God seems to me mean-spirited. When there are so many gods, believing in only one is an excess of economy."

While mocking writers and artists of his own times who tried so hard to shock the middle classes ("the bourgeois have been shocked so often they are cured of any astonishment," he said), he amused himself by offending anyone who came near him. Even today, his comments about Israel would provoke seismic tremors if spoken by a living writer of similar stature: "I have been twice to Israel and, unfortunately, I noticed that they are almost Hitlerian. The difference is they don't insist on the idea of the German race, but of the Jewish people. The idea of the chosen people of Nazi Germany is no different to that of the chosen people of the Hebrews, which Hitler took from the Bible."

Or this, about the Qur'ran: The Koran is very inferior to *The Thousand and One Nights*. Allah was not as inspired as Scheherazade."

Borges was not afraid to think. And because he was not afraid to think, he was neither of the right nor of the left; he was someone who disturbed everyone. Today, unfortunately, there are lots of writers around who are afraid to think – or afraid of what others might think about their thoughts – and this is what causes such a repetition of ideas. Such a lack of ideas.

Many years ago, I wrote a short story about Borges, based on a well-known sentence of his: "I imagine paradise as a place for dialogue. Like a library." In my story, the writer closes his eyes in Geneva and wakes up surrounded by banana trees. Somewhere near him a naked woman is levitating. Borges, who had not the slightest fondness for tropical landscapes – nor, for that matter, beautiful levitating women – convinces himself that he has woken up in Hell. It then occurs to him that perhaps God has confused him with Gabriel García Márquez, and that this is the Colombian writer's Paradise. This makes him happy, for since Márquez's Paradise is clearly his Hell, his own Paradise must surely be Márquez's Hell. There is no Paradise, it would seem, that is not also Hell. What for some is wonderful, proves for others to be perpetual tedium or long, drawn-out horror.

I sincerely hope that Borges has woken up in an enormous library, containing all the books ever written or to be written. Mine will be there, too. I like to think that one day Borges will read that little story – and that reading it will make him smile.

Saturday, 24 June 2016

Early in the morning, the first item of news I read was about the result of the referendum in which a majority of British voters decided to quit the European Union. I then began to receive messages from shocked and dismayed British friends. One of them was calling for London to declare independence and stay within the EU. I assumed he was joking, then quickly realised he wasn't. There are others supporting the same idea. The British capital – famous for its ethnic and cultural diversity, whose mayor Sadiq Khan is Muslim of Pakistani origin – voted resoundingly for the United Kingdom to remain in the European Union: 2,263,519 votes in favour, 1,513,232 votes against. "Let's free London from the rest of the island and sail the city over to the continent," my friend added, in a remark that reminded me of José Saramago and his book *The Stone Raft*.

Fear of the Other, of immigrants, has been amply deployed by the British right wing to mobilise the country against the EU. But it so happens that the Other has long since become part of the whole, and even part of the norm. In recent days an extract from an English-language newspaper has been circulating on social media, reporting an incident that illustrates the reality of modern Britain (and Europe generally): at a train station, a passenger got worked up because a woman, her face covered by a *niqab*, was talking to her own son in a strange language. "We're in England," the passenger said. "You should speak English!" A passer-by interrupts him: "Actually, we're in *Wales*, and they are speaking Welsh [Cymraeg]!"

Mia Couto, who is white, used to tell a somewhat similar story. On one occasion, in Stockholm, he went into a shop where, to his great surprise, he ran into an old friend. The friend, a black fellow Mozambican, had been living in Sweden for decades, had a Swedish passport and spoke the language fluently. The two men embraced, remembering old times, talking loudly and laughing even more loudly, with a casual enthusiasm that to us simply expresses joy, but which in Sweden can be easily mistaken for some sort of disturbance. The shopkeeper came over, clearly irritated. He turned to Mia and started explaining to him, in Swedish, that this was no way to behave. Mia's friend smiled at the shopkeeper: "You'll have to speak to me, I'm afraid. I'm the one who's Swedish. My friend here is African and doesn't understand a word of our beautiful language."

The new Europeans have definitively changed the face of Europe. The idea that it is possible to stop this process, or even reverse it, strikes me as not merely foolish, but almost childishly naïve. Naïve, because no wall, no matter how high, can stop people who are truly desperate. For as long as there are places at war or devastated by chronic poverty, and also places that are relatively prosperous and at peace, there will be movements of people from one to the other. Foolish, insofar as it sees in destructive terms a phenomenon that, much to the contrary, has been revitalising an ageing continent in terms of demography and culture. In European countries such as Portugal, whose population is falling year upon year, immigrants are helping to rebalance demographics and public finances, and contributing to the renewal of their cultural environments. There are, for example, countless faces of African origin among the leading figures in Portuguese, French and British popular music. In the case of France, this isn't even new. A good deal of the extraordinary *chanson française* movement of the 1940s, '50s, '60s and '70s was led by musicians such as Charles Aznavour (of Armenian origin), Serge Reggiani (Italian) and Georges Moustaki (Greek) – and that's without mentioning the black singer Josephine Baker, born in the American city of St Louis. And what would modern English literature be without immigrants? The British wouldn't be able to boast figures such as V. S. Naipaul, Zadie Smith or Salman Rushdie, among many others.

It is feared that the attitude of the British could spur nationalist movements throughout Europe, leading to similar referenda and an eventual break-up of the European Union. I don't believe such a tragedy is going to happen. What happened in the UK, however, cannot be seen as anything other than an enormous step back in the ideal of constructing a world that is more united, free of borders and open to the whole of humanity.

A whole host of whites

I'm in Paraty. Just as I sat down to write this column, I realised that it's been twelve years since I first visited this city for FLIP, Brazil's most prestigious literary festival, to take part in a debate with Caetano Veloso, chaired by Cacá Diegues. It was one of those intense and wonderful moments that stay with us, echoing throughout our lives, and, in that sense never truly become 'the past'. I remember how I flew back from the festival to Luanda just in time to be present for my daughter's birth. Since then my little girl has grown so beautifully, and so has FLIP. Many of the writers who have been to FLIP have gone on to become closely involved with the festival and Paraty, its host city. Something like that has happened to me. I have to confess that many criticisms of the event, even the most justified, rather irritate me, as if they were levelled at a family member or close friend.

One criticism I always hear is about the absence of black writers. The accusation was repeated this year, with more grounds than on previous occasions. The festival curator himself, Paulo Werneck, acknowledged the problem. I'm a friend of most of the African writers who have taken part in the event in recent years. In 2008, I chaired a discussion there between the writers Pepetela (Angola) and Chimamanda Ngozi Adichie (Nigeria). In conversations with Chimamanda, plus Teju Cole and Uzodinma Iweala (both American of Nigerian descent), on different occasions and in different parts of the world, they all expressed surprise and even some indignation – not so much at the fact that there were so few black writers onstage, but rather because they had been speaking to an almost exclusively white audience in a country where the majority of the population is of African descent.

This should be the central question. Why aren't there more black people in the audience? The reality is that there is still a colour bar separating those who, in Brazil, have access to books, and the vast majority of the population. To educate writers, you first need to create avid readers. If we want to develop good black writers, we first need to educate many millions of black readers.

A few weeks ago I took part in another literary festival, much less talked about than FLIP but no less interesting – the Festa Literária das Periferias (FLUP). The panel discussion took place in the Mário Lago Theatre in Vila Kennedy, a working-class district on the edge of Rio de Janeiro. Teju and Uzodinma would have enjoyed being there, in front of that audience, made up *mainly* of young people of African descent. It was a gratifying experience. It isn't very often that you meet readers who are so interested and well-informed. The sophistication of an audience can be measured by the quality of questions. This one was a particularly interesting audience whose questions, in some cases, caught me unawares and led me to re-evaluate some of my convictions. An audience like that is everything a writer could ask for.

Julio Ludemir, the writer, cultural producer and one of the creators of FLUP, explained to me that many of those young people have joined literary workshops. It was from one of these nuclei, for example, that Jessé Andarilho emerged; he is the author of *Fiel* (*Faithful*), a novel written with the precision of a police witness statement, which tells the story of the rise and fall of a boy caught up in Rio's drug trade. The same surroundings have also given us Yasmin Tayná, the standout young screenwriter of *Kbela*, a film that explores a black woman's identity through her relationship with her hair. Yasmin is due to launch her first book soon.

Experiments such as FLUP can change – or probably already are changing – FLIP. The curator of a literary festival cannot be some kind of race inspector, such as once existed in South Africa in the days of apartheid. When people talk to me about race, I always remember the story of a jazz pianist in the United States who announced during a press conference that he had signed a new double bass player. "Is this new double bass player black?" one of the journalists wanted to know. "I don't know," replied the pianist. "I haven't asked him."

I myself curate a literary festival, the Festival Literário Internacional de Óbidos (Folio), which takes place each year in September. While I was writing this column, I decided to do the sums, and discovered that of the forty authors we shall have taking part in the main events in Óbidos this year, seventeen are women and eight are of African or Asian origin. The two best known authors, V.S. Naipaul and Salman Rushdie, are of Indian origin. None of this, of course, was planned. It just happened like that. I didn't ask anyone's race. It doesn't interest me. But the truth is that the end result does matter, and matters a lot. The lack of balance doesn't mean that the festival should be condemned as racist or sexist. But it is an indication that society, as a whole, is unwell.

Keep calm: it isn't the end yet

We are living at a moment of ebbing tides. Caught amid turbulent waters, struggling to breathe, it's only natural that this all seems to us like the end of the world. Perhaps it's some other type of end, but not of the world. Nor even – indeed, far from it – of our present civilisation. If we could only manage to lift our heads above the water for a moment and wipe the foam from our eyes, we would see how far we have come. Only a few decades ago, the planet was an infinitely darker and more dangerous place. At the end of the Second World War, there were only four independent countries in Africa. When I was born, in 1960, apartheid was firmly entrenched, and democratic regimes seemed like delicate and precarious eccentricities. Half a dozen stars shone in a dark night. Many democracies were at risk, especially in Latin America. In various countries, including Brazil, the military ended up taking power and imposing totalitarian regimes. Wars were breaking out all over the place. Not least, the 1960s marked the beginning of the armed struggles in Angola, Mozambique and Guinea-Bissau.

Looking only at the Portuguese-speaking world, we are living today in unprecedented peace. For the first time in history, there is no declared state of war in any of the territories where our language is spoken. What's more, all these countries are formally democratic. I'm well aware that the Angolan regime is far from constituting an authentic democracy, but even so, I think it's preferable to have a dictatorship disguised as a democracy than a dictatorship that is proud to be so. In a dictatorship disguised as democracy, there is at least the widespread and public recognition that democracy is the superior model.

I'm not saying we don't face risks. The risks are many, and reversal is a reality. In Mozambique, confirmed confrontations (more or less hushed up) have taken place in recent months between the army and guerrillas belonging to the main opposition. It is utterly unacceptable that a party with seats in Parliament maintains armed soldiers so many years after the end of the civil war. On the other hand, the renewed contempt with which the country's urban elites insist on treating the rest of the population, ignoring the demands of the northern provinces, is also incomprehensible. The new Mozambican president, Felipe Nyusi, seems to be honest, idealistic and untainted by corruption. His greatest challenge will be to manage to control the corrupt and conservative wing of his own party, FRELIMO, which sees in the growing social unrest an opportunity to get rid of him and take back power.

In Angola, President José Eduardo dos Santos is preparing to hand over all of his unlimited power to his eldest daughter, Isabel dos Santos, who has the proud distinction of being the richest woman in Africa. The first step has been her appointment as chairwoman of Sonangol, the (still) prosperous, albeit very badly managed, state-owned oil company. Isabel's appointment was received with deep dismay, provoking discomfort even within the ruling party, the MPLA. In recent days the Angolan government has freed seventeen young activists in an attempt to stem the general unrest. The days and weeks ahead will certainly be very stormy.

Both within and beyond the Portuguese-speaking world, Portugal and Cape Verde resemble two tiny oases of tranquility. Boredom. A blessed boredom.

A large part of the anxiety and turmoil of these times, whether in Brazil, Angola, Mozambique or beyond, has the same origins: the democratisation of information, imposed by new technologies and resulting in greater transparency. The political class in all the countries in question, corrupt to its very bones, feels threatened and confused. It snarls, shows its teeth and occasionally bites. In the medium term, however, it is doomed. It will not survive.

When all is well, it is possible to ignore the dreamers, cast them aside, treat them like lunatics. But in times such as these, when so much is at stake, only our dreams – that is, our imagination – can save us. The things we are able to dream of are the things that can be done, and must be done.

Two views on Brazil

In the space of a week, I read *Autoimperalismo*, by Benjamin Moser, and *Trópicos Utópicos*, by Eduardo Giannetti. These texts are convergent, yet, at the same time, almost antagonistic. Convergent, because they deal with present-day Brazil; almost antagonistic, because they do so from different perspectives and often arrive at opposing conclusions. The former is a foreign view, an elegant and provocative pessimism; the latter, a Brazilian view, scattered, passionate and hopeful – perhaps because it is impossible for a Brazilian view not to be always equal parts passion and hope.

The view of a visitor has virtues and limitations. It is a view like that of a child exploring the world, in such a way that it can often see what, for being so obvious, locals no longer notice. On the other hand, the foreigner runs the risk of acting as a discoverer, when his discoveries are only a surprise to himself. In Moser's book there are brilliant moments, where you think *damn, that's so true!*, however much it pains us to agree. Moser, for example, looks at Brasília with genuine horror. Studying its important architecture, which he considers to be a poor, out-of-place imitation, he concludes that Brazil is an imperialist country, or rather, auto-imperialist, as it invades and colonises itself.

Moser is right, of course. I do not see anything new in such a conclusion. What he calls "auto-imperialism", others – a long time ago – called "endo-colonialism". There is no difference, in this respect, between the United States and Brazil. The US also colonised itself, and with a great deal of violence. And if there are, as Moser insists, those in that bizarre country without a name of its own who are horrified by that history, there are also as many who revel in it. Just ask Trump.

The difference is that throughout that complex process of endo-colonisation, Brazil managed to create its own culture, based on the cultural expressions of the colonised peoples – the indigenous and

African population. Giannetti mentions this in his book, almost as if he were responding to Moser. "Modern genetic mapping techniques allow us to quantify what is plain for all to see. While in the US just 1 percent of the white population has any African ancestry, in Brazil the majority of whites – around 60 percent – are of African or American Indian lineage," writes Giannetti.

Instead of "white population", it would be more accurate to write "population that sees itself as white". The majority of 'white' Brazilians are not considered 'white' in the US. The same happens, incidentally, with the Portuguese. My sister married a Portuguese man of Goan descent. They had a daughter in the US. When the father went to register the birth, he was given a document in which he had to select the "race" of his daughter, from a wide range of possibilities. My brother-in-law had no doubts: white. The American bureaucrats exchanged glances, caught between shock and amusement: "White?!" Eventually they convinced him to register the girl as Hispanic or Latina. The rich heritage of my niece's genetics did not fit onto that form.

"The genetic intertwinement," writes Giannetti, "is reflected in the way Brazilians self-classify when asked to declare their skin colour: from *Galician* to *fair* and from *half-black* to *cinnamon-coloured* and *leaning towards white*." For the economist from Minas Gerais, "there is a way of life embedded in our language – *language talks*. Hence while the presence of afro-indigenous terms and expressions in North American English is scarce, they feature ubiquitously in Brazilian Portuguese."

If there is a difference between Brazilian and North American endo-colonialism, it is here. By colonising itself, Brazil became decolonised. There is nothing, or almost nothing, indigenous or African in the vast majority of descendants of European North American colonists. Brazilians, meanwhile, can repeat what Cape Verdeans say about themselves: "Here, from pure white to ink black, we are all mulattos." If we remove the focus from *race* and place it on *culture*, as it should always be, the statement is even more accurate. In cultural terms, no Brazilian is 'white'. They are all mixed. All are, also, more African than European. Perhaps that is why Brazil – unlike the US – has managed to establish itself in the world without any violence, just relying on the extraordinary force of its mixed culture.

A ghost ship

The British paper *The Guardian* recently published the curious history – perhaps I should say *story* – explaining the sudden emergence of electronic music in the Cape Verde islands. According to *The Guardian*, somewhere around March 1968 there landed at the Cape Verdean island of São Nicolau a mysterious ghost ship. The ship – its name is never mentioned – is said to have set sail from Baltimore, bound for Rio de Janeiro, carrying Hammond organs. Halfway, it lost its crew (under what strange or fantastical circumstances it is not known), but not its cargo. Still according to *The Guardian*, which in this instance seems not to have bothered to check its sources, the Hammonds were distributed among all the archipelago's schools, on the order of the Cape Verdean and Bissau-Guinean nationalist leader Amílcar Cabral.

The year of the supposed event, 1968, should immediately prompt serious suspicion; it was a year so full of extraordinary events that it becomes difficult to believe in it. Let's see: in April, Martin Luther King, Jr was assassinated. In May, students set Paris ablaze. In June, Robert Kennedy was assassinated; in the same month, dramatist and feminist Valerie Solanas fired three shots at Andy Warhol, but only landed one. (Warhol survived.) In August, Soviet troops invaded Czechoslovakia, putting an end to the so-called Prague Spring. *Et cetera, et cetera.*

I am afraid that one more extravagance, however minor, however irrelevant in the grand scheme of worldwide developments, could result in 1968 losing all credibility. A bigger reason for suspicion is the reference to Cabral. In 1968, Cabral ran, with great success, the military operation against the Portuguese from the humid forests of Guinea-Bissau. Unlike Guinea, the islands of Cape Verde are almost entirely deserts or semi-deserts. They are not suitable for harbouring guerrilla activity. There was never any armed conflict in Cape Verde. The Portuguese always maintained absolute control of the archipelago. It is impossible, therefore, to imagine a situation like the one put forward in *The Guardian*, with folk storming an abandoned ship, taking possession of its cargo and distributing it to local schools under the command of one of the most famous guerrilla leaders of the time.

Cape Verde was, in the '60s, a poor and abandoned colony. The central power in Lisbon seemed not to have the slightest interest in those ten small islands punished by easterly winds. The Cape Verdeans were, already back then, among the most musical people in the world (and also some of the friendliest and most welcoming). However, no one had noticed that yet.

I imagine the electronic invasion, the Hammonds shining in every school in the driest, dustiest corners like shimmering metal UFOs. Such an invasion would, doubtless, have provoked an extraordinary musical revolution in the archipelago.

The pretext for the *Guardian* article was the release of a collection of Cape Verdean electronic music, *Space Echo – The Mystery Behind the Cosmic Sound of Cabo Verde Finally Revealed*, from the German label Analog Africa. Of the fifteen tracks on the album, eight are by Paulino Vieira. I tried to speak to Paulino to see if there was any truth, even a faint aroma, in the story *The Guardian* took as authentic. I am not asking for a romantic ghost ship. I would be happy with a regular cargo ship. I am not demanding a musical uprising led by a legendary guerrilla fighter. I would be content knowing the distribution of the Hammonds was a simple commercial operation.

Unfortunately, I did not manage to find the musician. I had interviewed him years ago. Paulino became known to a wide audience outside Cape Verde for accompanying Cesária Évora on piano. However, he was a legend on the islands long before that. He played any instrument – piano, harmonica, clarinet, *cavaquinho*, guitar – as if he had done nothing else for centuries. He had a reputation for being eccentric. When he took to the stage, anything could happen – including nothing. Such unpredictability terrified producers, though audiences loved him. One day, he simply stopped appearing.

If, one of these days, I find him in a Cape Verdean bar in Lisbon, I shall ask him how electronic music arrived. I suppose he will shrug his shoulders, distracted, and speak to me about the enormous Cape

Verdean community in the US. Those emigrants will have been the ones who brought the first Hammonds to those Creole islands.

If there was a ghost ship responsible for not one but several musical revolutions in Cape Verde, the name of that ship is Paulino Vieira.

Magnificent losers

I enjoy following the Olympics, not so much to surprise myself or marvel at the sporting results and much less to cheer for this or that flag, but rather for the life stories that emerge on that great stage. I am not interested merely in stories of resilience and victory. As a chronic loser, in the sporting arena – and not only there – I feel great empathy with the defeated. Not those who lose by a fraction of a second, the almost-winners, but those who are overtaken spectacularly – who fall like others rise, who are left behind and transform the defeat into the greatest of triumphs.

My hero, the champion of losers, is, since the Sydney 2000 Olympics, the great Eric Moussambani. Moussambani, from Equatorial Guinea, was twenty-two at the time. He learned to swim, with the help of a fisherman, just four months prior to the historic afternoon he dived, for the first time, into a 50 m pool (until then he had swum in a river and a 12 m hotel pool), finishing the 100 m with the worst time ever recorded: 1 minute, 52 seconds.

My father was a teacher and swimming coach in Angola. I must have been his worst student. I was the worst swimmer in the official history of Angolan swimming. Even so, I never managed a time as bad as Moussambani's. I never liked straight lines (I am of the Niemeyer school), so I made my advance swerving, bumping into the lane dividers. My house was full of trophies and medals: my dad's, my mum's and my sister's. Eventually I, too, won a medal: second place in breaststroke. Context: there were just two of us competing.

Eric's story: he was sweeping the house when he heard an invitation from Equatorial Guinea's Olympic Committee on the radio. They were looking for swimmers, in a country where few know how to swim. Eric was the only man to volunteer. Four months later, he landed in Sydney, in flowery Bermuda shorts. The South African team's trainer lent him a swimming costume and some goggles, and taught him how to turn. After his glorious defeat, which made him known the world over, Moussambani could have retired. He did not. He took up an offer from Spain, and decided to learn how to swim. And he learned.

Four years later, Moussambani achieved the minimum prerequisite to compete in Athens (he swam 100 m in 54 seconds), but he was ultimately unable to participate owing to an administrative error. Today he is the coach of Equatorial Guinea's swimming team.

Similarly famous Olympic losers, so famous that their magnificent defeat inspired a film, were the Jamaican bobsleigh team at the Winter Olympics in Calgary, Canada, in 1988. The story of this four-man sled team is even more extraordinary than Moussambani's: at least water *exists* in Equatorial Guinea, though Moussambani could only use the 12m hotel pool first thing in the morning, for an hour, before the guests woke up. In Jamaica, however, there is no snow. Ever. The four brave Jamaicans were foiled in their first attempt, but managed to survive the disaster – and the cold.

This year, in Rio, two losers also made history: the Egyptian beach volleyball players Doaa Elghobashy and Nada Meawad. A photo of Doaa next to one of her German opponents went viral – Doaa wearing a traditional hijab, leggings and a long-sleeved top, the German Kira Walkenhorst wearing a bikini. It was the first time Egypt had entered a team in the event. The photo served as a pretext for an intense discussion about cultural differences, religious fanaticism and women's freedom. Curiously, few photographers took interest in Nada, who chose to compete without the Islamic headscarf. Both showed enormous courage, but Nada probably more so. Harassed by the press, Doaa stressed that the hijab did not affect her game. She did not say – but I suspect – that the curiosity from journalists and the public was more uncomfortable.

With or without the hijab, the joy both women expressed at being at such an important event, competing with the best (even if they had no idea who the best were), represents the brightest side of what is often called the "Olympic spirit" – which, we almost always forget, is not about triumphing over the other, but about ensuring that it is humanity that triumphs.

Crazy season

According to recently released figures from NASA, 2016 will be the hottest year on Earth since at least 1880. Prior to that, no global records exist. This past June was already, on a planetary scale, the most scorching ever.

Almost three years ago, *Science* magazine published a study claiming that a direct link exists between weather and violence. A team of researchers from Princeton and Berkeley, led by the latter's Dr Solomon Hsiang, compared data on the weather with data on human violence over the course of several centuries. The scientists claim to have found strong evidence that rises in temperature, particularly when linked to more rainfall, tend to increase levels of individual and group violence.

I remembered, on reading this study, a conversation I had many years ago with Angolan novelist, poet, filmmaker and anthropologist Ruy Duarte de Carvalho. It was on the long balcony of his apartment, in Luanda's Maianga neighbourhood, during rainy season. The whole city was like a ship about to be wrecked in the heat. Ruy, an extraordinary poet as well as a most uncommon and intriguing individual, grew up amidst the endless horizons of southern Angola, where his father, a Portuguese adventurer, wandered, hunting elephants, and ended up making this early experience the centre of a whole life. He did nothing else, whether as a poet, filmmaker or anthropologist, but dwell with curiosity and passion on the world of the Namib Desert's nomad farmers. On the afternoon I am recalling today, he wore only a colourful cloth around his waist – the traditional dress of these farmers – as well as the necklaces and bracelets he always had on.

"Have you noticed that the biggest passions, almost all the great disasters of love, just like the worst crimes, happen in rainy season?" he asked me.

I must have looked at him with ill-disguised incredulity, as he then reeled off half a dozen examples – some intimate, others general and public. I began to look myself for stories of fierce conflicts and grand follies of love. The majority had happened, in accordance with Ruy's thesis, in the warmest months, which, in Angola, are also those of the big storms. I became intrigued: "And why does this happen?"

Ruy believed the excess energy in the air, resulting from the combination of heat and rain, produced crazy moods. It was as if people were under the effect of a powerful drug, one they could not escape. Around that time, I had begun to write a novel about the extreme violence which followed Angolan independence, in particular that which arose from a supposed attempted *coup d'état* on 27 May 1977 (the end of the rainy season), in the aftermath of which many thousands of dissidents were executed. My conversation with Ruy gave me the title for the book: *Rainy Season*.

Ruy had no scientific basis to substantiate his theory. It was pure poetic intuition. As so often happens, poetry seems to have beaten science to it. In another interesting example, the team led by Dr Hsiang concluded that the hottest and driest phases of the El Niño Southern Oscillation doubled a tropical country's chances of beginning a new civil war.

If we are to believe the theories in question, we are living on embers. In the coming years, if global warming continues to worsen, we will see more wars.

The politicians who have been trying to discredit studies on global warming are, by coincidence, the same ones who often defend the interests of arms producers and dealers. Look at the example of Donald Trump. I am not suggesting that arms producers cause global warming, but I imagine they are alert to the phenomenon.

On an individual level, it is advisable to take care in love during the rainy season, which, in Rio, falls principally between December and April – which is to say, at the end of the summer and in that elusive, almost metaphysical season that Rio likes to call "autumn".

If we happen, during these months, to commit some act of madness, swept up by an overwhelming passion, pushed by a force greater than ourselves, we can always blame global warming. Was not an excess of heat, ultimately, Meursault's justification in Camus's *L'Étranger*, when on an Algerian beach, blinded by sunlight, he murdered an Arab man?

Life's Vanquished, under the sun of the tropics

A few years ago, a friend gave me *A Utopia Brasileira e os Movimentos Negros*. The book surprised me for the intelligence, courage and erudition with which Antonio Risério deconstructs myths and assumptions about the racial situation in Brazil. Risério unsettles us because he confronts us with our own preconceptions, while simultaneously offering us new outlooks on the world. You can tell, reading this book, the enormous pleasure the author takes in upsetting (almost) everybody.

There is nothing more irritating than another person's intelligence when it is not at the service of our own ideas. On the other hand, nor does there exist anything more important than finding someone able to challenge us, discomfit us, make us look at the world differently.

When I heard that Risério was writing a novel, I became curious. *Que Você É Esse? (What You Is That?)*, published recently by Record after Editora 34 rejected the original, is almost as surprising and unsettling as the author's essayistic work. It is an ambitious novel, set in Bahia, which attempts to reconstruct an entire era – the one lived through (always partying, always with lots of sex and lots of alcohol, whether fighting or grieving) by the generation of Risério, a sociologist, anthropologist, poet, lyricist and scriptwriter who himself was born in Salvador in 1953, and imprisoned for subversion by the military dictatorship.

Risério says he came upon the title after hearing someone let off steam during a beach football game. The man suffered a bad foul from a friend and, turning on the offender, enquired, indignant: "What you is that, man?" Which is to say, *what others are we, unknown to those close to us and ourselves? What others live, in their legions, within us?*

The title is a bad one, as it is so strange and difficult to grasp.

However, once we have learned its meaning, we understand the novel better: disorganised, chaotic, full of voices and echoes of extinguished voices, like a Candomblé temple.

Risério claims that he does not see himself in any of the characters. He also refuses to classify the book as a *roman à clef*; however, it is hard not to see in the protagonist Daniel Kertzman a kind of alter ego of the author, just as many readers will surely enjoy remembering certain events and characters. Risério himself considers the novel self-criticism by one who was actively involved in a certain ideological project, producing political marketing, and later became disillusioned. Not by coincidence, the most controversial pages are those dealing with the degradation of political marketing and the decline of the Workers' Party. Those will have been the pages that worried the decision-makers at Editora 34. Risério accused them of censorship. The editors reacted, claiming they rejected the work on purely literary grounds: "... Lack of tension in the narrative voice, excessive narrative diversions, confusion (literarily counterproductive) of narrator and characters' voices, as well as between characters."

At the end of the book, Kertzman returns to Salvador, but no longer finds the city of counterculture and "redefining Brazilian blackness" in which he had grown up. He finds a city in a constant state of partying: "Everything had become a carnival of lambs ... The slogan was: be joyful. Constantly. As if there were no places here called Solitude, Banishment and Belvedere of the Distressed."

Que Você É Esse? is not a novel of big twists, but rather of small situations, like most people's lives. There are moments when it seems a confused collage, where anything goes, including some (very good) stories by Kertzman. Some pages seem torn from a diary. Others hint at essay. In numerous dialogues and reflections, you can hear the anthropologist's voice in the characters' speech – Kertzman's in particular. The book is also a wonderful collection of aphorisms, some of which call Nelson Rodrigues to mind: "You know you're getting old when a woman sings that she's in the mood – and you're dead scared she really is." Or, on the next page: "No cowardice is sublime."

The *Vencidos da Vida* ("Life's Vanquished") is the name by which a group of nineteenth-century Portuguese intellectuals came to be known. Among them, Eça de Queirós and Ramalho Ortigão stand out. The name is said to have been proposed by one of the members as an exercise in self-deprecation, aiming to highlight the confrontation between the ideals of youth and the dilettante life that they all, to a greater or lesser extent, ended up embracing.

There are many similarities between those characters and the ones who walk the pages of Risério's novel. They are them, exaggerated by tropicalism: more alcohol and much, much more sex. In the end, as it happens, only sex can save them. Or not even that.

Castaways in the city

I like to stumble, when reading the papers, upon some small event or other that, although it might seem totally irrelevant to the general workings of the universe, makes me reflect. That was the case with a short piece about an individual in the US who earned a living by walking people. Chuck McCarthy, in his mid-thirties, is an actor, or would like to be one, but is rarely given work. Observing people walking dogs, it occurred to him to walk people. "Madness," he thought. Then he thought better, and went for it.

It worked. Big cities are an infinite collection of lonely people. There are more types of lonely people than varieties of beer. Chuck says a wide range of people look him up. Some hire him because they feel safer accompanied, especially when they want to walk at night. Others like having a friend, even if it is a hired one, to show their neighbours they are not as lonely as they think. Solitude is an unmentionable illness.

I recalled, as I read about Chuck, one of Gabriel García Márquez's best stories, "I Sell My Dreams". The writer tells us that, as a young man in Vienna, he met a professional dreamer. The woman, of Colombian origin, foresaw events in her dreams. She had lived for years, dreaming, with an Austrian family. García Márquez reencounters her decades later in Barcelona, and introduces her to Pablo Neruda. The poet does not take her seriously. The following day, however, he confessed to his friend: "I dreamed about the woman who dreams. I dreamed she dreamed about me."

García Márquez laughed: "Sounds like a Borges story." The self-deprecation is justified. "I Sell My Dreams" must be the most Borgesian of all García Márquez's stories. It examines a need that almost all of us feel: to look to magic (any kind of magic will do) for some comfort and security. But it is also about solitude. We do not find out if the dreamer was using the ruse of premonitory dreams to obtain room and board, or to have the comfort of a family.

Living in big cities, we are surrounded by castaways, each one on their desert island. From these islands they see the world; but the world does not see them. I cannot conceive of a worse solitude.

In 2012, after I published *A General Theory of Oblivion* – a novel about a woman, Ludovica, who walls herself up in her apartment, cutting all ties with the outside world – I received letters from people who identified with the character, or who knew someone in a similar situation. I recall the account of a Cuban woman who went to study in Bucharest, in the latter years of the communist regime. At eighteen she married an agent of the secret police. Months later, Nicolae Ceausescu was put up against a wall of a barracks square and shot. The secret-police agent disappeared amid the noisy tumult of those days, and the young woman, terrified, shut herself in the house for months. "I was Ludo!" she told me.

The truth is that while writing my novel I was inspired, in part, by the story of the Angolan nationalist writer Adolfo Maria, who having been an important figure in the fight against the Portuguese colonial regime, later founded a dissident group, Revolta Ativa, whose members were imprisoned or forced into exile following independence. Adolfo remained underground, hidden in a boarded-up apartment, for three years. In a state of extreme solitude, he said in an interview, madness is always just an arm's length away: "We see the walls closing in on us." Adolfo fought the isolation by practising yoga and meditation. Solitude brought him clarity.

What Chuck McCarthy does could be called 'castaway support'. He has just created – I suspect – a job with a big future; perhaps even a broad and revolutionary social movement. I imagine that a few years from now, the streets of big cities will be full of walkers with their clients. I imagine the clients exchanging opinions about their respective walkers while they catch their breath, for a few moments, on a park bench:

"How is your walker?"

"John?! Talkative and fun. Good pace. Yours?"

"Smart, discreet and patient. At my age, you know, I can't have someone who walks in a hurry."

Eventually, the clients will start to prolong these rest stops. They will start to talk to each other more than to their walkers. They will start walking with each other. They will discover it is possible to walk with other people without paying for it – and then we will have a true revolution, and the walkers will be out of a job.

Or perhaps I am being too optimistic. Try as I might, I always slip into optimism.

Uninventing the enemy

In the summer of 2014, the Portuguese police detained Her Calunga Gima, twenty-nine, Angolan citizen, naturalised Dutchman, for trespassing on the runway of Lisbon Portela Airport armed with a knife. Taken to trial, accused of terrorism, Calunga Gima confessed he had been in Syria with some "guy friends" and had "pretended to convert to Islam" so as not to seem rude. What had most shocked him, during his brief visit to Syria, was discovering that some of these friends of his, Islamist fundamentalists, were homosexuals. He came to Lisbon by train, because (as he tried to explain to the judges) he was being chased by bad spirits. He thought that in the Portuguese capital he would be more at ease. Newborn babies looked at him strangely wherever he went; they would shout his name and cry. After a series of bizarre ordeals and misfortunes, he found himself near Portela Airport. He jumped the fence, still chased by a legion of spirits, and approached a plane belonging to an Angolan airline, its engines running: "I wanted to stick my head in the turbines," he explained before the speechless judges. "I wanted to fill my head with turbulence, because maybe that way I'd confuse the bad spirits."

The episode above, which is completely true, served as the basis for creating the main character in the play *O Terrorista Elegante* (*The Elegant Terrorist*), which Mia Couto and I wrote in Mozambique in January, and which was staged a few days ago in Lisbon. The piece, a commission for the A Comuna theatre group, attempts to discuss the climate of fear that has taken hold across the West, justifying the worst high-handedness and creating an environment of intolerance towards immigrants and religious and ethnic minorities, which is, ultimately, what Islamist terrorism wants. Intolerance causes bitterness and anger, and anger creates new fighters – in a circle of violence that only serves to fuel Islamist fascism. Terrorism triumphs as soon as intelligence collapses.

Charles Poitier Bentinho, our elegant terrorist, seems, at first, as disorientated as the character who inspired him. However, unlike him, he is not fleeing the bad spirits: on the contrary, he makes a living fighting them. Once imprisoned, he quickly realises that the three police officers interrogating him – a man and two women, one of whom represents a US anti-terrorism agency – suffer, all of them, from various demons: fear, blame, jealousy, persistent colonial bitterness. Bentinho, the prisoner, realises that it is his mission to help the interrogators free themselves from these demons – and that is what he does.

Moving from the stage to reality, I believe we have great need of people like Charles Poitier Bentinho, capable of pacifying the spirits, showing it is only possible to beat violence by coming together. That is, when people come together to the extent that, looking each other in the eyes, each can see themselves reflected in the other's soul, as in a mirror.

To set a war in motion, first it is necessary to create an enemy. The initial act in this process consists of separating the Other from us; we need to make them alien: the enemy is not like us because it does not speak our language or share our religious beliefs; it does not like samba or *feijoada*. In the next stage, the enemy is already no longer quite human. Not being human, it can be exterminated. It *must* be exterminated.

To end a war, to pacify a country or region, we must unleash the inverse process: return the Other to humanity. Bring it closer to us.

Music, literature, cinema, theatre have forever been tools for connection. Perhaps that is why all these arts are so hated and repressed in territories still dominated by Islamist fascists. The best way to fight intolerance is through culture. Supporting writers, musicians, visual artists, etc. in countries with an Islamist majority and sharing this artistic expression in our own world. I am sure there would be some surprises. How many Brazilians know about new Algerian rap, for example, or the vibrant alternative rock scene of night-time Beirut?

Calunga Gima was condemned to four years and six months in prison for the crimes of threatening the security of an aircraft and possession of a bladed article. He was not proven to have links to any terrorist group.

Almost immortals

On 29 November, Emma Morano's birthday was celebrated in Italy. A biography of the birthday girl was released for the occasion. But what, after all, has she done? She has lived. She has lived a long time. At 117 years old, she is the last person in the world who still links us directly to the nineteenth century. Emma lived under the same sun that shone for, in other locations, Eça de Queirós, Machado de Assis, Princess Isabel and Buffalo Bill.

Emma Morano looked after herself without help until she was 115. According to her, the secret behind such a long life lies in the good, old grappa she drinks regularly, the three raw eggs she eats every day, and the sheer contempt with which she regards fruit and vegetables. Doctors, of course, are much more inclined to think Emma benefited from some simple genetic advantage, along with a bit of help from modern medicine.

If we had been born a thousand years ago, we could not aspire to grow old. Most likely we would have died while still children, victims of hunger or an infinity of diseases that, in the centuries since, we have defeated. If we managed to survive those first years, we would surely have died, a little later, in a very violent manner. Few people back then got beyond twenty-five years. Humanity lived in a constant state of hate and conflict.

Since then, many illnesses have been beaten, wars have lessened and life expectancy has tripled in most of the world's countries. When I was born, news that someone had turned 100 would be all over the papers. Today, to be newsworthy, one must try a little harder and reach at least 117.

There are those who think that, as much as science advances, it will never be possible to extend life beyond a-hundred-and-a-few years. However, an ever-increasing number of scientists are researching and arguing the possibility of prolonging life indefinitely. It is not a question of living *forever*, but about living without an expiry date, and without the horror of decrepitude. One of these academics is Michio Kaku, an American physicist of Japanese descent and the author of several scientific research books. In one of these, *The Future of the Mind: The Scientific Quest to Understand, Enhance and Empower the Mind*, Kaku has fun imagining ways to prolong human life. One of the possibilities is transferring all the brain's information to a computer. The conscience of that person would remain preserved for an undefined time, in a sanitised and remote place, much like what believers call Paradise, Hell or Purgatory (depending on a person's memories and sins). Later, it would be possible to transfer all this information to a mechanical or organic body, and the person would return and interact normally with the physical world and other living beings.

According to Kaku, this – or something similar to this – will definitely happen, so long as it does not break any of the laws of physics. The question, in his opinion, is not whether or not it *will* happen, but *when* – and that depends above all on the power of computers.

In 1949, the magazine *Popular Mechanics* published an article that predicted that "in the future, computers will not weigh more than a tonne and a half". Many people, reading that, thought it an incredibly optimistic prediction.

Sixteen years later, Gordon Moore made a prediction that proved to be much more accurate, and which has become famous under the erroneous name of Moore's Law: "The speed or capacity of computer processing doubles about every two years." So far it has held true. If this prediction keeps up, the admirable new world dreamed of by Michio Kaku could be right around the corner.

The sad paradox is that while we have never been so close to 'immortality', we have also never been so close to the end of everything. It is true that the number of armed conflicts in the world has decreased a lot, especially in recent decades. The nuclear arsenal, however, has not decreased. Russia, the US, France, China, the UK, Pakistan, India, Israel and North Korea all possess nuclear weapons. Iran is trying to produce them. As if it were not enough with Putin and the other madmen, soon the button to end the world will also be within Donald Trump's reach, and everything points to it being –

soon – also within that of Marine Le Pen. It is not an outlook that is at all calming. To the nuclear threat, add climate disaster.

The science that can give us 'immortality' is the same science capable of destroying us. Perhaps it would be better to invest more in civic, ethical and environmental education and less in technological development.

In the meantime, there is always *cachaça* and raw eggs.

The useless beauty of giraffes

Some years ago, I visited Kruger National Park in South Africa, in the company of Mia Couto. We went by car from Maputo, which is little more than two hours from Kruger. Mia, who as well as being a writer is a biologist, has always worked with the environment, and knows the park well. At one point, we saw two giraffes mating. I like giraffes, because they are an elegant improbability. There are many improbable beings, but almost all of them seem a little awkward, such as platypuses or kangaroos, and you remember what they say about camels: a horse designed by committee.

The giraffes wrapped their never-ending necks around each other, with a slow and loving tenderness, making any other nuptial dance, by comparison, seem coarse and dull. We all keep a box full of happy memories, which we turn to on dark days to reconcile ourselves with life. In my box of memories, there will always be that image of the giraffes dancing. I remembered it days ago, after reading an alert from the International Union for Conservation of Nature (IUCN) about the drastic decline in the giraffe population. In 1985 there were around 155,000; last year only 97,000 were recorded. These numbers signal, for the first time, the possibility of the species becoming extinct within a few decades. The destruction of the giraffe's natural habitat, along with poaching, explain – according to the IUCN – these numbers.

In 1962, Rachel Carson published *Silent Spring*, the book that paved the way for the global ecological movement. The title is a reference to the mass extinction of many species of birds, as a result of the triumph of the agricultural industry and the proliferation of pesticides. In the book, Carson accuses the chemical industry of hiding the environmental damage caused by pesticides, in particular DDT – a poison that, years later, would be banned almost the world over.

The pesticide industry's denial, at that time, is no different to current denials by the polluting industries responsible for the increase of the greenhouse effect. The plot is the same; only the names of the companies involved change (when they do change).

Donald Trump's recent nomination of Scott Pruitt to lead the US's Environmental Protection Agency (EPA) was a contemptuous spit in the direction of all those who care for the survival of life on Earth. While Attorney General for the state of Oklahoma, a role he still holds, Pruitt entered into a legal battle with the EPA, refusing to reduce coal plants' emissions of greenhouse gases. Pruitt even referred to the EPA as "unlawful and overreaching". It is as if Trump decided to invite a paedophile to take control of a home for abandoned children.

Many people in the US were outraged by this now-infamous appointment. One of them was the actor Leonardo DiCaprio, who a few weeks ago presented a documentary he produced, *Before the Flood*, about the consequences of global warming for the environment and for all our lives. The documentary also looks into alternative energy solutions. As soon as he heard about Pruitt's appointment, DiCaprio asked to speak with Trump. The actor did not try to convince Trump of the links between global warming, the greenhouse effect and polluting industries: it would have been a waste of time. Trump, like all deniers, is perfectly aware of the links. He just denies them. What DiCaprio tried to do was convince Trump that the American economy has everything to gain by choosing to invest in sustainable infrastructure. In other words, it is not a question of denouncing the stupidity and immorality of polluting industries, but of trying to persuade Trump and his business friends that they could make more money by *not* polluting than by destroying the planet.

I understand the strategy, but it reveals how downtrodden we feel, all of us, since Trump's victory. And the man has yet to even move into the White House.

I reckon I shall have to settle for living in a world without giraffes. Giraffes do not provide profit. Merely beauty.

Manoel and me

In 1994, I travelled from Luanda to Rio de Janeiro, and then by bus from Rio de Janeiro to Campo Grande, with the sole aim of interviewing Manoel de Barros. I had discovered Manoel's work by pure chance a few years earlier while leafing through a Spanish literary magazine, *El Paseante*. I remember very clearly the emotions I felt as I read those poems. They took me back to a happy childhood – or rather, to happy fragments of my childhood.

A few years later, I was interviewed at home by a Portuguese newspaper. At a certain point, I recall, the journalist wanted to know what I thought about the current state of Portuguese-language literature. I told him that the Africans and the Brazilians continued to have a less formal relationship with the language than the Portuguese themselves, and that maybe this explained the existence of a Guimarães Rosa, whose work helped bring about that of Luandino Vieira in Angola, which in turn inspired Mia Couto's early literary output. Portugal never had its own disciple of Guimarães Rosa, direct or indirect. I added that I had recently discovered a Brazilian poet – Manoel de Barros – whose reimagining of the language I found extraordinary. The photographer accompanying the journalist, who had barely spoken up to that point, let out a joyful, triumphant cry: "Manoel de Barros! Manoel de Barros is my neighbour in Campo Grande! He's literally my neighbour, his house is just on the other side of the wall!"

The photographer in question was Marcelo Buainain, responsible for the wonderful images that accompanied the article in *El Paseante*. I was so impressed by this coincidence that I decided there and then to travel to Campo Grande to interview the poet. Nobody knew Manoel in Portugal at the time. Even in Brazil, very few people outside Mato Grosso do Sul had read his poems. Naturally, no newspapers were interested. So I gathered what little money I had, bought my ticket and landed in Rio de Janeiro a few days later.

I stayed at Marcelo Buainain's parents' house in Campo Grande. Manoel must have been a little surprised that someone had travelled so far to interview him. That aside, he must have recognised that I was a fellow little boy. Little boys recognise each other, independent of their age. What's certain is that he welcomed me warmly into his home and, though he was known for his aversion towards dictaphones (he prefers to respond in writing), he allowed me to record the whole interview.

Afterwards, I spent three weeks travelling around the Pantanal. On my return I published a kind of poetic travelogue of the region, using Manoel's poetry along with the interview. The article won a prize, which meant that I eventually earned back the money I'd invested.

Over the years that followed I watched, with no surprise whatsoever, as Manoel's success grew and grew. It was no shock to me that he became one of the most widely read Portuguese-language poets. Nor was I shocked to see that his success was accompanied by a somewhat disdainful attitude on the part of certain sectors of academia and literary criticism. Critics are jealous creatures. Writers tend to lose so-called 'good critical fortune' as they gain more readers. For some critics, the idea of a pop poet is an almost intolerable concept.

When exalts the insignificance and greatness of small beings like slugs, moths and small birds, Manoel celebrates his own life – at every immense, absurd moment. I have read all his work many times over, but even now some of his lines and turns of phrase have the effect of secret explosions of light, taking me by surprise while I'm busy walking, cooking or playing with my children: *Behind the sunset the insects boil*, for example. Or: *Words / I like to play with them. / I've no time for being serious.*

A whole approach to living is summed up in that last line: being serious is such a bore. Totally unnecessary.

Today, Monday 19 December 2016, we celebrate 100 years since Manoel de Barros's birth. A century is a long time, but in poetry it's no time at all. I think I'd like to be out in the Pantanal, remembering old Manoel. So, at random, I open up his collection *Compêndio para Uso dos Pássaros* – and there I am.

The day the Virgin Mary lost her head

The thing I like most about Christmas is Nativity scenes. My father used to make them. He began by making small ones next to the Christmas tree, similar to the ones I'd see when visiting friends. His enthusiasm grew quickly, and because he was a man of great passion and creativity, the Nativity scenes grew as I did, so that after a certain point they no longer fitted in the living room; my father had to build them in the garden. The second generation of Nativity scenes had life-size figures inside what were almost authentic stables. They were so realistic and sophisticated that neither my sister nor I were authorised to enter the stables to play with Baby Jesus. But I always preferred the first generation. To the traditional porcelain figures – shepherds, oxen, donkeys, the Three Kings and their camels, Mary, Joseph and Baby Jesus – I would add my own plastic cowboys and Indians.

The last of the first generation of Nativity scenes collapsed one night during the Christmas holidays when I was eight or nine years old, probably owing to the innumerable characters spread all over the complex cardboard and wire structures. There was even a river, with a convoluted system to allow the water to flow, and barges and rafts moving along it. My sister had now added several of her dolls to my Apaches, Mohicans and cowboys, as well as a herd of elephants made from blackwood. All these beings were happily making their way to greet Baby Jesus when the disaster occurred. I was the only one woken up by the noise, and therefore the first to enter the room. I managed to save Baby Jesus, who was drowning in a rather undignified way in a pool of water and mud. Sadly, the Virgin Mary lost her head. We eventually managed to put the Nativity scene back together, but we never found the Virgin's head – so we substituted one of the shepherds for Jesus's mother, adding a blonde wig made of cotton wool. The cross-dressing shepherd played his part, and didn't look at all bad; it looked rather good, in fact.

I think of that Nativity scene as a model of the world in which I grew up, and in which I believe: a world that also seems to be tumbling down. A world of porous borders, be they of race, ethnicity or gender. A syncretic, multiracial, integrative world. A world that seeks – or sought – to imitate Brazil with regard to what Brazil does best: its extraordinary capacity to nationalise the Other.

What we are witnessing is nothing less than the past rising from the ashes, the sum total of all that we thought had been left in the past: the rank smell of the crudest forms of nationalism, the mildew of racism, xenophobia, machismo and religious intolerance. The movement has been building for several years; but with Donald Trump's victory in 2016 we can say that it has been made explicit in all its eccentricity and brutal obscenity.

Every December I like to collect the predictions of astrologers, scientists and political analysts for the year to come. Twelve months later, I compare the predictions with what actually happened. The conclusion is that almost no one, regardless of whether their predictions were based on magic or science, is ever right. The future continues to be inscrutable, something I consider to be both terrifying and comforting. We never know what lies beyond the curve of time. The future can bring us anything and everything – including the past.

Judging by what happened in 2016, we must be prepared for the return of more from the terrible past. That's what the majority of astrologers and political analysts predict. Given the obvious pleasure the future takes in defying predictions, perhaps 2017 could yet surprise us with its positivity. For those such as myself, who believe neither in astrologers nor in political analysts, there is always mathematics. Regression to the mean is a mathematical concept whereby in any random series of events there is a huge probability that, by pure chance, a trivial incident will follow an extraordinary one. In this example, it is likely that an extraordinarily bad and unsettled year will be followed by some relatively tranquil months. We shall see.

I return now to the day the Virgin lost her head. It was a terrible disaster – that is, of course, in the tiny universe in which it occurred.

But the following morning, we had a new Nativity scene that was even more beautiful than the previous one. Perhaps the moral of the story is this: sometimes the Virgin must lose her head in order for the world to move forward.

The cruel months

I fear December and January. I suspect that more people die across the world during those two months than any other, though I haven't found any data to confirm or refute my suspicions. I did discover, however, that in countries with pronounced winters more people really do die at the beginning of that season. In Portugal, for example, the highest number of deaths are recorded on 3 January. It is as if the Grim Reaper has a quota to fulfil. At certain points throughout the year he gets lazy, dozes off, chills out; then December comes, and he remembers he still has thousands and thousands of heads to cut off: he gets up, grabs his big scythe and off he goes, frantically slicing in every direction. January comes, and the Grim Reaper's in such a frenzy that he keeps going with his harvest of lives. It's only when February comes around that he finally eases off.

I imagine many sick people keep going until the end of the year from sheer stubbornness, like exhausted marathon runners whose eyes stay fixed on the approaching goal. Once they've reached it, they collapse.

Essentially, more people tend to die in December because the month carries the idea of an ending with it. But it is also the case that many people die in December and January because of natural disasters, and I doubt cataclysms check the calendar before they strike. For example, the day on which the most people died from a single event in the history of humanity was 23 January 1556, when a devastating earthquake hit Shaanxi province, in China. It is calculated that more than 800,000 people disappeared on that one day.

There is evidently no way of protecting oneself against the natural cruelty of certain months, nothing to be done. So I follow the example of the ostrich, and bury my head in the sand. I try to avoid the news. I take only the briefest glances at the headlines, focusing on the small items that get lost in the inside pages. Still, I am taken aback by the death of George Michael. I barely have time to recuperate before

Carrie Fisher dies, too. The following day it's Debbie Reynolds, who happened to be Carrie's mother. I hold off discovering the details, and instead come across a brief article about a Chinese scientist who has dedicated years to the study of Stradivarius violins.

According to Hwan-Ching Tai, from the National University of Taiwan, the unique sound of the original Stradivarius violins came not just from the particular way the violins were built and the wood they were built from, but also from the chemical products used more than three centuries ago to combat the insects that might have otherwise destroyed the instruments. I find this detail pleasing; it is a ready-made, beautiful allegory. What Tai is telling us is that the essence, the unique sound of Stradivarius violins, depends on something that, until now, no one had been able to see or appraise. That is, the essential seeks shelter in irrelevancies. I'm equally delighted by small mistakes that result in great achievements, such as the poison that, it turns out, gives that haughty levity to the sound of the Stradivarius.

This tiny discovery brings me back to the theme of the end and those two months during which we live constantly between mourning and celebration. In fact, as I was reading the article on the Stradivarius, I reflected that mourning and celebration are both part of the same process. In my country, Angola, as in several other African countries, mourning becomes a celebration, the *kombaritokwe*, during which the friends of the deceased come together to remember and celebrate, eating, dancing and enjoying themselves. Death, or the illusion of death, is what allows us to see life in all its glory.

As is well known, the Christian Christmas reused ancient pagan festivities related to the cult of the sun. By celebrating Christ's birth, we are, even if we don't know it, celebrating the sun. Or Horus, the ancient Egyptian god, son of Osiris and Isis, who has the sun as one eye and the moon as the other. Horus was conceived after the death of Osiris; Isis fell pregnant while coming to rest, in the form of a bird, on her husband's mummy. Horus carries the keys to life, death and fertility in his hands. Later, Horus kills his brother Set, god of darkness, violence, betrayal, envy, jealousy, serpents, deserts and war.

Horus, then, has been born and is expanding, though right now it may feel as if Set is winning. Yes, the month of January 2017, now making its debut, has made a sombre and violent entrance. There are dead people. There is war. There are expanding deserts, serpents, envy, jealousy and betrayal. But in the end, Horus triumphs – albeit, legend has it, blind in one eye (the moon). But still, he triumphs.

A strange fruit

To be invited to sing at an American president's inauguration ceremony tends to be viewed as a privilege. Barack Obama, for example, had to perform a complex juggling act to accommodate the many artists who supported him during his campaign in the 2020 election and then insisted on taking part in the victory celebration: Beyoncé sang the national anthem before the swearing-in; Kelly Clarkson and James Taylor came after it, and somehow there was still time for Alicia Keys, Marc Anthony and Brad Paisley, among others. Even Obama's enemies applauded the show.

This year, however, nobody wants to sing for Donald Trump. The businessman and new American president has been given one excuse after another – so many that it's become a joke. The most original, most sarcastic and most intelligent of all these rejections has to be the one given by the Jamaican-British singer Rebecca Ferguson, who announced that she would indeed be willing to perform at Trump's inauguration, but only on the condition that she could sing "Strange Fruit".

"Strange Fruit" was written by Abel Meeropol, a Jewish communist who adopted the children of Julius and Ethel Rosenberg after they were executed for spying for the Soviet Union. Meeropol wrote the song at the end of the 1930s, as a tribute to all the black people lynched in the US. It became immensely popular through Billie Holiday's interpretation, and some years later Nina Simone breathed new life into the song – so much life! – transforming it into a sort of anthem of the civil rights movement.

The lyrics were published in *The New Masses* (a Marxist magazine that was very close to the Communist Party of the United States of America), before being set to music. Do not think, however, that Meeropol's words were mere propaganda. Far from it. "Strange Fruit" is poem of sad irony and inconspicuous despair that, at times, almost seems to resign itself to the very horror it denounces. Decades have gone by, and Meeropol's lines (*"Strange fruit hanging from the poplar trees ... Pastoral scene of the gallant South"*) have not lost one bit of their disturbing power or their eerie light.

I would genuinely pay to see the expression on Trump's big, orange face as he listened to Rebecca Ferguson singing "Strange Fruit", though perhaps he wouldn't even understand the irony. Steve Bannon, on the other hand: now *he'd* be squirming in discomfort. Trump might even applaud. No one knows. The best thing about Trump is his unpredictability. It's also the worst thing about him. His reaction to this entire episode of serial rejections from the artist class was one of pure mockery: he pointed out that Hillary Clinton had had the support of every artist, and still lost.

It pains me to say it, but Trump is right. His victory represented the defeat of the world of arts, and of thought. Fans can be driven to buy a certain style of shoe if they see their favourite singer or actor wearing it, but that doesn't mean they will also buy their ideas. People want their favourite artists' songs (and, yes, their shoes, cigarettes and underwear), but not their thoughts. Writers are even less relevant. They don't even sell shoes.

I naïvely believed that literature was a different story. At the end of the day, when you buy a book, you're buying ideas. Books have a transformative power that is harder to achieve with other art forms. Trump's victory has made me reassess this, and other old certainties. Do books change the world? Yes, of course, some have done and continue to do so. Just think of the Bible, the Qur'an, *The Origin of Species*, *The Communist Manifesto*, *Lolita*, *The Satanic Verses* or Dona Benta's cookbook, *Comer Bem* (*Eat Well*). Sadly, though, to change does not mean to improve. Most of the books mentioned above did not bring about peace and prosperity – quite the opposite. Not that they are intrinsically bad. It just so happens that many people look at books as if they are mirrors: they aren't interested in seeing other people in them (which is the best thing a book can give us), only themselves; they aren't looking for challenging ideas; instead, they look to books to confirm their own preconceptions.

On the 20th of this month, when Donald Trump is inaugurated, the national anthem will be sung by a sixteen-year-old blonde girl,

Jackie Evancho. The other performers include the Mormon Tabernacle Choir, the Mississippi State University Chorale and New York's Radio City Rockettes. It looks, then, to be a festival of whiteness – and of decrepitude, as well. If this is Trump's great, triumphant America, then I prefer the one that lost.

Cannibalism, expanded

I've spent the last few weeks listening to new albums by Carminho and António Zambujo. The first is called *Carminho Canta Tom Jobim*. On the second, *Até Pensei Que Fosse Minha*, Zambujo reinterprets a selection of Chico Buarque songs. What an intriguing coincidence: two of the biggest names in contemporary Portuguese music have both released albums that pay tribute to Brazilian popular music (MPB). No, I don't think this is simply a coincidence.

I met Carminho several years ago, at a private party in Lisbon. She was singing some very well-known MPB songs – not with a Portuguese accent, not like a *fado* singer, but as if she herself were a Brazilian singer. So I assumed she was a Brazilian singer. Back then, Carminho hadn't yet released any albums, but she was already considered, I was told at the time, to be the elegant future of *fado*: a prediction that has since come true.

As for Zambujo, it was Marília Gabriela who first told me about him. Hearing her speak so enthusiastically, I assumed Zambujo was also Brazilian. "No!" Gabi replied. "He's Portuguese." I wasn't convinced. Surely I'd have heard about such an interesting Portuguese singer. Gabi then gave me Zambujo's third album, *Outro Sentido*, and I had to concede that she was right: the guy was Portuguese, and sang in a way I'd never heard a Portuguese person sing before. A vocation for all things Atlantic was already evident on that album, and it has only kept growing and deepening over the albums that have followed.

Zambujo never went down well with the *fado* purists, nor – happily – did he ever worry about pleasing them. His greatest virtues have always been a cheerful disrespect for frontiers, a taste for adventure and a natural affinity with Brazil and Lusophone Africa, Cape Verde in particular. On some of Zambujo's albums, the presence of a *cavaquinho crioulo*, magnificently played by John Luz (one of the many secret geniuses of Cape Verde) stands out. It's as if the singer, originally from the Alentejo, were founding a new territory, an independent musical republic, open to the many different sounds of Lusophony. To create this effect, Zambujo has surrounded himself with a first-class team, with a special mention for the double-bass player Ricardo Cruz, who writes many of the songs and has also been responsible for the production and musical direction of Zambujo's most recent albums. On *Até Pensei Que Fosse Minha*, Cruz splits the production with Marcello Gonçalves (of Trio Madeira Brasil), who is responsible for the musical direction and arrangements.

At first sight – or rather, first hearing – both Carminho and Zambujo seem to be going down the same path with their new albums. But on closer inspection, it is clear that this is not the case: Jobim's songs, sung by Carminho, remain Brazilian even if interpreted in a *fado* style. Zambujo, however, has fully claimed Chico's songs as his own. The album is anything but obvious. It's not just the arrangements that are surprising; the repertory itself goes in directions that aren't always predictable. I didn't expect, for example, to encounter *"Até Pensei"*, the song from which the album's title is taken, nor *"Sem Fantasia"*, sung in collaboration with Roberta Sá (whom I also love). Zambujo even invites Carminho to sing on *"O Meu Amor"*, the song that comes closest to *fado*. His choice of *"Geni e o Zepelim"* didn't surprise me so much. That song was very popular in Portugal during the '80s, as well as in Angola and Mozambique, having been recorded by the Portuguese singers Sérgio Godinho and Geninha Melo e Castro.

Carminho, always respectful whether singing *fado* or singing Jobim's songs as if they were *fado*, gives us an elegant, radiant album. It was recorded with Banda Nova, which was the last group to accompany Tom Jobim, consisting of his son and grandson, Paulo and Daniel Jobim. With musicians like these two, quality was guaranteed. On the other hand, the album perhaps lacks the joy of discovery and appropriation that is in such ready supply on *Até Pensei Que Fosse Minha*. What's more, the title of Zambujo's album – *I Even Thought that You Were Mine* – wonderfully sums up this whole process of happy assimilation.

It is clear that these two albums being released so close to each other was not just a coincidence. Carminho and Zambujo are the only Portuguese singers who have managed to have much impact in

Brazil recently. The two records represent an attempt to increase their existing audiences. But they also represent – I want to believe this – one more contribution towards the construction of a common territory of Portuguese-language culture and shared feeling, a construction that is entirely independent from political logic and governmental structures and which constantly devours and assimilates the other. Where the Indians once devoured Pero Fernandes Sardinha, today it is Pero Fernandes Sardinha who is devouring the Indians. Everyone is eating everyone, and it's a beautiful thing to behold.

Zambujo's album was the second-highest seller in Portugal during 2016, despite having only been released in October. In Brazil, his show in support of the album was considered one of the year's best.

A garden of memory

The possible creation of a Museum of Slavery, an idea put forward by Rio de Janeiro's culture secretary Nilcemar Nogueira, was received with enthusiasm – but also with a certain level of discomfort. Some believe that such a space would reopen wounds and deepen stereotypes, doing more harm than good to the community it seeks to honour. The argument takes us back to an ancient debate: should we remember pain and humiliation, or should we do the opposite and exercise forgetfulness?

There are several spaces on the African continent whose purpose is to remember the monumental crime of slavery. The most famous is situated on the small island of Gorée, in Senegal, which is believed to have been one of the main African ports for the shipping of slaves between the fifteenth and nineteenth centuries. At Elmina Castle in Ghana, the oldest European (Portuguese) fortification south of the Sahara, visitors both white and black, most of them American, are put in the shoes of slaves and led through the dark cells and narrow corridors towards the quay, as if they themselves were captives. The experience is intense and unsettling. Outbursts of tears and anger are fairly common at the end of the visit, with black visitors turning against white, reproving them for the suffering of their ancestors.

A few kilometres from Luanda, the noisy, chaotic Angolan capital, one can also visit a Museum of Slavery, which is more notable for the harsh beauty of the building that houses it and the lush countryside that surrounds it than the physical memories it holds inside, which are sadly scarce and of poor quality. On the Island of Mozambique, from where I write this, there is a kind of secret garden, the Garden of Memory, which commemorates in a simple way and with a certain elegant sadness (one of the main Mozambican personality traits, in my opinion) the thousands of Africans who were kidnapped, sent to this island and then sold as slaves and taken to Brazil.

I spent a year living in Berlin. On one occasion, I joined a group of writers on a visit to an old concentration camp. It was winter, I recall. The silence spread out over the frozen courtyards. I felt shame. I felt despair at being a person. I felt nostalgia for a time before I was a person. I felt a desire not to be anything at all, to be a tall stone surrounded by grass, an indifferent river, a tree rising up in the middle of the forest.

I am a writer. I advocate for memory. But this is less about actual remembering than it is about understanding. Spaces that help people put themselves in others' shoes, which make them experience their suffering, can be important for this process of understanding. To understand evil does not mean to accept it. On the contrary – it's important to understand in order to prevent. It's also important to understand in order to forgive – and then, yes, to move on.

The writer and composer Nei Lopes argues that, instead of a Museum of Slavery, it would be better to build a cultural centre dedicated to African heritage. I agree with my friend Nei, though I wouldn't say *instead of* – I'd say that the story of slavery is part of a bigger history, one formed not only of darkness but also of a great deal of light: all the extraordinary things that emerged in Brazil, thanks to what the Africans brought there hidden under their skins … a vast cultural heritage.

Brazil's African heart is immediately evident to even the most unprepared tourist. The face that Brazil shows to the world – the face the world loves to see – has always been black: popular music, Carnival, capoeira, *congada*, Candomblé. Even Brazilian Portuguese – as Nei continues to demonstrate with his distinguished research – is in large part distinct from Portuguese in Portugal thanks to the contribution of African languages (especially Quimbundo and Quicongo, both of which are spoken in Angola).

The only issue with Nilcemar Nogueira's proposal is its tardiness. It's unbelievable that Rio de Janeiro doesn't already have a living, dynamic space capable of helping us to see how Africans have contributed to the invention of Brazil over the centuries, a space that would also allow visitors to share in the suffering of millions of men and women who were forcibly removed from their countries of origin, wounded, exploited and oppressed, yet managed to establish a cultural territory built from love and tenderness, one that has given us *cafuné, calulu* and the Mangueira Samba school (founded, it so happens, by Nilcemar's grandfather Cartola, descended from the slaves of the Baron of Carapebus).

What is truth for?

The first positive effect of Donald Trump's election was philosophical: it caused huge numbers of people, all across the world, to begin discussing *truth*. What is truth? What is truth for? Does truth exist?

The second positive effect, directly related to the first, occurred after Trump's adviser Kellyanne Conway defended the White House press secretary Sean Spicer's barefaced lie that more people had attended the new American president's inauguration than had attended that of any president before Trump. Spicer was not lying, Conway explained; he was simply using "alternative facts". Over the following days, dozens of commentators pointed out that the expression could have come from the mighty pen of George Orwell, in his novel *1984*. That was reason enough for readers to flock back to Orwell's novel: the book has been at the top of the Amazon sales chart for several days now.

Orwell wrote *1984* in 1948 on the island of Jura, in Scotland, while battling persistent tuberculosis. It was published the following year, to great success. It's always difficult to explain the reasons behind the triumph of a certain book. In this case, however, I believe it has much to do with the author's desire to understand the way a totalitarian society structures and imposes itself, at the very apogee of the Communist dystopia. In Orwell's novel, the control and manipulation of information plays an essential role in the whole process. In the vast country dreamed up by Orwell, all of it subject to the rule of Big Brother, there are four ministries: the Ministry of Peace, responsible for war; the Ministry of Love, responsible for maintaining law and order at all costs; the Ministry of Plenty, responsible for economic matters; and, finally, the all-powerful Ministry of Truth, which has all information at its disposal, recreated from 'alternative facts'.

The Ministry of Truth's supreme achievement is Newspeak, a language that shrinks as it expands. It is "the only language in the world whose vocabulary gets smaller every year", one of the ruling party's bureaucrats states. The objective, he explains, is to narrow the range of thought: "In the end we shall make thoughtcrime literally impossible, because there will be no words in which to express it."

The impression that stays with me whenever I listen to Donald Trump is that he communicates in a rather advanced form of Newspeak. The current President is already at *1984* levels, or perhaps even beyond them, having reduced the English language to half a dozen basic adjectives – *sad*, *big*, *bad*, *horrible*, *incredible*, and a few wretched verbs and nouns – with the result that there is no longer any risk of displaying one iota of intelligence, even by accident. I don't think we have ever, in the world of politics or of spectacle (which are in this instance one and the same), had such indigence of thought, so solid, so blond and so pleased with itself.

Trump has not read *1984*. Trump doesn't read. If he did, we could be led to believe that he had seen in Orwell's dystopia not a warning and denunciation of totalitarian systems, but a manual for the destruction of democracy.

Let's return to truth, because, in the end, it's important to distinguish truth from "alternative facts".

Or is it? I'm sceptical about the idea of a single 'truth'. I believe each person has their own version of events, and that the sum total of these versions brings us close to the 'truth' – assuming, of course, that the versions are not completely at odds with one another. My coat could be green for me, dark green for another person and a yellowy green for a third. But if someone came to me saying that the same coat was pink, then I would doubt their honesty. On the other hand, each of us should stay faithful to our respective versions. For Trump, however, my coat is not only a fabulous pink – if that suits him – but it could easily become yellow if that turned out to be of more use.

The idea that politicians are naturally dishonest in the same way that slugs are naturally slimy is extremely dangerous: it implies the capitulation of intelligence and of the people themselves. Democracy is failing because we are giving up on it. The great challenge of our day is to revitalise democracy. To reinvent it. One of the first steps towards that goal is to demand more of those who represent us, to better choose who represents us, so that the expression *lying politician* ceases to be a cliché and becomes an oxymoron.

My new obsession

Over my life as a writer, I have fed a number of obsessions. Obsessions are a fundamental part of the creative process. Writers must not be afraid of repeating themselves. In literature (or in art, cinema or music), repetition has a pretty name: it's called style.

Whenever I hear someone talking about a writer's creative process and the part obsessions play in it, I remember what the Spanish writer Rosa Montero once told me. I met Rosa some ten years ago in Rome, when we were both on the jury of a literary prize. It was a case of friendship at first sight. We discovered that we shared several obsessions, beginning with lizards. The narrator of one of my first novels is a lizard; in one of Rosa's novels, one of the main characters has a lizard as a pet. What's more, Rosa has a lizard tattooed on her right wrist.

Dwarves are another of Rosa's obsessions, which has annoyed one or two literary critics. Perturbed by this response, Rosa promised herself that she'd write a novel with no short people in it. She had a few ideas, and began developing them. Yet the novel resisted. It wasn't going anywhere. The weeks slipped away as she battled unhappily against it. Finally, the knot came undone and the novel began to move along. The book was published, and in one of the first interviews, a journalist commented: "Not another dwarf, Rosa?" Only then did the writer realise that one of the characters had made her first appearance in the novel as a person of average height, but had kept losing centimetres as the pages went on. By the end of the book, the woman was tiny.

Conclusion? First, don't take malign critics too seriously; second, we must never battle our obsessions. At the end of the day, they are what pull us towards writing.

Great artists who never repeat themselves are rare. The exceptions have always scared me a little. The Brazilian director Heitor Dhalia is a case in point. I saw *Drained* in 1996, and was very impressed by its iconoclastic vigour and formal boldness. Three years later, I went into a cinema on a whim and saw the sweet-natured *Adrift*. I didn't know who the director was. I supposed – from the rhythm, the warmth of the colours, the gaze it cast over Brazil – that it was some European director from the old guard, a Frenchman, surely. I couldn't believe it when, leaving the cinema, a friend assured me that the film's director was the same person responsible for *Drained*. More recently, I saw *Serra Pelada*. I like all three films for different reasons, which is unsurprising given that they don't bear the slightest resemblance to one another. It is as if *The Autumn of the Patriarch*, *Waiting for the Barbarians* and *The Last Flight of the Flamingo*, to name three books by authors with hugely different styles (García Márquez, Coetzee and Couto), had been written by the same person.

I imagine three different guys, each one with a strong, exuberant personality, co-existing inside the roomy spirit – for it must be very spacious – of Heitor Dhalia. Either that, or he rents out his spirit to different identities. (I don't know Dhalia personally, though I'd love to meet him.)

All this to say that I recently found myself prisoner to a new obsession, and it happened to be a particularly obscene and disturbing one: Donald Trump. The truth, I confess to my shame, is that every morning when I get up, the first thing I do is go and look up his latest scandals. I read all of it, in Portuguese, English, French and Spanish. I even use Google Translate, with tragic consequences, to try to understand what the Russian papers are saying about him. My partner has banned me from mentioning Trump's name in front of her, especially at mealtimes. I can't. I know things about Trump that I can't claim to know about myself. Just today, as I was writing this column, I discovered that the reason Trump's hair has that strange look about it is that, according to one of his doctors, he takes anti-androgens daily in an attempt to combat baldness. The medication can have unpleasant secondary effects, which I shall not mention here.

Luckily or unluckily, I am not alone in my obsession. I am certain that over the coming decades Trump will be used as a character in many hundreds of books and films. It occurs to me that the world would benefit immensely if it were possible to read those books and watch those films today, rather than fifty years from now. I imagine the past would have been far more pleasant if, back then, humanity had been able to read what people are writing today about Hitler, Mao and Stalin. Mad tyrants can make great literary characters. Ideally, they would only be fictional. Call it preventative fiction.

He's back

I'm rereading *Look Who's Back*, by Timur Vermes, the German writer of Hungarian origin, an intelligent, unsettling and extremely topical political satire that allows us to view our present age through the eyes of Adolf Hitler. The novel was released in 2012 to the great surprise of many in Germany, where it provoked an intense debate. That year it sold more than one million copies in Germany. The film, directed by David Wnendt and with a screenplay written by Vermes himself, came out in 2015. Good books that inspire even better films are very rare. This is one of them.

Look Who's Back begins with Hitler waking up in the middle of a field in Berlin, close to the bunker where was meant to have killed himself. He was fifty-six at the time, and that's the age he looks when he comes back to life. He doesn't know how he's ended up there. Later he will tell one of his followers that it may be due to his vegetarian diet. Hitler takes a while to realise that he's no longer in 1945, but has entered the twenty-first century. Finally, he has an epiphany: if he is alive seventy years after the end of the Third Reich, it can only be because he has been given a second opportunity to bring greatness back to the Germans – even though, as he repeatedly makes clear without making any attempt to hide his resentment, they have shown great ingratitude towards him and deserve every punishment they get.

To start with, people take him to be an impersonator, a poor street clown, and they laugh at him. The tyrant is not put off. He has a plan: to make Germany great again. And he knows how to achieve it: through television, the Internet, and all the other new means of communication. He begins by accepting a small role, playing himself, on a comedy show on a popular TV channel. The audience laughs, it's an enormous success … but Hitler isn't fooling around. Hitler never fools around.

Adolf Hitler's onscreen speeches are taken simply as amusing attempts to subvert tedious, politically correct thinking. But then, little by little, they begin to be taken seriously. Some people react with indignation and horror. Unfortunately, they are outnumbered by those who see themselves reflected in Hitler's hatred and bile, and feel sufficiently bold to call publicly for the expulsion of immigrants, the persecution of independent journalists and the building of walls.

The film mixes fictional scenes with real, prankster-style moments in which the main actor, Oliver Masucci, engages with unsuspecting citizens on the streets of Berlin and other German cities. The most unsettling moments in the film, which turn what could have been just another burlesque satire into a terrible denunciation, are those in which some of these citizens approach the actor, dressed up and in character as Adolf Hitler, and congratulate him – at which point we realise that they are not addressing Masucci, but the dictator. It's impossible not to laugh at Wnendt's film, but it is a terrified laughter.

These scenes are also important because they bolster the main point being made by the book and the film: it's easy to transform any old clown into a populist leader with a huge following. The clown just needs to know how to voice the key fears and concerns that afflict people, and then amplify that voice. The next step is the degradation of the free press and then, as a general rule, of all contrary opinions.

"To all intents and purposes, it was like the early Twenties all over again," Timur Vermes's Hitler says of his brilliant TV career. "With the difference that back then I took possession of a party. This time it was a television programme."

I shall close with something trivial and amusing, and mention that I was somewhat unsettled by the German writer's surname, which means "worms" in Portuguese. It might even affect his success in the Portuguese-speaking universe. It happens. Some years ago, at a gathering of writers in London, I came across the author of *The Last King of Scotland*. When we were introduced to each other, he grabbed me by the arm, took me to one corner of the room and asked me why all the Portuguese-language authors had laughed after reading his name (we were all wearing nametags). "Giles," I told him, "your surname is a whole approach to life. Unfortunately, there is a small spelling error in Portuguese. That must be why people are laughing."

I borrowed a pen and changed the *n* in *Foden* to an *m*. *Fodem* – meaning, *they fuck*. Now it was just right.

Muhamed's choice

On the Island of Mozambique/Muhipiti, where I've been living for the past few months, the overwhelming majority of people are Muslim. When Vasco da Gama arrived here in 1498, the island was already an important trading hub and centre of the Swahili language, populated by Arabs and black Africans whose *sheikh* was subject to the powerful Sultan of Zanzibar. A gentle form of Islam predominated, adapted to a mixed-race society of great travellers and traders. Slaves, wax, marble and blackwood were traded for Indian cloth and beads.

Along with the Portuguese came Christianity. Catholic churches were built next to the mosques. Indians came later, building Hindu temples. Over hundreds of years, right up into our own time, the Island has been a magnificent example of religious, ethnic and cultural tolerance. During Catholic festivals, it's common for the drummers playing on the steps of the church to be Muslims. Both Catholics and Muslims, in turn, never fully abandoned Bantu religious and magical practices, creating the kind of healthy mystical mishmash that is so familiar to Brazilians.

Until a few years ago it was difficult, on a day-to-day level, to distinguish Muslims from Christians. This has started to change. Today it's not unusual to see young women in the city's narrow streets wearing the *hijab*, and sometimes even heavy, black *burqas*. The "ninjas", as some call them, face the mockery of the younger citizens and the horror and distrust of the elder ones. The truth is, however, that their numbers grow with each passing year.

Speaking to some locals, it is possible to understand the origin of the phenomenon. For example, I spoke to eighteen-year-old Muhamed B., who spends his afternoons behind the counter of a stand in the bazaar selling traditional *capulanas*, the beautiful coloured cloths worn by all Mozambican women regardless of their origin and social rank. Muhamed is ambitious, but he knows he'll never get out from behind that counter unless he leaves the island. He tells me he has been invited to study in Saudi Arabia.

"To study what?" I ask.

He answers, almost embarrassed: "Islamic theology."

Clearly, studying Islamic theology in Saudi Arabia is not the same as studying Islamic theology at the Sorbonne. Saudi Arabia is both the heart and the head of radical Wahhabi Islam. Do not forget that, of the nineteen terrorists who killed themselves by launching two commercial planes into the Twin Towers in New York, fifteen were Saudi.

"Why Islamic theology?"

"Because the grants they offer are only to study Islamic theology," Muhamed says. "But I hope that once I'm in Riyadh, I'll be able to switch to another course. I want to study medicine. I'd really like to be a doctor."

Islamic fundamentalism spreads by taking advantage of poverty and the inefficiency of state apparatuses in Mozambique and in many other Islamic countries. What it essentially does is occupy empty spaces. Because there are no public schools, people have no alternative but to send their sons to *madrasas*, many of them financed by Saudi Arabia, with teachers who advocate the most radical versions of Islam.

In the years following independence in 1975, Mozambique received strong support from Northern European countries, and from Sweden in particular, which explains the residual presence of a small Scandinavian community on the Island of Mozambique and in other cities in the country. In the past decade, with the global economic crisis, the majority of programmes aimed at assisting development have ended up being cancelled and dismantled. It's no surprise that it is precisely now, as the West is pulling out, that Islamic fundamentalism is on the rise.

What many – starting with the current US administration – still have not understood, is that in a global world, the fight against Islamic fundamentalism and all the barbarity associated with it, including terrorism, can also be fought by promoting development. Muhamed could be studying medicine in Paris, Lisbon or São Paulo. Tomorrow he'd be saving lives in some hospital in Mozambique. Instead, he's going to Riyadh. The money wasted on a single day of fighting the self-proclaimed Islamic State in Syria would undoubtedly pay for Muhamed's entire education, as well as that of hundreds of others like him. It's a question of doing the maths and making the choice.

After the end

Writers can be divided into the ones who claim to suffer as they write, and those who say they have fun doing it. They can also be divided into those who write to find out how the story they've started ends, and those who only sit down to write after they've sketched out the entire structure in their heads and determined the plot down to the very last detail. I'm the kind who enjoys it; I'm also the kind who writes in order to learn what will happen next. The best part of the writing process – at least for those writers who enjoy writing and do it in order to know the ending – is the last few pages. What happens on those pages, when different and distant threads are tied up and the entire plot suddenly gains form and coherence, is a wonder that will never cease to astonish me.

There are many writers who let themselves be overcome with melancholy after finishing a new novel. For months we have watched the characters grow. We talk to them. We live with them. We learn with them. And then a page turns, and all those lives reach their conclusion. There is nothing left but an enormous silence, and a huge amount of empty time to fill.

It's true, though, that for the readers, those same lives whose endings we have just witnessed are only just beginning. They're always just beginning. They begin every time a new reader opens the book and starts to read. And as each reader creates a new book as they read, one determined by their own world, these lives are never exactly the same for any two people.

It's often the case that I only understand what I have written after a reader tells me their version. I find it harder and harder to talk about a book I've just finished writing. I'm pained by that fatal question journalists always ask me when I'm promoting a new title: "Can you tell me what the new book is about?"

I feel like telling them the truth: "Read it, and you tell me."

Many years ago, when I first started writing, I used to pretend I *did* know. I probably believed it. Now, if I'm lucky, I find out whenever a reader talks to me. Thus I am capable of expounding at length on the topic of my older books, as if I had in fact written them – but not my more recent ones. I feel like an impostor. If no one has read them yet, I haven't written them yet.

It is difficult to escape 'creator's melancholy' after the end. Writers opt for different ways of trying to elude it. In a recent interview, the Portuguese novelist Patrícia Reis explained that before submitting a new book to her publisher, she begins another: "The other book allows me to survive the necessary mourning of the characters." Patrícia joins one novel onto the next, like anxious smokers who keep lighting one cigarette with the butt of another until the whole packet – or life itself – is over.

I tend to do the same thing. Weeks before finishing a novel, I begin making lists of projects. I used to take no notice of the impossible ones. Today I note everything down, then leave out whatever seems too easy, and then begin to sound out just how possible the impossible ideas are. The impossibilities, the frightening ones, are the only ones that are worth exploring. Writing, just like living, means actively seeking to be surprised.

I know writers who try to bat away the sadness that fills this sudden void with other forms of artistic expression: they paint, take photos, compose *fados*, create maps of imaginary cities. Some are highly competent at their parallel activities. Bruce Chatwin was a pretty good photographer. Nabokov drew butterflies. Ferreira Guilar made collages and copies of famous paintings. Mia Couto plays violin. Valter Hugo Mãe sings *fado*. Afonso Cruz spends his time producing craft beer and blues music. Ruy Duarte de Carvalho, one of the greatest names in Portuguese-language African poetry, used to paint beautiful watercolours of oxen: I have two of them, properly framed, in front of my desk. When I look at them, I travel straight to southern Angola.

I have finished a new novel. I shall spend several months more inside that world, working with editors and copy editors and correcting proofs, but I've already begun to say goodbye to it. Yes, melancholy is inevitable, along with the fear of never being able to write again. I make lists of projects. I take photos. I paint watercolours (though without the talent of a Ruy Duarte). One of these days I hope to go back to writing, as if it were the first time, with the same sense of surprise, the same unease, the same inability to understand exactly what it is I'm doing – until it's over, until someone reads it and tells me.

Wonderful cultural appropriation

Africa's greatest wealth is its extraordinary ethnic and cultural diversity. Along with this, there is its curiosity towards others and its capacity to assimilate and integrate external cultural expressions, reinventing them, renewing them, giving them more colour and energy. This is also one of Brazil's great virtues. An African inheritance, perhaps.

I thought about this again while listening to the new Orchestra Baobab album, *Tribute to Ndiouga Dieng*, a glorious return reminiscent of the group's best work in the '70s and '80s. Orchestra Baobab began in Dakar, the capital of Senegal, as the resident band in a club of the same name. All of Africa danced to their Cuban rhythms. The band's two singers were originally from Casamance, a part of Senegal where they still speak a Portuguese-based creole, and perhaps that is why they felt inclined to sing in Spanish, or in an invented language they believed to be Spanish. They also sang in Casamance creole, Wolof and other Senegalese languages. Between 1970 and 1985 (when the group broke up), they released twenty albums with some of the happiest and brightest songs the continent has ever produced, mixing Cuban rhythms with the local tradition.

The group resurfaced in 2001, in the wake of the success of Buena Vista Social Club. Not by chance, British producer Nick Gold, who was behind the launch of Buena Vista, had, in 1987, released *Pirate's Choice*, a compilation of Orchestra Baobab's best songs. Ndiouga Dieng, to whom the new album pays tribute, was one of the longest-serving members of the band and passed away last year.

Orchestra Baobab was not the first African band to reinvent Cuban sounds, rumba or merengue. Along Africa's west coast, the mix of Latin rhythms and local traditions has spawned, in recent decades, countless musical genres, such as the powerful Zairian rumba or the Angolan merengue.

What happens with music, in Africa, happens with all other forms of cultural, creative and artistic expression. Angola's rich cuisine integrates harmoniously with Portuguese and Brazilian traditions. In Mozambique, Indian cuisine merges and becomes entwined with local flavours. The magnificent headdresses of Herero woman in Namibia, one of the country's postcard images, are nothing if not reminiscent of Victorian times: Namibian women appropriated the style from the wives of British missionaries, who arrived in the country at the beginning of the twentieth century, and gave it colour and glamour. Cultural appropriation, some would say, although in this case, I think we could also call it intelligence, generosity, creativity and openness to others.

A few years ago, I was invited to a small literary festival in a German town. I discovered, on arrival, that the festival was organised by a young black German of Congolese origin. At the end of my talk, the young man got up, thanked me and explained he had not only invited me because he liked my books, but also to show German readers that in Africa there exists a great ethnic diversity, which includes many communities of European, Indian and Malayan descent (in Madagascar, in the latter instance). He added that in Germany, his compatriots rarely viewed him as an equal: "Whenever I say I'm German, I have to face a certain surprise. I plan on going into politics, but I know I'll have many difficulties owing to the colour of my skin. I only wish Europeans were as open and generous to immigrants as Africans are."

The truth is that in Africa, strong xenophobic tendencies do also exist. You only have to look at the recent demonstrations in South Africa against mainly black immigrants from Mozambique, Congo and Mali. That, however, is not the norm. The norm is what we can see in Orchestra Baobab's work: an immense curiosity and generosity; a desire to experience everything; a world of hunger; that power of taking what is different, giving it its own look, making it an undeniable part of the national whole.

I cannot explain where this African talent for integrating and assimilating came from. I like to think that as Africa is the mother continent, the cradle of humanity, there remains in every African's heart a desire to embrace the whole planet. More than that – the capacity to see in every person all of humanity, exiled throughout the world. Either that, or I suffer from a dangerous excess of romanticism. Which is quite likely.

While the earth shakes

My son Carlos was four or five when he watched a video of my wedding for the first time. For a few minutes he followed the images with rapt attention. He laughed, amused, when recognising cousins, uncles, aunts, family friends. At a certain point, however, he fell into a deep silence.
He called for me: "Daddy, where am I, at that party?"
"You're not there."
"I'm not?" He was a picture of indignation. "So, you got married and didn't invite your own son?!"
I told him that back then, he did not exist yet. It was the worst thing I could have said. He looked at me, more than outraged, horrified: "I didn't exist?! What do you mean I didn't exist? I have always existed."
I share my son's indignation. The idea of not always having existed scares me even more than that of one day no longer existing. Worse than ceasing to exist is not having existed for all eternity, or almost all of it – which, really, comes to the same thing. So the Universe has been partying for millions of years, stars exploding in endless space, worlds forming, Earth gaining life, the first man opening his eyes in Africa – probably Angola, I suspect even in Huambo, right where today the yard of the house in which I was born and grew up is – and they are only inviting me now?
I never saw Nefertiti, Mistress of Upper and Lower Egypt, Lady of All Women, Sweet of Love, dancing by the Nile. I never saw Nebuchadnezzar wander the hanging gardens of Babylon at twilight, or, in old age, suffer from lycanthropy, spitting and howling like a wolf at full moon. I never saw Qin Shi Huang, First Emperor of China, walking along what would become the Great Wall. I never saw Queen Nzinga strut, dressed as a man, among her harem of more than fifty men, whom she dressed as women. I never saw Zumba ruling Quilombo dos Palmares. I never had the chance to

talk to Eça de Queirós, both of us seated at a table in La Columnata Egipciana café in Havana, where he wrote some of his first stories. I never travelled by zeppelin. I never heard Louis Armstrong play trumpet on the streets of New Orleans. I never witnessed the surprise of the French when they heard the music of Pixinguinha and the Oito Batutas in Paris in 1922 (it is hard to understand how no Brazilian writer has yet immortalised this journey, nor any filmmaker shown interest).

I think, by way of consolation, that I did get handed a curious time: I witnessed the moment Armstrong (not the one with the trumpet; the other one, Neil) planted his foot on lunar soil, while speaking a phrase that he had rehearsed dozens of times on Earth: *That's one small step for man, one giant leap for mankind.* I followed from a distance, through the pages of *Paris Match* magazine (to which my mother subscribed), the joyous outbreak of May 1968. Although I was very young, I remember the mocking blue eyes of Daniel Cohn-Bendit, holding the gaze of a police officer. I bore witness to the independence of Angola and the other Portuguese-speaking African countries, and I was in the Grand Parade in Cape Town when Nelson Mandela spoke, celebrating the end of apartheid and the foundation of a new South Africa, the Rainbow Nation he tried to establish.

The fast-paced days of the present are even more interesting. More unsettling, too. We are going through a patch of turbulence, and it is no use looking for the safety belt at your seat, because there is no belt; there's no seat, either, and we can't be sure whether or not there is even a pilot in the cockpit. We are living in the midst of a storm, in a volatile and dangerous time. We go to sleep, and when we wake up the world has changed:

"Have you read the papers? They arrested someone else for corruption!"

"And the president?! Didn't they arrest the president?"

In Angola, not yet. In Venezuela, not yet. In South Africa, not yet. In Brazil, not yet; but in some other country, they probably have done. It can be scary, so much news, so much turmoil ... it's so relentless. However, we cannot but feel a certain excitement, too. The truth is that this present points to a better future. Tomorrow there will still be corrupt politicians, I am sorry to say. But there will be fewer than today. They will be less protected, and they will live in fear.

I shall never reconcile myself to the idea of not always having existed. However, if in the time I have left I might be able to witness the end of major corruption, globally, I shall be content.

Tiradentes' lice

Joaquim, the Marcelo Gomes film that came to Brazilian cinemas last week, proves that intelligent life still exists in the world of Portuguese-language cinematic fiction.

The first sign of intelligence was the refusal by this director from Pernambuco to tell Tiradentes' life story. The film begins at the end, with Joaquim José da Silva Xavier (or, more precisely, his severed head) lamenting his sad misfortune, declaring that he had ended up like this for being, of all the Minas Gerais conspirators, the poorest and most unfortunate.

Many historians think the same, disagreeing only about that severed head having been unlucky. Tiradentes did not achieve hero status, glory and posterity for how he lived, but for how he died. The Portuguese wanted to make an example of him to discourage future conspiracies, and turned his execution into a grand public spectacle. Had they transported him to Angola or Mozambique, quietly, as they did with his co-conspirators, there would not be a public holiday in his honour today in Brazil; most probably, the story of the Minas Gerais Conspiracy would be unknown to the majority of Brazilians.

Gomes shows us Joaquim before he became an agitator against the monarchy and Portuguese rule: a common man, in the midst of a cruel, harsh and confusing time. The scene in which Preta the slave inspects the young officer's long hair, looking for lice, and, later, when she cuts it roughly with a knife, nicely sums up the protagonist's ideological confusion. At one point, Tiradentes warns the slave – about whom he is crazy – not to criticise the Portuguese, as he considers himself one of them.

The icon of the long-haired, bearded hero is a more recent creation of republican Brazil. Even after independence, while the monarchy was maintained, Tiradentes remained in relative obscurity. The revolutionary republicans remembered him for the way he died, and resurrected him with the body of an improbable Baroque Christ.

Nothing new there. All countries invent their founding heroes, some of whom have only the remotest connection to the nation that claims them. That is the case of the 'Portuguese' hero Viriato, a tribal leader who fought the Roman legions. Viriato, naturally, did not fight for Portugal, or even an idea of Portugal. Quite the contrary: if his warriors had won, today there would *be* no Portugal – a country that, culturally and ethnically speaking, is a direct consequence of first the Roman then Arab presence on the Iberian Peninsula.

The choice of African actors to play African slaves, as well as Portuguese to play the Portuguese and indigenous actors to play indigenous characters, also seems to be an intelligent and courageous one, adding truth to the film. Truth, it is important to remember, is different to credibility. The excellent Zezé Mota is credible playing an African woman; that is, she looks African. Isabel Zuaa and Welket Bungué, the two actors of Guinea-Bissauan origin who bring the main black characters to life, however, do not just look African – they *are* African.

In a recent interview, Gomes explained that it was not simply a question of accents: "I need Portuguese actors to play the Portuguese, because even the way they walk is different."

One of the most interesting aspects of the film has to do with the idea of incommunicability between the various ethnicities that make up Brazil: indigenous, African and Portuguese. This idea is even more interesting for opposing the sacred cliché of the mixed-race *mestiço* country, the cultural melting pot. In the film, the Portuguese do not understand what the indigenous people and Africans are saying – nor do they care; in fact, they do not even understand the Portuguese-speaking Brazilians, who, though speaking the same language, are conveying different worlds. The director's decision not to translate speech in Guarani or Guinea-Bissauan creole puts the viewer in Joaquim's shoes. What was strangest for me was hearing all the Africans talking among themselves in beautiful and musical Guinea-Bissauan creole, a language that only began to resemble its current form in the nineteenth century; not to mention Preta's inexplicable Lisbon-accented perfect Portuguese.

Here and there, moments of sharing and communication do occur, and it is then that we see Brazil being born – for example, in the scene in which the indigenous guide (Karay Rya Pua) sings and dances with Joaquim's slave (Welket Bungué). I love the idea that it was music, and not any spoken language, that united the various founding ethnicities of Brazil. If it was not so, it should have been.

Thursday, 4 May 2017

Political Identity and Conflict in Central Angola, 1975–2002 by Justin Pearce has just been launched in Lisbon. Pearce is a former journalist and currently a Fellow in Politics and International Studies at the University of Cambridge, England.

The book presents itself as being "the first major piece of research on the Angolan Civil War". That does not seem entirely true: first, it is modestly sized for such a vast and complex saga. Second, there are already several other works that deal with the issue, accounts from people involved in the war, above all on the UNITA side, such as *Memórias de um Guerrilheiro* by Alcides Sakala and *Angola, a Segunda Revolução: Memórias da luta pela Democracia* by Jardo Muekalia. These two titles are, first and foremost, insider accounts by people who lived through the war, but also include reflection and consideration. I still remember *Jogos Africanos* by the Portuguese academic and businessman Jaime Nogueira Pinto, who similarly mixed essay and eyewitness testimony; it includes a series of extremely interesting accounts of life within UNITA during the civil war, throwing light on some of the key crises the movement faced.

In his book, Justin Pearce shows how the MPLA seized power after independence, capitalising on the splits in UNITA to legitimise itself internally and externally. The book's key strength is its use of interviews with ordinary citizens in an attempt to understand lengthy, complex processes such as the appropriation of the state apparatus by the MPLA. Based on these accounts, Pearce proposes various controversial theories: for instance, that the MPLA (or the government, as the party is conflated with the government and the state itself) supported migration to the cities, emptying the countryside, with the sole aim of depleting the guerrillas.

Pearce also appears critical with regard to UNITA's ability to create a parallel state. The party of the black cockerel imposed itself on rural communities more through force and fear than by persuasion, and in all areas under its control took more than it gave to the inhabitants.

For an Angolan, Pearce's book offers nothing new. It is useful, however, in giving a view of the country that is not limited to Luanda and the big cities, serving, also, as a pretext for a more in-depth debate about the way the civil war 'constructed' and 'deconstructed' Angola. I hope that in the coming years other books can add to it with both internal and external viewpoints; the greater the number of versions and perspectives that exist, the better we will be able to understand the terrible tragedy the country went through.

Sunday, 7 May 2017

I was fascinated by the blend of naïveté and fearlessness – almost provocation – displayed by the businessman and art collector Sindika Dokolo in a recent interview in *Novo Jornal*, in which he spoke of Luaty Beirão as an example of Angolan sincerity: "Even though I don't love what he does, or his ideas, which are almost anarchist, he has that very Angolan quality: bravery in his fight."

Some might explain Sindika's words by saying that with the imminent departure of José Eduardo dos Santos, those who are close to him are looking to assure their own survival by praising people they previously criticised. In other words, they now want to be on good terms with both God and the Devil. I do not think so. I believe in Sindika's sincerity. Ultimately, the president's son-in-law is merely saying out loud what, in the privacy of the Presidential Palace halls, his family, friends and associates have been whispering among themselves. I am sure that, like Sindika, the majority of the regime's supporters admire Luaty for his courage and dignity – and what's not to admire? Moreover: they all know Luaty's cause is just. The bat knows the night. The traitor knows betrayal.

In any case, we tend to admire in others what we lack ourselves. Citing Luaty as an example of Angolan honesty, Sindika is also trying to extend that quality to those within his circle, like those indigenous tribes in Brazil that devoured their enemies, hoping to assimilate their bravery.

I was also fascinated by the reference to Luaty's supposed anarchism. Anarchism reached its zenith a century ago, advocating a world without governments, gods or borders. That early anarchism supported terrorist tactics to destroy the bourgeoisie, capitalism and the Catholic Church. I do not believe Luaty supports those methods. On the contrary, he and his comrades always deploy non-violent strategies to defend their ideals. That our predatory bourgeoisie fears and trembles before potential anarchist movements is, I believe, a funny and wonderful irony of history.

The good news is Luaty will be at the FLIP festival in Paraty at the end of July, in a debate that is part of the event's official programme. Luaty will use the event to present the Brazilian edition of his prison memoir, *Sou Eu Mais Livre, Então* (*Am I Freer, Then?*), as well as a collection of his song lyrics, *Kanguei no Maiki*.

It will be worth going to FLIP this year just for that panel. I shall be there to see, in the flesh, a display of that Angolan honesty so praised by Sindika Dokolo.

The European explorer financed by an African king

I've been working on the script for a film set in the nineteenth century, in which some of the action takes place in Angola and touches upon the incalculable crime of slavery and the horrific abduction of millions of Africans to Brazil. While researching old documents, I stumbled upon a name that has fascinated me for many years: Ladislau Magyar.

Throughout the nineteenth century, Europe went through a period of intense curiosity about Africa. Explorers from England, France, Portugal, etc. crisscrossed the continent and recounted their adventures in widely circulated newspapers and books. In doing so, they became celebrities, almost as famous as today's film stars.

The majority of these scientists and travellers relied on the support – at times very generous – of newspapers, their respective governments or institutions such as the Royal Geographical Society in London. Ladislau (the Portuguese form of the Hungarian name László) Magyar took an infinitely more interesting and original path: he married a princess from the Ovimbundu people and obtained the support of his new father-in-law to carry out his expeditions. I suspect he was the only one of his type: a European explorer financed by an African king.

In his writings, Magyar describes some curious aspects of life among the Ovimbundu. He writes, for example, that his father-in-law used to send young slaves to Luanda to learn how to read. Once they could read, the young men would return to the central plateau of Angola and become secretaries in the royal household. Paradoxically, it was their status as slaves that allowed them access to books, and perhaps even liberation.

This practice reminded me of a similar one in Mauritania. A large expanse of West African desert wedged between Morocco to the north and Senegal and Mali to the south, Mauritania was the last country in the world to make slavery illegal. In fact, it did so several times, most recently in 2007. For hundreds of years, nomadic, light-skinned Moorish tribes – the so-called "white Moors" – dominated the country, enslaving the blacks. The French, who colonised the territory from the beginning of the nineteenth century onwards, tried to impose a sedentary lifestyle and European education on the local population, without great success. The wealthier "white Moors" refused to send their children to school; instead, they sent the children of their slaves. In 1960, France agreed to the country's independence. Many of these black, slave children, who had received a formal education, succeeded in obtaining important positions in the government and civil service, to the consternation of the light-skinned minority. In 1989, on the pretext of a war with Senegal, thousands of black Mauritanians were put on buses and expelled across the border. I became friends with two black Mauritanians who lived through that tragedy. One day they were Mauritanians; the next morning, they found themselves in a strange land without passports and without a country. Both of them ended up studying in Lisbon as stateless persons supported by international institutions, until eventually they regained their nationality and returned home.

A few months ago, in Maputo, I took part in a debate with a Mozambican writer who uses the pseudonym "Deusa de África" – Goddess of Africa. Deusa had written a novel titled *Equity in the Celestial Kingdom*, in which people reawaken after their deaths in a world where whites are slaves and blacks support slavery. Some readers were clearly uncomfortable with the theme of the novel. I have to say I feel rather envious of the writer, not only for her self-esteem (I try to imagine changing my name to "God of Africa"), but above all for succeeding in causing discomfort.

I like stories, both real and fictional, that turn the world upside down, break with the comfort of moral standards and preconceived ideas and put us in the place of the Other, obliging us to experience the world as if we'd been born in a stranger's body.

The Angolan poet Ana Paula Tavares has written a long poem celebrating "The Love Story of Princess Ozoro and the Hungarian Ladislau Magyar". Ozoro's voice alternates with that of her betrothed;

a chorus of old women; a chorus of young girls and a chorus of sorcerers. At a certain point, Magyar asks for Ozoro's hand:

> I bring some drowsy wine from the interior of the
> land and the strategy of a Hungarian game, I move the bishop by
> a straight line to the house of the king, my lord. So here
> I am and I introduce myself, my name the same as the name of my
> people, Magyar, they of the journeys, Magyar, they of the gypsies.
> My lord
> I brought my horses and I offer you my knowledge of
> wheat; in exchange I ask for guides to new paths, food
> for my caravans, permission to enter Ochilombo, and the hand of
> Ozoro the more-than-perfect.
> My lord, let her heal me from the fever and pain I bring
> from the mountain beyond the Carpathians.
> My lord, let her teach me to be of the land.

As told by Ana Paula, it is the most beautiful love story I know.

The ideal kleptocracy

A Protestant pastor was recently kidnapped in Luanda by a gang of young criminals. The terrified pastor initially thought they intended to rob him or demand a ransom from his family. No. Pointing a pistol at his head, they insisted that he pray for them while other members of their gang carried out a major robbery in another part of the city. The criminals wanted God as their accomplice, and, by the way, they also wanted His forgiveness – even at gunpoint.

The method adopted by these Angolan thugs – kidnap a priest to get God's attention and blessing – may be unusual, but their intention isn't. Throughout human history, we find hundreds of examples of devout criminals who believe they are acting in God's name, and even criminals who, following their deaths, come to be worshipped as saints. Lampião, the nineteenth-century king of Brazilian banditry, prayed a lot. He liked to carry round his neck grubby little pouches containing prayers and superstitious charms. Jararaca ("Snake"), one of his henchmen who was captured and summarily shot at the age of twenty-six, is now a very popular saint out in the arid interior of north-eastern Brazil. I visited his grave in Mossoró, and found dozens of candles lit around the hard lump of rock. Thousands of pilgrims come from far away to pray for miracles and blessings. Jararaca may have failed as a bandit, but as a saint his career is going from strength to strength. Being a popular saint is one of the very few career opportunities after death.

What's new is that today's bandits don't only want God as their accomplice; they also demand to have the law on their side. They seek, by every available means, the respect of society and the approval of the masses. While never renouncing their banditry – robbing, threatening, blackmailing, possibly killing – they want to be treated with the respect due to honest citizens. They want honest citizens to welcome them into their homes and to take genuine pride in them as fellow citizens.

Previously, honest folk enjoyed certain perks compared to big bandits. For example, what my grandmother used to call "the sleep of the just": a privilege reserved exclusively for honest people. An enormous privilege, we can all agree. Bandits would all supposedly suffer from terrible insomnia, and honest people would sleep soundly. It no longer works like that. Today's bandits are born without a conscience. The few who still come equipped with that archaic spiritual mechanism take Xanax. This has made it impossible to distinguish bandits from honest citizens by the dark circles under their eyes.

The *Houaiss Dictionary of the Portuguese Language* defines kleptocracy as "a socio-political regime in which corrupt practices with public money are implicitly permitted or even celebrated". Those are the ordinary kleptocracies. There are quite a few around the world. Brazil – its more fervent patriots may be disappointed to hear – is not the only one. Let's now try to imagine the perfect kleptocracy. In an ideal kleptocracy, the one all big bandits dream of, they would succeed not only in taking control of the apparatuses of state, including the judicial system, but also obtain the respect and admiration of the people. In this perfect kleptocracy, there would be nothing to distinguish a big bandit from an honest person other than wealth and the source of that wealth.

In the ideal kleptocracy, honest citizens who are sufficiently courageous to speak out against the bandits who have seized power risk being tried and imprisoned for defamation or treason. In the ideal kleptocracy, honest citizens secretly envy the big bandits, and aspire to become big bandits themselves. In the perfect kleptocracy, the big bandits tailor the laws to fit their respective illegalities, thereby preventing unforeseen judicial prosecutions and protecting themselves against the emergence of unexpectedly honest judges. At the very pinnacle of perfect kleptocracy, every law would serve the interests of the big bandits. Corruption would then be global, endemic, ingrained and irreversible.

This does not, however, mean that the 'golden age' of such a system would entail the enrichment of everyone in society (illicitly, of course). Quite the opposite. The ideal kleptocracy, at the very peak of its glory, would be a society consisting of an infinitely small minority of extremely rich robber barons, and a vast majority of incredibly poor petty thieves – petty thieves, then, like the ones who kidnapped a Protestant pastor in Luanda to get God's attention and obtain His forgiveness.

The end of miracles

On a fine July morning in 1518, in the main square in Strasbourg, a woman began to dance. Anyone watching her would have thought it a little strange: there was no music, and she was moving very vigorously but without a hint of elegance or joy. By nightfall, a handful of people had joined her. A week later, there were around thirty dancers. By August, more than 400 dancers filled the square with their strange and unruly masque. The civil and religious authorities were mindful of other, similar occurrences. In Aachen (Aix-la-Chapelle) in the summer of 1374, dozens of people had danced in silence, for weeks, in an epidemic that spread to other towns and cities.

It was thought that providing musicians might bring some order to the chaos and contain the mysterious outbreak; but that only made things worse. The crowd grew, and carried on dancing. Some of the musicians even joined the dancers. Many of them whirled round and round, until they fell down dead.

At the time, people spoke of witchcraft. Today it's believed that the dancers may have been victims of poisoning from ergot, a type of fungus commonly found on rye and other cereals. For centuries, hundreds of women were persecuted as witches, in a series of tragedies such as those described above, which the wisdom of the time was incapable of explaining. Mysterious events were usually classified as either the work of the Devil, i.e. witchcraft, or the work of God, i.e. miracles.

As science advances, God and the Devil tend to become less active. This does not necessarily imply the collapse of religions. As a matter of fact, in recent decades we have witnessed the strengthening of various religious currents, and there are even cases, such as Iran, where societies that were largely secular have returned to theocratic regimes. When I talk about the gradual lethargy of God and the Devil, I mean merely that room for prodigious events, whether miracles or witchcraft, will tend to diminish.

As I write this piece, Pope Francis is visiting the Sanctuary of Fátima, in Portugal. There were a million people waiting for him. A large proportion of the foreign pilgrims came from Brazil. The Pope travelled to Portugal to canonise Francisco and Jacinta Marto, two of the three children who, in 1917, claimed to have seen and spoken with the Virgin Mary while tending their family's sheep. The two children died the following year, victims of the terrible "Spanish flu" pandemic that, between 1918 and 1919, took the lives of millions of people around the world. (The precise number isn't known; the estimates vary between 50 and 100 million.) The surviving child, Lúcia dos Santos, died in 2005 at the age of ninety-seven, having spent her whole life behind the high walls of various convents.

In the early years, the Catholic Church refused to accept the children's account. It only did so in 1930, leading to the Sanctuary of Fátima's rapid expansion. The town's name is Arab in origin: Fátima was one of the Prophet Muhammad's daughters, and the only one to give him descendants. For this reason, to this day, it is one of the most common names for Muslim women. According to an old local legend, the town was given the name in honour of an Arab princess at the time of the so-called "Moorish" colonisation of the Iberian Peninsula.

It isn't surprising that many Muslims feel an affinity for, and even venerate, Our Lady of Fátima. The Portuguese newspapers recently reported the story of a young Lebanese Muslim man called Sami Aoun, who travelled from Beirut to visit Fátima, covering the last couple of hundred metres on his knees. Sami thinks the Western news media do not understand Islam and the relationship between Muslims and Jesus Christ: "A Muslim must believe first in Christianity, and only then in Islam. Because Christianity came first and opened the way for all peoples to believe in a single God. I believe in the Virgin Mary. As a Muslim, I believe in Jesus Christ, and I love him dearly."

On the other hand, many Catholics show no inclination towards the cult of Our Lady of Fátima. According to Father Mário de Oliveira, author of *Fátima, Never Again*, the Sanctuary of Fátima is a "circus act", a "puppet theatre of apparitions". In his opinion, the three children were victims of an outdated Church that terrorised the faithful by disseminating the image of a cruel, sadistic and vindictive God.

In his most recent novel, *In Your Womb*, the writer José Luís Peixoto has chosen not to take sides, neither validating nor contradicting the "apparitions" theory. Instead, he concentrates on the difficult day-to-day lives of three children in a village lost to the world. It is literature trying to comprehend the incomprehensible.

It could be, as I suggested earlier, that scientific advances will take away room for miracles. The human fascination with mysterious events, however, is something I think will never go away.

Monday, 19 June 2017

A trip to Dublin. There was a lady waiting for us at the airport and another one at our hotel, with strict instructions for us to remain in hiding. And so here we are, like secret agents, fleeing from journalists. Nevertheless, we went for a stroll around the city, which is very beautiful, full of young and charming people, and bought a couple more amusing T-shirts and a dress for Yara. I'd already bought her two at the airport. She looks stunningly beautiful in all of them.

In Portugal, all the talk is about fires. It's a big deal. I hope it may help us to rethink how we manage our forests. We'll see. In Dublin it's a beautiful day, mild temperatures. Lots of sunshine.

Wednesday, 21 June 2017

An incredibly intense, tiring day. The ceremony for the handing-out of the International Dublin Literary Award was complicated, ostentatious and vaguely preposterous (there was even a fanfare), and my feet were hurting horribly – but it all ended up working out fine. Daniel translated and delivered my speech. We did yet another interview in the afternoon, for radio, and at night we had to sit through another formal dinner, with all the dignitaries and members of the judging panel. We've already got the cheque.

Without Yara's support, the whole thing would have been awful. As it was, we both managed to laugh about it, even at dinner – though by then we were both very tired.

Here's my acceptance speech:

> Good afternoon.
>
> My name is José Eduardo Agualusa.
>
> *Agualusa* is a word that has almost completely disappeared from the Portuguese language. As a surname, it's rarer still. Old sailors used to use the word to describe a sea that was calm and luminous. I imagine it started out as some sailor's nickname – a distant Portuguese grandfather, no doubt.
>
> I believe certain names impose their destinies. Perhaps that's why, despite having been born in Huambo, a city in Angola's central plateau, almost 300 kilometres from the coast at an altitude of 2000 metres, I've always felt drawn to the sea.
>
> I chose to live beside the sea in Luanda, in Lisbon, in Rio de Janeiro, or on the Island of Mozambique. All these cities are characters in my books – but most of all Luanda, Angola's capital, a port city founded in 1575, a place both beautiful and awful, ferocious and sweet, a place of unlikely encounters and

the stage for the wildest stories. Luanda is the main character in *A General Theory of Oblivion*. The other is an old Portuguese lady, Ludovica, who is terrified by the city and its inhabitants, and walls herself off in an apartment.

The novel's subject is the fear of the Other. It seems – I'm sorry to say – that the subject is even more current today than when I wrote it. In the troubled times we're going through, in this world in search of new political thinking and new ideals, the fear of the Other is a kind of conflagration started by pyromaniacs that threatens to consume us all.

In my novel, Ludo is saved by a boy who allows her to see what is obvious: there is no Other. The Other is always ourselves. Each man is all of humanity.

This is also a book about the fear felt by those who live under totalitarian regimes. I once spent a year in Berlin, thanks to a literary bursary. The Wall had been brought down some years earlier. At that time, however, it was still possible for any foreigner to recognise which neighbourhoods had been on the side of the defunct German Democratic Republic. You always knew you'd crossed over the moment the city started losing its colour. One evening, as I walked the grey neighbourhoods of East Berlin, I remembered an example of environmental adaptation studied by most biology students: a type of butterfly in an industrial English city that lost its original colours so as better to hide, to escape its potential predators. In places subjected to totalitarian regimes, something similar happens to their citizens. Fear steals away the colour. People start preferring shades of grey. They lose their originality, their irreverence, their exuberance. They force themselves to disappear into the crowd. In a dictatorship, nobody wants to attract the attention of their predators. Fear immobilises, and it degrades. People aren't just afraid of being arrested for having made a sour comment about the President of the Republic in a public place, or because they were reading a particular book. People are afraid of losing their jobs because they were seen in public with somebody who didn't look afraid. They're afraid of expressing any opinion outside the norm. They're afraid of talking out loud, laughing out loud, thinking out loud. They're afraid, then, of existing too much. So they exist on a small scale, disguised, invisible. Fear steals our individuality. Fear steals our lives.

The greatest writers are able to put their readers into another person's skin. I think that's the greatest virtue of reading. By entering the skin of different narrators, by feeling a part of other lives, a reader increasingly finds himself part of the rest of humanity. In my view – and I'll venture to share this belief with you, naïve though some will find it – great readers have less propensity to violence and hate. First, because violence is always a surrendering of intelligence, a retreat of thinking. But mostly because reading, as an exercise in otherness, brings people closer.

I come from a country, Angola, which has suffered a long and cruel civil war. I experienced this war as a citizen and as a journalist. I've learned a bit about wars. I learned, for example, that in order to generate a favourable climate of hysteria, creators of civil wars start out by de-nationalising the enemy. Then they go on to question the enemy's humanity. The enemy is first a foreigner, then a monster. And a monster, and a foreign one at that, can be killed. *Should* be killed.

Great literature, meanwhile, almost always works in the opposite direction. It allows us to see the humanity in others, even those foreign to us. Even those who seem like monsters to us.

I was glad to learn that a book of mine was chosen for this prize for many reasons, but particularly because of the selection process – because the books are chosen by public libraries – and because the whole award process is run by Dublin City Public Libraries. I became a writer in public libraries, not only because if I hadn't had access to books in some of these libraries as a child, I never would have started writing, but because, to a great extent, my first book was actually written in a public library.

If literature develops our empathy muscles, makes us better people, then you might think of public libraries as weapons of massive construction: powerful tools for personal development and the development of societies.

The fight for democratisation, for pacification and for the development of countries such as Angola undoubtedly entails the creation of good networks of public libraries capable of bringing books to their readers. My very best dream – and I dream a lot; I have epic, grandiose dreams – is to contribute a network like that to my country's development. I dream of the day when all Angolan children, all Angolan young people, can read – just as I read when I was their age – the great writers of universal literature.

I'm also delighted that this prize is not just for authors but also for translators. Translators are writers, too, writers who are generous, sometimes almost invisible and largely responsible for a book's success.

And so I want to take this chance to thank my translator into English, Daniel Hahn. We started this adventure in English-language publishing together, some years ago, with a little novel called *Creole*.

Books have given me a great deal. Best of all, they have given me some friends. Danny is one of those.

I was also pleased to learn that there were two African writers on this year's shortlist: Chinelo Okparanta and Mia Couto.

Mia is more than a friend to me. For many years, he's been my big brother. He phoned me a few days ago, from Maputo, in Mozambique. "Hey," he said, "apparently I lost the Dublin prize."

"I'm really sorry – they told me that my book won," I replied, breaking the rule that I was supposed to keep the news secret till today. Then Mia laughed. I heard the laugh of my best friend, my big brother, like an explosion of light: "In that case, I didn't lose. We won!"

Yes, we both won. So from this place I send my greetings to my Mozambican brother Mia Couto; I send my greetings to my Nigerian sister Chinelo Okparanta. I send my greetings to all African writers, those who came before me and shaped me and made me a writer, and those who journey with me today, in this common project of rethinking our continent and making it known to the rest of the world, with all the pains and tragedies that afflict us, yes, but also with all our great joy, creativity, hope and love.

Thank you very much.

Secret authors

I'm in Dublin for the first time. I don't know much about the city beyond what I've read in the books written by some of the most important names in world literature, who were born and lived here, names such as James Joyce, Oscar Wilde, George Bernard Shaw and Samuel Beckett. There cannot be any other city in the world of a similar size that has produced so many great writers. As we wandered through the city we spotted a pub, Davy Byrne's. Yes, they assured us, it's the very same one where Leopold Bloom drank a glass of wine and ate a cheese sandwich. Only a few days ago, 16 June, the city celebrated "Bloomsday", named in honour of this famous character in *Ulysses*. Leopold Bloom is, as it happens, the only literary character to have a day named after him.

Daniel Hahn quipped that all the statues in Dublin are of writers. Not all, but certainly a majority. In any event, a city that has more statues of writers than politicians is certainly to be highly recommended.

In recent days I've been talking with Daniel about translation. A book can be said to be well translated when the readers don't even notice the presence of a translator; or, to put it another way, when the book seems to have been written directly in that language. The best translator, therefore, is invisible. But is that really the case? Perhaps not entirely. Daniel argues – and I think he's right – that the translator creates the author as he translates him.

The Spanish writer José Manuel Fajardo, who, like many other writers, has proved also to be an excellent translator, told me something similar: "I think of every writer I translate as if he were a character, with a particular style. I strive to be that writer in the same way that, when I write a novel, I strive to be a particular narrator."

Daniel became a translator with *Creole* (2002), one of my first novels, and since then he has translated a further four. After all these years, it's highly likely my books have acquired their own distinctive voice in the English language. Clearly this would not have happened if each novel had been worked on by a different translator.

Ulysses is itself a good example of how translators reinvent books. In Brazil, there are three translations: Houaiss's from 1966; Bernardina da Silveira Pinheiro's, published in 2005; and Caetano Galindo's, from 2012. The book is the same. And no, the book is *not* the same. Each one of these versions has its own characteristic colouring, the voice that Daniel refers to, whether more Gongoristic or mannered (Houaiss), reserved and academic (Pinheiro) or colourful (Galindo), which gives the book a varied personality.

Let's imagine, for a moment, a writer with an extensive, complex but cohesive bibliography, such as António Lobo Antunes. If I've counted correctly, he already has some twenty-seven novels under his belt, in addition to his excellent books of journalism and non-fiction. Reading all these books translated into another language by the same person would be a very different experience from reading them translated by different translator–authors. I imagine that a reader who tried to read all these books one after the other, each by a different translator, could end up with a sense of misgiving, a subtle, almost unconscious impression that the books could not have been written by the same person – or that the author suffered from multiple personality disorder.

At the time his translation was published, Galindo gave an interview in which he takes on, with remarkable courage, the role of translator–author:

> When I give somebody one of my translations as a present, I usually write in it that it's "a book by so-and-so, written by me". A translation, in several very important senses, is written by the translator. It is the translator who is responsible for the choices that define the final text. Clearly, you try to prevent your own idiosyncrasies from creeping into the text too much. But to begin with, you need to "know" what they are! But this *Ulysses* is mine. It has my features, some of my faults and, I hope, something or other that can be assessed positively.

I think Galindo's position is courageous because, for a large number of readers, the translator must not under any circumstances impose their own voice. To such readers, a novel is a finished object, sacred, that should be transmitted from one language to another without anything in it being altered. At the end of one of the panel discussions I took part in alongside Daniel, a lady came up to me, very irritated: "When I read one of your books I want to hear *your* voice, not the translator's." At the time, dragged along by the scrum of people wanting to speak to me, I didn't know what to say to her. So here's my reply: A translated book is always a joint effort. It can't *not* be. Normally, writers don't choose their translators. If you're lucky, the partnership is for life. If you're really lucky, as I was when Daniel came along, the books resulting from that partnership are just as good or even better than the originals.

Neural lace

Recently, someone took me for ten years younger. At that instant I understood, to my horror, that it still doesn't make the slightest difference: even a decade younger, I am still much older than I think I am.

When I thought about the incident, I also realised that without children I might perhaps have aged even more – not only physically, but because I would have lost some connection to the present. Over and above physical decline, growing older is reflected in the difficulty that many people experience in acknowledging the present as being 'their' time – hence the expression *in my time* or *in my day*.

It isn't yet possible to stop or reverse physical decline. One day it will be, but chances are I'll be dead by then, or, failing that, shall have aged beyond the point of no return. Bear with me. I'm trying to come to terms with it. I can, however, battle against the ageing of the mind, by which I mean trying to ensure that the present continues to be "my" time. As I said, children help a lot in this process. Children keep us citizens of the present, active and attentive.

If it wasn't for my twelve-year-old daughter Vera, I wouldn't know who Ariana Grande was. If it wasn't for my son Carlos, now twenty, I might not know anything about Drake or Kendrick Lamar. Much more importantly, I'd have missed out on a bunch of good films and TV series. Carlos, who is studying cinema in the UK, keeps me up to date on the audiovisual world.

It was my son who drew my attention to *Sense8*, the series directed for Netflix by the Wachowski sisters, Lilly and Lana. It's an exuberant fantasy, shot in garish colours, the action of which takes place in very diverse settings from Kenya to South Korea via Mexico, India and the US. For those who may not remember, Lilly and Lana were Andy and Larry before deciding to change their names and gender. As men, they wrote and directed *The Matrix* trilogy; *The Matrix* must be one of the films that has most inspired books and other writings about philosophy. In 2012, the brothers also directed *Cloud Atlas*, adapted from the enormous novel by the English novelist David Mitchell. As with the *Matrix* trilogy and *Cloud Atlas*, *Sense8* departs from an extremely provocative and intelligent premise, and then proceeds to destroy this promising beginning in action scenes that descend to varying degrees of absurdity while still being very well filmed.

The premise is that there exists, among us, a more advanced species of the *Homo* genus called *Homo sensorius*, whose members are able to share thoughts, feelings and sensory experiences no matter how far apart they are from each other; their brains function like computers connected by a network. In *Sense8*, this has become possible due to genetic mutation. It isn't conceivable that this could ever happen in such a way. However, only recently, the billionaire Elon Musk announced that he has set up a company called Neuralink to develop technology intended to connect human brains to computers. The new company is concentrating on the technology of *neural lace*, implanting electrodes into the brain that are capable of transmitting or "importing" thoughts to a computer. In a few years' time, it may well be possible to connect brains to each other and to supercomputers, in one gigantic network.

In *Sense8*, the eight members of the *H. sensorius* group benefit from one another's skills, thereby becoming almost superhuman. Unfortunately, they use this shared knowledge more to fight, kill or deceive other people (the group includes fighters, thieves and actors) than to make ethical, cultural or scientific progress.

It's possible to imagine a group like them making better use of such shared knowledge. One of the most interesting questions the series poses, but doesn't develop, is the loss of individuality. In a permanent neural network, each person would give up their privacy, even their personality, to become part of a larger and infinitely more ambitious project. The individual would end up dissolving themselves into the whole. This would indeed be something new and revolutionary for *Homo sapiens*, but not for life on Earth. After all, bees and ants as well as many plant species already do this. A bee or an ant does not exist – cannot exist – in isolation. A beehive is made up of bees in the same way that we are made up of cells. The individual is not the bee, but the hive.

The good news is that in such a society/entity, I would not have to worry about getting old. But I still might not be ready to give up my individuality. I think I'd still prefer to see myself looking old, in the mirror, than to see all my other selves.

Improbable happiness

In Lisbon, I went to see the première of *Félicité*, a film by the Franco–Senegalese director Alain Gomis that won this year's Jury Grand Prix at the Berlin International Film Festival. The film tells the story of a Congolese singer, Félicité (whose name means *happiness* in French), as she struggles to save the life of her adolescent son following a motorbike accident.

Alain was born in Paris in 1972 to a French mother and a Senegalese father. He studied cinema at the Sorbonne and has directed four feature-length films. I met him minutes before the showing started, in conversation with the Angolan director Zezé Gamboa. Alain is a tall fellow with long, greying dreadlocks and the elegance and serenity of a yoga instructor. Zezé, a prodigious teller of stories in the finest Angolan tradition, was holding court, telling old tales and infecting everyone with his roars of laughter. His latest film, *The Great Kilapy*, with Lázaro Ramos in the leading role, tells the true story of Joãozinho das Garotas, an Angolan 'loveable rogue' who gets rich through a series of swindles, thereby pulling himself up a few notches in 1960s Luanda society and irritating the white colonists by driving around in luxury cars and dating the city's most beautiful women, including the daughter of the Portuguese governor. I can remember hearing Zezé tell this story dozens of times before, finally, turning it into a film.

Alain's film is the polar opposite of Zezé's. Instead of flashy convertibles, glamorous parties and shimmering beaches, i.e. all the deceptive splendour of a certain colonial Africa, what we see is the devastating reality of the slums of Kinshasa. What unites the films – and the two worlds – is the systematic power of corruption.

I passed through Kinshasa a few years ago. I was robbed twice by the police before leaving the airport – once because, according to one of the policemen, I was not wearing suitable shoes for the occasion (I was wearing trainers). Later on, in the same airport, I had my return ticket refused without explanation and was forced to buy another one. However, the US $100 notes I handed over were themselves rejected: "We only accept the ones with the big head," they told me. (The $100 notes all feature the portrait of Benjamin Franklin, but on older banknotes, his head is slightly smaller.) I therefore had to change my dollars for other dollars in order to pay for my new ticket.

In Alain's film, doctors refuse to operate on Félicité's son, who has fractured one of his legs, until she pays them an absurd amount of money. Félicité endures a string of ordeals – paying a police officer to help her recover some old debts, begging for money from rich people, etc. – until she gets the necessary sum together. However, by the time she's done this, her son has lost his leg. The boy survives, but must use crutches for the rest of his life.

In the hands of a European director – in particular, a Portuguese director – this would be the moment at which everything would become even worse, likely culminating in the breakup of the family unit and the protagonist's suicide. Pessimism, as I like to recall, is one of the luxuries of happy nations. In the Congo, as in Angola or Brazil, there isn't much room for pessimism. And so, instead of the family unit dissolving, it ends up stronger. In the final scene, Félicité and her boyfriend are sitting in their living room with the crippled boy. They look at each other in silence, and then begin to laugh.

Alain Gomis's great feat is to combine a harsh and unforgiving story, in a setting crying out with despair, with sudden moments of pure poetry. For example, the snippets of conversation between patrons of the bar where Félicité sings are, to my mind, simply extraordinary. Some are genuine haikus. The night-time images of Félicité's dreams are similarly remarkable.

Alain chose to film in Kinshasa rather than Dakar, the capital of his own country, because he was fascinated by the city's unusual energy. The film succeeds in showing the reasons for this fascination: Yes, Kinshasa is a nightmare, a city ravaged by cruelty and corruption. But it is also the home of a wonderfully creative people, who, as they cannot count on the support of the state for anything at all, learn to improvise. Alain recalled, by the way, an old Congolese joke in which the country's former dictator Mobutu Sese Seko proposes adding a rather illuminating Article 15 to the constitution: "Everyone should just get by as best they can."

Watching the film, I am sure many Brazilians will recognise something of themselves in its story. It's set in Kinshasa, but it could be Rio.

The art of falling

Among the various disciplines children should study at nursery school is the art of falling, the importance of which is often ignored by the majority of educationalists. First of all, the real fall: how to fall down without injuring your head and your dignity. Second, and just as important, the metaphorical fall: how to handle a downfall, how to face a defeat, without injuring your dignity.

It's only when we trip and fall that we remember this. It happened to me, yet again, this morning. I was walking absentmindedly, looked up at a veranda (I like verandas), and the next moment I was flat on my back on the pavement – and people were laughing. A few days earlier, a friend who is a former jujutsu champion also tripped while we were walking together. But as he was falling, he tucked in his head, rolled his body, and, in a single, elegant movement, regained a standing position as if he hadn't even touched the ground. He looked like a dancer. He looked like a demiurge. He looked like a jujutsu champion. People applauded. What should have been a mishap turned into a victory.

"Where did you learn that?" I asked, impressed.

"At jujutsu, of course," he replied. "For an athlete, it's important to know how to fall."

For everyone, in fact. In the case of metaphorical falls, major defeats, this goes without saying. Let's consider Michel Temer. The world looks at him and see a man falling without the slightest elegance, looking stupendously ridiculous, and with a tremendous and cacophonous display of incompetence as he goes down. The world is laughing. The only reason it isn't laughing harder is because, unlike my physical fall, which lasted for the blink of an eye, Temer's metaphorical tumble is being dragged out over long, excruciating months. The world isn't laughing harder because this endless fall, so absurd, so crude, so disgraceful and so despicable, makes other people feel ashamed.

There comes a point when the world stops laughing completely, because when the fall is very nasty, it stops being comedy and turns into tragedy. This is what is happening right now in Venezuela, with Nicolás Maduro. There is nothing funny about Maduro's downfall, because in the process he is dragging down the entire country. People are dying almost every day because of Maduro's incompetence and obstinacy. Venezuela is on the verge of civil war.

It is also what happened with Muammar Gaddafi. The last images of the Libyan dictator, pursued by an enraged mob through the streets of Sirte on 20 October 2011, are a real-life horror movie. Gaddafi's fall, however, began long before, on Friday 17 December, 2010, when the young Tunisian Mohamed Bouazizi set himself on fire and triggered a series of protests that culminated in the downfall of President Zine El Abidine Ben Ali. The Libyan dictator had lots of time to prepare an exit – an elegant fall, let's say – but he preferred to close his eyes and cling to power.

Lesson Number One: *shutting your eyes doesn't stop you from falling.* Nor does it hold back time. We continue falling, but as our eyes are shut, it's likely we shall injure ourselves even more. Gaddafi could have called free and fair elections, overseen by the international community. If he had won the elections (which wouldn't have been at all impossible, as Libya had good social and economic indicators), he could have continued in power. There would have been no downfall. If he'd lost, he would still have left in glory. It would almost have been a victory.

Nicolás Maduro has already left it too late to depart in style, but he is still in a position to avoid Gaddafi's unhappy fate. As for Michel Temer, he can at least prevent democracy falling with him. He can prevent the country falling with him. By resigning the presidency and agreeing to face justice, Temer would display at least a hint of dignity, even patriotism, which, while it wouldn't save him from his fall, would at least spare him from ridicule. He might even receive some applause.

Lesson Number Two: *if you are falling, accept that it's happening.* As it isn't possible to defy the laws of gravity (or, in Temer's case, laws in general), the best thing is to try and minimise the damage: tuck your chin into your chest to protect your neck, bend your knees, curl your torso, stretch out your arms and let yourself go.

Unfortunately, I don't think this is going to happen. People like Gaddafi, Maduro or Temer tend to confuse their own downfall with a general disequilibrium in the universe: it is not they who are falling, it is Planet Earth that has slipped off-course. They cling to whomever happens to be nearby, desperate to survive at any cost.

Final lesson: *don't stand too close to anyone who doesn't know how to fall, and who has a propensity to stumble.*

The secret poetry of chance

I am a compulsive reader of poetry. As I read a lot and am interested in new writers, I sometimes find myself stumbling upon some very *bad* poetry. This is how I ended up confirming Borges's thesis that even the worst poets manage to write, in the course of their lifetimes, one or two extraordinary lines. This shouldn't surprise us when we bear in mind that poetry is, to a large extent, a matter of chance.

As a child, I travelled a lot by train. My father worked for the Benguela Railway, a British firm that, until Angola's independence in 1975, was the most powerful and profitable company in the country. My father gave classes to the workers along the entire route from Benguela to the border with Zambia, a distance of more than 1,300 km. To do this, he travelled in a specially converted railway carriage that, in addition to a classroom, had a couple of sleeping compartments, a dining room and a kitchen. During the holidays, my mother, my sister and I used to accompany our father. For us, it was an adventure. I remember waking up at dawn with the train stopped in the middle of the savannah, and peering out of the window to see gnus and gazelles licking the dew that had formed on the railway tracks during the night. To pass the time, my mother, who was a Portuguese teacher, organised a variety of word games. One of my favourites was the "Exquisite Corpse". Many years later, I discovered that the game, as *Cadavre exquis*, was invented in France by the first Surrealist poets.

The object of the game is to surprise – to create poetry! – through the intervention of chance. Looking back on those long, hot afternoons punctuated by the hypnotic rhythm of the train, I think that my passion for poetry, and for literature in general, began with those bits of paper my mother cut up, on which each of us in turn would write down nouns, adjectives and verbs, folding the paper and then writing the next one. We would then unscroll and read, to shrieks of laughter and surprise.

The name of the game came from the first sentence it produced: "The exquisite corpse shall drink the new wine." In Portugal, the game became very popular among the early Surrealist poets. In 1961, the poet Mário Cesariny published *The Surrealist Anthology of the Exquisite Corpse*, which gathered together some of these experiments. Among them is an amusing collection of new proverbs. For example: "Many planes – itchy typhoons."

Baudelaire used to say that it is God who provides the first line. *Chance* is the name agnostics give to God. *God* is the name that believers give to Chance. Each to his own. It can be said, therefore, that great poets seek out the illuminating mistake. Bad poets, on the other hand, are always trying to find the 'right' answer. In the case of these plodding and consistently mediocre poets, it seems fair to suppose that their good lines come not from an admirable moment of epiphany, but from a genuine misunderstanding – the real mistake, the pure accident. A sort of Exquisite Corpse of the unconscious.

It gives me even more pleasure to discover the best lines of lesser poets than the best lines of great poets, because everyone knows the latter, whereas the former – as well as being particularly unexpected – are almost entirely secret. For some time I seriously considered putting together an anthology of these magnificent mistakes that few people will ever read, but I gave up on the idea when I realised that, in all probability, their authors would not give permission. How would I explain the project to them? "Dear poet, I would like to publish your best mistakes." No, it wouldn't work.

In their eagerness to err, some great poets give in to stealing from those who have a natural talent for mistakes: children, or adults who have come to our language from another and haven't yet fully mastered it. Manoel de Barros, for example, used to steal the most beautifully contorted words from his children. On the other hand, many Portuguese-speaking African poets such as the Mozambican Mia Couto or the Angolans David Mestre and Ondjaki, among many others, seek or have sought inspiration in the Portuguese spoken by rural people in their respective countries. For several years, I used to cut out death notices from the *Jornal de Angola*, some of which were ready-made poems. Unfortunately, I lost the cuttings. But I remember one of them to this day, from a son grieving for the death of his father, knocked down by a truck: "We hung your portrait on the living-room wall, Daddy. Your portrait is the mirror of our house." Unintended poetry – or perhaps not.

Tuesday, 18 July 2017

I disembarked in São Paulo today on an icy morning, as groggy and unsteady as a zombie, though less alive and with less soul, after ten hours shut away in the suffocating economy-class cabin of a TAP plane. It's moments such as these when we understand the value of a good night's sleep.

Planes nowadays are the territories where the class struggle is at its most explicit. A few weeks ago, I fully understood the phrase – which does feel somewhat old-fashioned now – "class choice". Before the flight had even taken off, I was approached by one of the cabin crew. The captain – a compatriot and reader of mine – was inviting me to move up into business class. I asked her whether or not my girlfriend could come with me. She couldn't, as there was only one business seat free, so naturally I said no. My choice of class was, as it turned out, really a choice of love. I admit that if I had been flying alone, faced with the prospect of a ten-hour overnight flight, I would have chosen to travel with the bourgeoisie. That's what I most envy the bourgeoisie: *space*. Oh, to be able to move my arms freely! To be able to recline my seat, straighten my legs, stretch like a feline in the sun.

I arrived in São Paulo exhausted, and that same night I had to face an attentive audience of readers. I'm rather mistrustful – while also admiring – of people who hardly need to sleep. I have even more admiration for those who, having a great need for sleep, like me, manage to drop off anywhere and in any situation. Marcelo Rebelo de Sousa claims not to need more than four hours' sleep a night, taking the most of the rest of the time to read and write. There's no way I could not envy him. But I've always been more envious of another Portuguese president, Mário Soares, who gained a reputation for being able to fall asleep in any context – even while he was being interviewed.

Terribly sleepy, sitting in front of the intrepid readers who had travelled through that icy São Paulo night to hear me, I remembered a South African poet I had met many years earlier in Berlin. They were three poets, really. Each one was sitting at a small, white table. The hall was in darkness, apart from three spotlights, one on each of the tables. There was a German journalist there too, and she was introducing the poets with a long, dry, monotonous speech that reminded me of those never-ending highways across the Namibian desert. After fifteen vast minutes, the whole audience was nodding sleepily. I was just about ready to fall asleep myself when I noticed, astonished, that one of the poets had put his head down on his arms and was snoring. The sheer unexpectedness of the situation woke the audience up. The host finished her speech and addressed her first question to the sleeping poet. The poet retorted with a harsh snore. The journalist, alarmed and on edge, raised her voice, repeating the question. Nothing. The poet was dreaming, unresponsive, spread across the total splendour of the table. It was then that the woman got up and shouted in the poet's ear. He woke with a start, looked her up and down, and said, "I do not answer that question."

I stood up and clapped.

For centuries, sleep was considered an incomprehensible waste of time, almost a vice, and its most besotted worshippers were despised as idlers. In recent years, fortunately, science has been rehabilitating sleep. Lab rats deprived of sleep died within ten days from a failure of their immune system. Not at all surprising. We shouldn't have to murder little rats to prove something so obvious. Sleep torture has long been used by totalitarian regimes and alleged democracies as a way of breaking prisoners without leaving any physical marks.

In a study conducted by the University of Chicago in 2015, a group of healthy men, aged between eighteen and twenty-seven, were prevented from sleeping for more than four hours for six days. After this time, their bodies were as worn out as those of people forty years older. The insulin in their blood had dropped to levels like those of diabetics.

Not sleeping ages you. That is the main conclusion of most studies on the subject. The other misfortune, though it is not mentioned in any of these studies, is that if you don't sleep, you don't dream. Because I sleep a lot, I dream a lot. And dreaming, as I am always trying to explain in interviews and in conversations with my readers, is a part of my job: I tend to dream plots, characters, pieces of dialogue and even titles for my novels. Deprived of sleep, deprived of dreams, I don't just risk getting old ingloriously, but – worse still – I would wither as a writer.

Oh, all I want is a good bed, a goose-down pillow! Let me sleep, sleep, sleep. Let me sleep till summer comes.

The book thief

Some returns are more returns than others. Returning to Paraty, for FLIP, is like coming back to your childhood home and finding the whole tribe reunited. The tribe, in this case, is that of literature.

To Jorge Luis Borges, Paradise was supposed to resemble an infinite library. I think a library is important, but I wouldn't pass up many other benefits – namely, a huge tropical ocean, palm-lined beaches, a distant chirping of birds. You couldn't have a Paradise very far from the sea. On the other hand, I also can't imagine an infinite library as an image of Paradise if it did not have readers to serve. A book doesn't start existing the moment the writer finishes it, but only the moment the first reader starts reading it. And it dies when the last reader gives it up. In this Paradise of mine, therefore, many books would have to exist, with many readers to read them, drinking beer (coconut water, in my case), and talking animatedly to one another on a tropical beach. I see now that my image of Paradise is very like FLIP.

This year, 2017, FLIP was even more interesting than usual. The crisis would seem to have improved it. On one hand, the official programme, under the charge of Josélia Aguilar, managed to achieve a gender balance in addition to putting more writers of African heritage on the stage – a long overdue recognition. On the other, the unofficial programme has grown. This, actually, seems to be a trend. The parallel programme has become ever more central, enriched, gaining in robustness and coherence. This year the Jorge Amado House joined forces with the Fundação Saramago, bringing to Paraty, among other important names in Portuguese-language literature, José Luís Peixoto and the Luso–Brazilian Andréa Zamorano. Also at the Casa Amado / Saramago, Lívia Nestrovski and the guitarist Fred Ferreira did a show based on the letters and books of Amado and Saramago.

At the Casa Santa Rita de Cássia, the discussions, sponsored by KDP, Amazon's self-publishing platform, focused on the importance of literary blogs and self-publishing, with many independent authors present. Casa Sesc offered a huge, lavish programme, with an emphasis on workshops in creative writing and illustration. It also stood out for the attention paid to cinema, theatre and popular music. (Siba and Caio Prado, two singers I like very much, both showed up there.) The Casa Libre focused on the connections between reading and development. There I attended a lively discussion about social education and books, with Lázaro Ramos arguing for the importance of community libraries and the desacralising of the writer.

It was Lázaro Ramos, by the way, who opened the festival, alongside the historian Lilia Schwarcz, reading passages from the work of Lima Barreto – the special-tribute author for this fifteenth incarnation of FLIP. "The worst criticism of all for a writer is silence," Barreto recalled at one point, through the mouth of the Bahian actor. Barreto knew what he was talking about. Many of his writings were totally ignored by the press of the day. His work was only really discovered – that is, it only began to be read – after his death.

One of the most devastating, albeit rarely discussed, consequences of the global collapse of journalism has been the disappearance of spaces for critical reviewing. This discreet agony has been hurting readers and writers badly; readers, for reasons that are obvious, as they no longer have where to discover and read about books, and writers, because they suffer from that silence. The emergence and growth of literary festivals has been helping to overcome this, generating discussion and enabling direct contact between writers and their readers. FLIP is a good example. What I most like about Paraty is the informality of the encounters: the possibility of being approached by ordinary readers who, by commenting on what they have read, help me to understand my own work, and the possibility, too, of literally tripping over one of my favourite writers on those uneven pavements.

In Paraty, I read the moving story in the papers of Flávio de Oliveira, an eighteen-year-old native of Itapólis, a small municipality in São Paulo state, accused of stealing nearly 400 books from a variety of public libraries. Yes, I do know we shouldn't be encouraging the pillaging of public libraries; but how could one not have some sympathy for a young book thief? How lovely would Brazil be – what an amazing country! – if all of its thieves only ever stole books?

It would appear that Flávio's story had a happy ending. The libraries recovered their books. However, the young man also started receiving donations from all kinds of sources, and he has been reconstructing his library.

The language of the alchemists

This week I learned from the newspapers that one of my favourite languages is on the verge of extinction. Sfyria, a whistled version of the Greek language, is, according to UNESCO's *Atlas of the World's Languages in Danger*, the one with the fewest speakers in the world – only five.

Whistled languages are, as a general rule, very ancient and very rare. Almost all of them, like Sfyria (which is whistled in Antia, an absolutely tiny place in the southeastern corner of the Greek island of Euboea), are or were used by rural populations, especially by shepherds, who needed to communicate between two valleys. There are some who argue that whistling was brought to the island by Persian soldiers 2,500 years ago. The last whistlers of Antia managed to communicate with one another at distances of more than four kilometres. When we shout, we cannot make ourselves heard beyond 400 metres, and we quickly lose our voices.

Fortunately, Sfyria is not the last of the whistled languages in the world. In La Gomera, in the Canary Islands, the Silbo Gomero remains. Like Sfyria, the Silbo Gomero was on the verge of extinction when, in the final years of the last century, the local government decided it ought to be taught in public schools. In 2009, the Canaries' whistled language was recognised by UNESCO as part of the Intangible Cultural Heritage of Humanity, and today its future seems secure. In other words, if the political will is there, it's almost always possible to reverse a language's decline.

The collapse of whistled languages is connected to the proliferation of mobile phones. We might say that whistled languages prove the practical usefulness of poetry. On the other hand, the example of Sfyria also shows us just how fragile poetry is.

Many of the whistled languages we know about are inspired by birdsong, which should not surprise us. Many years ago, when I was a journalist, I interviewed an Angolan poet and musicologist called Jorge Macedo. Like almost all Angolan writers, Jorge was an incredibly interesting character. He had studied marimba in Kinshasa, in what today is the Democratic Republic of the Congo, one of the craziest and most musical cities on the planet. He told me that many of the traditional melodies for the marimba had been inspired by birdsong. He gave examples, playing marimba, while at the same time imitating different songbirds. He also showed me how some words in Quimbundo and Quicongo also had their etymologies in the secret language of birds.

Just a few years later, in Campo Grande, in the Brazilian state of Mato Grosso do Sul, I recorded an amazing interview, filled with laughter and tears, with the singer Tetê Espíndola, who explained to me how jazz had its origins in the songs of certain birds. Having previously heard Jorge Macedo, I didn't think this unlikely. Tetê, moreover, knows what she's talking about – she talks birdish. In 1991, she recorded the album *Ouvir / Birds*, in which she combines her famous high-pitched voice with the songs of various birds from the Amazonian basin.

Later still, in the interior of Angola, I chatted with an ex-soldier from UNITA, the movement that for many long years fought the governing regime in Luanda. He told me that in the bush, during the war, the guerrilla fighters communicated with one another by whistling and singing like birds. He told me they had developed a whole complex language, just by listening to different birds' songs.

These conversations with Jorge Macedo, Tetê Espíndola and that old, nameless guerrilla fighter helped me to write *Milagrário Pessoal* (*Personal Notebook of Miracles*), a novel the main character of which is the Portuguese language, but which is really about the fascinating mystery of speech. I discovered, while writing it, that various cultures – which are geographically remote from one another – retain countless myths about the role played by birds in the creation of human languages. One of the most interesting is the myth of the "green language", the bird language, used by alchemists and considered a perfect language, the only one in which it is possible to express the deepest mysteries of existence. This "green language" was whistled, too.

Perhaps Sfyria, the Silbo Gomero and any other of the rare

whistled languages that survive are actually the lost language of the alchemists. What I do know, with absolute certainty, is that whenever a language dies, what we lose with it is not only words, but unique ways of expressing feelings and emotions – and one gets wiped out every fourteen days.

Maybe technology threatens some of these languages the way mobile phones did with whistled languages; and yet, technology is also the thing that might help to save them: Google, for example, has created a platform, the Endangered Languages Project, on which anybody can put audio and video recordings along with documents relating to languages that are on the way to extinction. It seems to me that a lot more is needed. But it's a start.

Three divers and a dwarf

My son Carlos took me to see the new Christopher Nolan movie *Dunkirk*, an ambitious, extremely noisy and expensive war epic – a genre I don't usually enjoy – in which the Anglo–American director seeks to show how it is possible to be great in defeat.

While I watched the movie, I remembered an episode from a long time ago. When Carlos was three or four, he caused a small flood in the bathroom. I had to call a plumber to unblock the bathtub. After half an hour of work and a lot of noise, using a variety of tools, the plumber came over to show me the cause of the disaster: three small plastic frogmen and one of the Seven Dwarves (I think it was Dopey). I paid an arm and a leg for this business, said goodbye to the plumber and then, right away, with the four little plastic creatures in my hand, went to talk to Carlos: "What does this mean?"

The boy looked right at me, frightened. He told me he'd been playing with Dopey while he was having his bath, and that the poor wretch had disappeared down the drain. Then he sent a frogman on a mission to rescue him, but he never came back. He was compelled to send a second frogman to rescue the other two. But he didn't come back, either. And so he sent a third.

There was no way I could punish him. There are some blunders that are generous, just the same way that occasionally correct things do happen that are motivated by nothing but hatred or bitterness.

Christopher Nolan's movie reproduces, almost as a documentary, one of the greatest defeats of the Allied Forces in the Second World War, when more than 400,000 British soldiers were surrounded by German troops on the beaches of Dunkirk in the north of France. The operation's success was only possible thanks to the involvement of thousands of civil seafaring craft.

Nolan ignored the important contribution to the whole historical drama of countless soldiers and sailors from India and Africa. In the British merchant navy, for example, one in every four crew members was a Lascar, an Indian sailor (the same people referred to by Sir Richard Burton in the mid-nineteenth century as "Portuguese blacks"). It's hard to imagine Nolan's forgetting was accidental, not only because he himself has always showed a paranoid obsessiveness about details, but also because a film with a hundred-million-dollar budget must surely have had an army of historians and researchers.

What, then, could such an extraordinary act of forgetting mean? To some critics, Nolan was contributing to the building of an image of a United Kingdom that is ethnically pure and self-sufficient, an image so pleasing to the English nationalists who support Brexit. I don't know what Nolan thinks about this. His movie, though, albeit practically without any dialogue, and developed before the referendum in which those who wanted to leave the European Union were victorious, seems to speak for its director in support of that disastrous idea. It's no surprise that it's been received with great enthusiasm by the British far-right.

So what we have is a movie that tells the story of a defeat transformed into an almost-victory thanks to the generous impulse of common citizens – those fishermen who mobilised to rescue the soldiers. At the same time, we have a movie that, through an error (intentional or otherwise), risks serving a political project that made selfishness its banner.

These contradictions mirror the crazy times in which we're living. We recently saw, in Charlottesville, South Carolina, how a group of guys waved swastikas and little Confederate flags as they shouted anti-Jewish slogans: a "collection of clowns", in the unexpected and well-informed opinion of Steve Bannon, President Trump's guru (and presumably his ex-guru by the time this column is published), the same Bannon whom Anthony Scaramucci, the White House's meteoric former communications director, accused of acrobatic practices of sexual self-satisfaction. (Scaramucci, naturally, went too far: nobody can imagine Steve Bannon, a man now of a certain age with the decadent, sloppy physique of someone who has never practiced any sports, engaging in such complex exercises in contortionism.)

As it happens, however, the collection of clowns in Charlottesville had received authorisation to march, citing the massacre of other

North American citizens. The generous young people who confronted them, however, had not. In other words, the Nazis had the law on their side. The people with the courage to oppose them didn't.

It's a world all topsy-turvy, as my grandmother would have put it. I think about Dopey now, and feel a strange kind of nostalgia.

A wondrous discord

It is possible to measure a country's index of happiness and social stability by studying the great controversies dividing them. A country arguing about whether it is under a dictatorship or a democracy, as is happening in Angola, still has a long and painful road ahead. The same can be said about Brazil, where almost all the great controversies of recent months have originated in the extreme corruption of their political class. In the two Koreas, war is being discussed. In the US, there is the connection, or otherwise, between the terrible storm that flooded Houston, global warming and the pitiful political choices being made by President Trump. All these arguments are serious, urgent, fundamental.

What can we say, however, about a country engaged in a lively and enthusiastic debate – bringing to it all the emotion and soul of the most dramatic ethical dilemmas – about the qualities and defects of two school workbooks for children aged between four and six? This is what has been happening in Portugal the last few days. The publication of two school textbooks, one aimed at girls and the other at boys, including similar text by the same author but illustrated by two different artists, unleashed a vigorous exchange of arguments between enemy currents: on one side, those speaking out against the publishers' unbearable chauvinism; on the other, those who defend the rights of girls to like princesses more than toy cars, and boys, football more than embroidery.

One exercise in particular annoyed feminists. It involved a maze. The thing was, the maze in the boys' book was slightly more intricate than the one in the girls'. The page with the two mazes was reproduced in a number of newspapers, leading some of the most respected Portuguese columnists, both men and women, to produce violent columns criticising the publishers.

Alarmed by the huge outcry, the Portuguese government, through the Commission for Citizenship and Gender Equality, advised the publishers to withdraw the books, which they did, hurriedly, not even bothering to defend themselves.

It was then that the comedian Ricardo Araújo Pereira popped up on television on a political satire programme, *Governo Sombra*, holding the two books. He started out by saying he had read the books and felt cheated, but contrary to what all the critics had said, he had not found in them any explicit suggestion of male chauvinist prejudice. The different mazes had not been the result of a deliberate choice, but pure chance. Indeed, in other pictures, girls appeared in situations suggestive of greater intellectual inclination: reading books, for example, while the boys were playing with toy cars.

Pereira accused the many detractors of the now famous (or infamous) schoolbooks of not even having read them. Some of those he was targeting responded, confirming that yes, it was true they hadn't read the books, but insisting on their objections.

This wondrous Portuguese strife not only amply proves my initial thesis, about the possibility of evaluating different countries' happiness index via their main controversies, but it also alerts us to the excesses of so-called politically correct thought.

Countries struggling with big problems argue over big problems. Countries without problems argue over how many angels can dance on the head of a pin – boy angels or girl angels. Before this very serious question about the schoolbooks first arose, I had already been surprised to witness epic arguments in the Portuguese newspapers and on social media about such great dramas as significant as some young singer's alleged flatulence.

Happy countries are, as a rule, dull countries. Happiness is the sibling to tedium. The list of the happiest countries in the world, in the *World Happiness Report* produced by the United Nations Sustainable Development Solutions Network, is topped, unsurprisingly, by Norway, Denmark and Iceland. It is clear, of course, that even these countries can witness brutal outbreaks of irrationality, such as in 2011 when the extreme-right terrorist Anders Breivik murdered seventy-seven people; in general, however, you are more likely to die of boredom than from a gunshot wound.

I recall that in Sweden, in March 2017, an unusual corruption scandal exploded; a Member of Parliament from a conservative party made personal use of the points accumulated on the cards that the state offers parliamentarians for free travel on the country's public transport. It seems the corrupt deputy used the points on his card to buy a packet of peanuts.

Perhaps the ideal scenario would be to live in Oslo (or Lisbon) and read Brazilian or Angolan newspapers. That way, you wouldn't run the risk of dying of boredom – but not from a gunshot wound, either.

The Doomsday Clock

There is a new date for the end of the world: 23 September 2017. To go by my experience, which by this point is quite huge in matters of ends of the world, I'm sure this one is going to be another enormous failure. I can't think of any other event that has been announced so many times, for millennia, without ever having been accomplished. Current predictions assure us that the planet will explode following a collision with an asteroid. The fact that there is no asteroid approaching us does not seem to dishearten the prophets. This particular asteroid, according to them, is invisible.

As for me, while I don't believe the world is going to end on 23 September, destroyed by an asteroid, I'll admit I do worry a little. Until recently, the end of the world didn't depend on us human beings. Only a terrible cosmic disaster could extinguish life on Earth. However, we have made a great deal of progress in techniques of large-scale destruction and killing. In the days when men killed one another through the practice of swordsmanship, you could even see the point of that old expression, "the art of war". A duel with swords had something of a dance about it. Men killed each other while looking each other in the eye. Technological progress has led us to kill at a distance, an ever greater distance, at the furthest limit, through drones or remote-controlled missiles. Whole populations get killed as if you were exterminating cockroaches. In war, all progress is barbarism.

Today we have the capability to destroy the planet. I am more afraid of man than I am of stars. I trust any asteroid more than I trust Donald Trump or Kim Jong-Un.

In 1947, a group of scientists created a symbolic clock, the Doomsday Clock, which aims to warn us of the likelihood of a nuclear cataclysm taking place. When it was created, it was seven minutes to midnight – with midnight being the moment of the great disaster. After that, the timepiece was adjusted backwards or forwards, depending on whether the prevailing winds were those of good sense or idiocy. In 1953, when both the US and the Soviet Union carried out nuclear tests, it showed two minutes to midnight. In the years that followed, it moved back. In 1991, after the Soviet Union and the US signed the Strategic Arms Reduction Treaty, the minute hand pulled back to seventeen minutes. Since then, it has not stopped moving ever closer to midnight. It is now, once again, very close to the two-minute mark.

My daughter Vera, then thirteen, asked me upon hearing of the trial explosion of a hydrogen bomb in North Korea what we can do to avoid a nuclear war. The question took me by surprise:

"What can we do?"

"Who – us, or the politicians?"

"Us, normal people. We can't blame the politicians if we don't do anything. You, for example – you think you do enough?"

I thought about it. Nowadays there are already people devoting themselves to coming up with strategies and devices to prevent the Earth from being destroyed, one day, by an asteroid. I've got nothing against that. In the short term, however, it would make much more sense if we tried to answer my daughter's question: what are we doing to prevent a nuclear conflict? What can we do?

Becoming aware that doing something is a matter of urgency already feels to me like a good start. A few days ago, I rewatched *Wild River*, a movie made by the American director Elia Kazan in 1960. The movie tells the story of a US government agent, played by Montgomery Clift, who is sent to a small town on the banks of the Tennessee River that is in the process of being submerged because of the building of a dam. Clift's character's mission is to persuade an old woman to abandon her house on an island, taking the rural workers with her. She refuses to leave, and one of the workers remains by her side. Near the end of the film, as the river waters rise, Clift sees the field worker ploughing the earth as though nothing were happening.

I fear that, right now, we are that field worker: the hands of the clock move forward and we just go on, indifferent, with our usual daily routines. Unfortunately, as an Angolan proverb reminds us, "blindness doesn't save the blind man from the lion's attack". Whenever I hear arguments for a nuclear deterrent – *we've got to have nuclear weapons to prevent our enemies from using nuclear weapons* – I feel it's an insult to our intelligence. Trying to prevent a war by producing ever more deadly weapons is like trying to prevent fire by distributing flamethrowers to pyromaniacs. If the weapons exist, one day somebody is going to use them.

The world is not going to end on 23 September. But as long as we aren't able to dismantle the whole nuclear arsenal, it is always going to be on the verge of ending.

The curtains of censorship

Art history is a story of scandal and censorship. All great art can unsettle by questioning dominant thinking and values. That is art's purpose – to make us think. What Fernando Pessoa wrote as advertising material intended to promote Coca-Cola could also be used to define most great works of art: "First it seems bold, then it takes hold."

If a work does not surprise (before drawing us in), perhaps it is because it will never take hold. With luck, the work will take hold – which is to say, it will become part of the canon, and even then continue to unsettle. With a lot of luck, it really will continue to *épater la bourgeoisie*.

Censorship emerges to try to contain the fire, but almost always works to throw petrol on it. Sometimes it is hard to say to what extent censorship is, deliberately or not, part of the censored work's promotional campaign. As Paul Valéry said, "violent censorship makes credible the opinions it attacks".

Not all art shocks, of course. Many artists desire scandal, not because they really want shake up the system, but simply with the aim of earning their daily bread – and, while they're at it, a house with a pool.

Nudity, as incredible as it seems, after so many centuries of artistic (and non-artistic) exhibition of the human body, continues to provide many a good scandal. Religious issues are another sure thing, although in this field too, everything has been done already, from the celebrated Andres Serrano photograph, *Piss Christ* to the British artist Chris Ofili's *The Holy Virgin Mary*, which incorporates elephant faeces, via the caricatures of the Prophet Muhammad published by the French satirical magazine *Charlie Hebdo*.

If only for its shock effect on the bourgeoisie, I still prefer Nerval, who took his pet lobster Thibault for a walk on a blue leash around Paris's parks. Salvador Dalí was also photographed walking an anteater. In my hometown, when I was a child, I met an old elephant hunter, since retired, who used to take his snake for a walk. If the old hunter were an artist, it might have been one for the art *hiss*story books. As it was, it was just a man with a snake. I don't think the creature even had a name. At that time, in my remote little town, lots of things lacked names, especially snakes. Also, no one else was surprised by it.

It is worth noting that *L'Origine du monde*, Courbet's hairy canvas, ended up being hidden behind a curtain in the bathroom of its first owner, Turkish diplomat Khalil Bey. Anyone who wanted to see it had to open the curtain. Naturally, everyone who used that bathroom did so, to see the origin of the world. The curtain was not intended to hide it; it merely pretended to, in a sort of erotic game for the guests. I see now, in the wake of the censoring of the exhibition "Queermuseu – Mapping Difference in Brazilian Art" in Porto Alegre, some museums such as the MASP will also be hiding works of art behind curtains. In this instance, I do not think those responsible for the museums want to play erotic games; I am left with the impression they underestimate the intelligence and maturity of their visitors. No visitor, I assume, is forced to enter the areas where the exhibits are displayed, much less forced to take young children. Visiting an exhibition is always a choice.

I am the son of a very conservative man. My father is so conservative that he still calls Ethiopia "Abyssinia" and Iran "Persia", and never came to terms with the end of communism. All true conservatives are really closet communists. I have also never met a communist who was not deeply conservative.

Being the son of a conservative man perhaps helps me to understand Kim Kataguiri and other members of the Movimento Brasil Livre (it is curious how so many repressive movements use the word *free*), which boycotted the exhibition. I suspect that Kim, who is twenty-one, thinks like my father, who is ninety. If I could put myself inside Kim's head, when I opened my eyes I would be in 1948.

For a conservative soul, sex is scary, because it is an impetuous, indomitable and unpredictable force; because it is a force for change.

The bad news is we will never manage to placate a conservative mind with regard to sex and displays of it. That fight will continue for centuries. The good news is that sex always wins.

A wolf in the mirror

James Fallon, a neuroscientist from the US, became widely known after revealing he has the brain of a psychopath. Fallon spent years studying the brains of murderers. One day, rather by accident, he discovered his own brain had all the common traits of a psychopath's. After talking to his family, he discovered he came from a long line of criminals.

Fallon was in Porto, in northern Portugal, last week to talk about neuroscience, drawing a large and diverse audience. If he had not had the benefit of a particularly happy and protected childhood, Fallon could have destroyed many lives – as well as his own. Those were his words, spoken during the aforementioned event. Beyond having a brain that does not allow him to be moved, to feel real empathy, the American neuroscientist carries the infamous "warrior gene" (MAOA-L), which seems to be present in people with a history of violence, making them more likely to act aggressively. On the other hand, it is true that such aggressiveness, depending on how it manifests itself, and the circumstances, could even be seen not as a defect but a quality.

Fallon's case has come to be used as an argument for the dominance of nurture over nature: in the same way an individual may have an immense talent for writing but will never be a writer if they are not taught to read and write – and, by the way, if they do not have good libraries available to them – a person with a psychopathic brain will likewise only become a ruthless murderer if they suffer considerable violence as a child. Growing up surrounded by love and affection, as Fallon did, it is not likely this will happen.

It is a comforting theory, but, sadly, far from being confirmed. The surest thing to say is that nurture counts for a lot – and so does genetics. A wolf does not become a lamb if brought up in a flock of sheep. It is likely, though, that its wolf nature will be somewhat pacified, and it will not eat the sheep.

But I would not sleep too soundly if I were them.

I think about Fallon working. I imagine him exploring the darkness (that murky source of evil), and I can conceive of no more terrifying task. Then I imagine him discovering, first bewildered (he says he laughed), then with growing horror, the similarity between his own brain and those of the murderers he was studying: a wolf seeing itself in the mirror.

I know little of my ancestry. I am ignorant of the shady faces beyond my great-grandparents. No doubt there will be cruel men, whispering threats in some distant bend in the river of time. There will be scoundrels, thieves, rapists, supporters of slavery. What darkness will I have inherited from them? I do not know. On reflection, we are all wolves and all lambs. On the other hand, although there are forces pulling us, this way and that, we still have some freedom of choice. That choice makes us human.

Fear of nudity

A few years ago, travelling in Malaysia, a cartoon published in a local paper caught my attention. The first panel showed group of European explorers descending from their ships 500 years ago and complaining, horrified, about the shamelessness of the natives who greeted them naked. The second panel showed these same natives, 500 years later, covered from head to toe, shouting angrily at two or three European women tourists, topless on the beach.

I spent a year in Berlin at the turn of the century on a literary scholarship. Close to the apartment where my wife and I, and our four-year-old son lived, there was a pleasant, very green park with a big lake. I do not know its name. We always called it "the Green Beach". In summer, occasionally, the sun came out and the day warmed up. Then we would abandon whatever it was we were doing and descend upon the Green Beach. In those miraculous moments of light, the expanse of grass filled with people. There were whole families, grandparents, parents and small children; young couples; sweet old ladies, arriving in small steps, sometimes in groups, and offering us water and biscuits; the Senegalese man who sold us fruit; the Romanian writer who lived on the floor above; the muscly Russians we knew from the gym. All of them naked.

I took some Brazilian friends visiting Berlin to swim in the lake. For the first few minutes they found the widespread nudity strange. Some did not hide their discomfort. However, they soon forgot. Several ended up taking off their clothes and enjoying the sun and freedom.

Now and again a photo crops up on social media of three naked young women, supposedly on some beach in the former German Democratic Republic. One of them looks very much like German chancellor Angela Merkel. The image is usually accompanied by derisive comments from Brazilians or Portuguese, as if the fact Merkel practised nudism in her adolescence and youth like millions of her compatriots might compromise her qualities as a human and political leader.

I think all my readers, on the left and right, will agree with me if I say the majority of German politicians, not to mention those from Sweden or Denmark (countries that also enjoy collective nudity on beaches and in saunas), are, as a general rule, infinitely more trustworthy than their Brazilian counterparts.

Nudity is a display of confidence in others and in oneself. When nude, there is nowhere to conceal weapons, money or a wire. My trust in politicians would increase if they began to appear naked in public. Televised debates would not be a pretty sight, I know, but the country would gain in transparency.

Naked, the politicians would be forced to think, to defend their ideas, instead of simply reciting speeches. Those who showed themselves incapable of thought, and the openly wicked, whose thoughts rest solely on hate and bitterness, would then be left truly exposed.

Ultimately, the gymnophobia of certain sections of Brazilian society, and of some of its more notorious politicians, has much to do with the fear that others might see them for what they are.

A few years ago, I wrote a short story based on the real experience of a friend of mine, who one morning found himself naked in the corridor of a large hotel in London. In an episode of sleepwalking, he had got up in the middle of the night, gone out into the corridor naked and slumped onto a chair. He woke at first light. Horrified, he tried to return to his room, but the door was closed. Then he remembered his grandmother. This friend's grandmother was born and grew up in a small village in Angola, without electricity. She believed the artificial light in big cities, by preventing us from seeing the stars, made us too arrogant. Under starlight, confronted with the vastness of the universe, humankind understands it is insignificant and puts everything into perspective. Having understood the tremendous irrelevance of his state and condition, my friend went down to the lobby, explained what had happened to him and asked for a copy of the key to his room. The receptionist did not even notice he was naked. They just saw a dignified man, and gave him the key.

The people in the Green Park, in Berlin, likewise were not *naked people*. They were people enjoying Nature. The same could be said of the actor Wagner Schwartz, interacting with the public in São Paulo's Museum of Modern Art. He was an actor interacting with his audience.

Knowing that this taboo exists in a country where, like Malaysia, people walked around naked before the arrival of the first colonisers, seems to me gloriously ironic.

The elegance of silence

I went to see *Blade Runner 2049*, directed by Denis Villeneuve. Ridley Scott's original *Blade Runner* came out in 1983 and is set in 2019. The latest version, as the title suggests, takes place thirty years later, in a setting every bit as sinister as the previous one.

We are now almost in 2019. We do not have flying cars. Nor are there human replicants, made to measure and used as slave labour. Nor do I believe these will exist in 2049. The future is always extraordinary, much more so than in our imagination, but it appears to practise the good habit of discretion. Just think: the greatest technological innovations of our times are the Internet and smartphones, which no sci-fi film managed to predict. If we could pick up someone from 1983 and drop them on the Copacabana boardwalk, in that exact moment I suspect our time traveller would notice few differences. Nothing too spectacular. Looking closer, they would spot people talking into a small black device. Maybe they would give this little importance, confusing it with a simple voice recorder. And, at first glance, they would not see the Internet.

Likewise, no sci-fi film managed to predict the collapse of the Soviet Union, *Blade Runner* included. Some imagined an epic, dramatic ending such as a nuclear holocaust. No one was able to suggest that the Soviet Union would simply dismantle, almost silently, ashamedly, like an ash city in the afternoon breeze.

Blade Runner is dystopian fiction. Dystopian fiction imagines what could go wrong and intensifies the dark tones. In *Blade Runner* old and new, all the landscapes are darkened by a curtain of rain, snow or dust. Such dystopias are the utopias of pessimists. They are useful, just like pessimists, because they warn us of future disasters. They are not useful, just like pessimists, because disasters rarely happen the way we imagine them.

Consider the replicants: the main philosophical questions raised by the film concern the existence of these perfect, or better than perfect, copies of human beings, created by a powerful businessman, Niander Wallace (Jared Leto), a sort of blind and angry God. I do not believe there will be replicants in 2049 – not for technological reasons or even moral imperatives, but for simple economic motives: a replicant, such as the ones that appear in the two films, would be an incredibly expensive item, and there will always be wave upon wave of cheap people ready to fill the same roles.

In the new film, the replicant-killing replicant K (Ryan Gosling), unable to have one of his kind at his service, buys a virtual companion (this calls to mind the case of some slaves who, as soon as they could, bought other, cheaper slaves). Both K and his companion Joi (the Cuban Ana de Armas) face serious identity problems. All replicants possess artificial childhood memories. Wallace believes that, this way, they will feel less lost, more authentic, more human. The problem is, they know these memories are all false. What is the identity of an individual whose memories are scarce, false and intermittent?

It is an age-old question. And it is so because ultimately, we are closer to those replicants than Niander Wallace imagines. We also build ourselves on memories that are often false and almost always scarce and intermittent. I speak for myself. As I write this, I am trying to gather all the memories I retain from when I was seven, eight, nine and ten years old. I cannot find more than a dozen. Some are not even original memories. They are memories of photos or videos my father took, which I viewed many times as an adult. If they had shown me fake videos, with myself as one of the characters, eight or nine years old, I would remember those moments as if I had in fact lived them. My ninety-year-old father has been writing a never-ending autobiography full of extremely detailed stories from his childhood. Perhaps he is human, and I am an adopted replicant. That would explain my sympathy for the replicants and the permanent identity crisis.

I enjoyed *Blade Runner 2049*, but I would prefer there not to be any more. The best part of the original film comprised the questions left unanswered. Certain films, like certain people, are only interesting for the ellipses, the silences, what is not shown. There are no inelegant silences. But answers? Oh, yes.

On books and revolutions

I returned to Folio, the international literary festival in Óbidos, in 2017, this time not in the role of event curator but as a writer, to participate in a conversation with Milton Hatoum chaired by Ondjaki.

In the long summer that settled over Portugal, the small town of Óbidos felt like Paraty, only with more Brazilians, more sun and less rain. This on the threshold of November, when it was supposed to be cold, wet and dismal every hour of the day. What scares me most about this massive disaster we call global warming is, sometimes, its friendliness. It is hard to fight against an apocalypse that softens winter. This Portuguese winter, anyway.

The audience for the discussion seemed to be made up entirely of Brazilians. At times I even forgot I was in Portugal. The majority of the questions were about the political situation in Brazil: how to exit the crisis?

A difficult question. I am Angolan. For decades, whenever any Brazilian friend complained about Brazil, I said they should look at Angola. Now, for the first time, I have more hope for Angola than for Brazil. In Angola, at least, there exists a possibility of change – with or without revolution. There are politicians in the democratic opposition who appear serious and trustworthy, even if I do not share their ideas. Whereas in Brazil, I see politicians behaving all very much like one another, brazenly robbing, shielding one another and mocking those who do not steal. Swapping the politicians in power for those who are currently in opposition and hoping something changes is like painting a rock yellow and believing that, if you just squeeze it hard enough, it will give you lemonade.

Milton Hatoum proposed a long-term solution: invest in education. I agree with Milton, of course, but I do not know how it will be possible to improve the public education system without first replacing the entire political class with one that believes in such an investment, and then with one that has itself been well educated.

I left the session in Óbidos thinking about this question. I still do not have a good answer. Maybe, however, part of the answer lies in the theme of Folio's latest edition: "Revolutions, Revolts and Rebellions". Curiously, FLUP, which will take place between the 10th and 15th of this month in Vidigal, has a similar theme.

Literary festivals such as the ones in Óbidos or Vidigal, and the hundreds of similar events popping up all over Brazil, help to develop readers. They are part of a true revolution in thought, elegant and silent, through books and education. The same can be said of the hundreds of community libraries that have been opened in recent years in Brazil. On a journey across the country to present my latest novel, I discovered two of these libraries: one in São Paulo, another in Olinda. Talking to the people behind them, I heard, for the first time, about the Rede Nacional de Bibliotecas Comunitárias (National Network of Community Libraries).

I was moved, in one of these libraries, listening to accounts from readers. On a future visit to São Paulo I would love to visit the Caminhos da Leitura community library, which operates in the Colony Cemetery in the far south of the city. This is the Brazil I believe in, the one that gives us hope again: the one that manages to turn a cemetery into a place of reading and learning.

I feel a boundless admiration for the ordinary people who create and run libraries. This year, during a panel discussion in Oslo, Norway, somebody asked me what I think about the Scandinavian countries' support for development programmes. Sweden, Norway and Denmark have spent decades supporting development in countries of the South, particularly in Africa. I answered that if the money was mine, I would invest it first and foremost in creating a network of public libraries. If there was no interest on the part of the relevant government bodies in the receiving country, I would seek out independent organisations.

Libraries never disappoint. A good reader is a more informed and responsible voter; in developing readers we are also building empathy and interest in others. In the long term, this effort will translate into a more demanding and engaged society, and, by extension, into a slightly less crude political class than the current one.

But it will always be a slow revolution – if you will allow me the oxymoron. After all, it is a beautiful oxymoron.

The gold of the islands

Last week I revisited the sunny streets of Cidade da Praia, the capital of Cape Verde, where I'd been invited to attend a literary festival. On the final day of the festival, writers were taken to see a show featuring young local artists.

The show took place at the Palácio da Cultura, an old colonial residence recently done up to serve as a nursery for the initiatives of young creators. Music is one of the main art forms practised here. Less well-informed visitors are always surprised by the rich musical tradition of a country with a total area of only 4,000 square kilometres and fewer than 500,000 inhabitants. How can this be explained? It's simple: children grow up inside the music. In any house you visit, even out on the most remote, forsaken wasteland, you will always find a guitar, a cavaquinho or an old violin handed down by some distant relative.

Cape Verde is proof of the artificiality of the distinction between classical and popular music. I understood this many years ago while watching a performance by the legendary Travadinha on one of the stages of the Gulbenkian Foundation, in Lisbon. Travadinho, or António Vicente Lopes, was a timid, fragile-looking man, always hidden behind a pair of large, dark glasses. He'd received no formal education and could barely read, exchanging his Cape Verdean Crioulo for Portuguese only with a degree of discomfort. However, he descended from a long line of violinists. When he took to the stage on that overcast Lisbon afternoon, the majority of his audience cannot have been prepared for what happened next: as soon as he began to play, that subdued and hesitant little man was transfigured; from one moment to the next he became a kind of incandescent flame, dominating the entire stage with the authority of a general and the elegance of a dancer, irradiating dense, sophisticated music, at once classical, highbrow, popular and profoundly contemporary.

Before he died, in 1987, Travadinha was able to record an album. Legend has it that he did so while burning with fever. I couldn't say. That strange record is a long way from encapsulating all of his considerable genius, but it's enough to rescue him from oblivion – that final death.

For years I wrote about Brazilian and African popular music for a Portuguese newspaper. I was a mediocre music critic, partly through sheer incompetence, but also because, as Thelonious Monk is claimed to have put it, "writing about music is like dancing about architecture". Nevertheless, writing (or trying to write) about music did lead me to some happy experiences. The best of these all related to the discovery of a new voice at almost the exact moment when it was emerging.

Last week, at the Palácio da Cultura in Praia, I experienced a similar feeling as I watched the procession of young musicians. I was particularly impressed by two singers, both still in their teens: Ellah Barbosa and Mayra Neves. What unites these two young girls, markedly different in style and voice, is the joy with which they flaunt all the rules and subvert some of Cape Verdean popular music's most sacred songs. Ellah does this in a more discreet, elegant manner, with a voice and posture that, from the start, awaken a sense of wonder. Mayra, still only seventeen, shatters convention with a big, powerful voice, that you would think impossible to contain inside such a slender body. Both sing as if they were inventing this music themselves. And they are.

Astonishment can dilate time. When we were children, time seemed to go on for longer because each day offered us a new surprise. After a certain age, it becomes increasingly difficult to find anything that still surprises us. I'm not sure whether, after having lived for many years, we end up dying of old age or simply from boredom.

You often hear it said that for every ten Cape Verdeans, eleven are musicians. Some argue that Cape Verdeans have a genetic predisposition for music. This may, in part, be true. Musical talent is something that gets passed down through genes. But what Cape Verdeans certainly have, beyond any doubt, is a sophisticated musical culture honed across generations and generations of singers, composers and instrumentalists. When the day comes that we can enter any house on any of the ten islands that make up the archipelago and discover not just a guitar, a violin or a cavaquinho but also a bookstand filled with books, this will be the day that Cape Verde boasts as many exceptional writers as it currently does extraordinary musicians.

It's also said that Cape Verde is like a small Brazil. And it is, in terms of all that's best about Brazil: a mixed-race culture that responded to the hatred of a cruel and violent colonial system (which they all are) with forgiveness.

Hero and traitor

Dictators always resemble one another. Those that manage to reach old age begin to look even more alike. In the end, they all become indistinguishable from the decrepit Latin American despot Gabriel García Márquez portrayed so effectively in *The Autumn of the Patriarch*: imprisoned within the bitter solitude of their respective palaces, as in the wreckage of an intimate nightmare, reminding themselves of the brilliance (and the crimes) of their past. Nobody is listening.

Robert Mugabe is the best example of this fate. He first became known in the 1960s when he joined the movement struggling for the independence of what was then Southern Rhodesia, a prosperous British colony dominated by white farmers. In 1964, some of these farmers, led by Ian Smith, proclaimed the independence of Southern Rhodesia, which was renamed "Rhodesia". Mugabe, who had been imprisoned a short time earlier, was not released until 1974. A year later, he sought refuge in Mozambique. At this point, he was a very elegant and intelligent man, with a degree in administration from a British university and interests ranging from Elvis Presley to Karl Marx.

In the film *The Interpreter*, directed by Sydney Pollack in 2005, Nicole Kidman plays Silvia Broome, an interpreter working at the headquarters of the United Nations in New York. Silvia was born in an African country with a history very similar to that of Zimbabwe. The president of this fictional country, Edmond Zuwanie, is an obvious representation of Mugabe – a former hero of the struggle against British colonialism, who is loved and followed by many, but who has transformed into a vicious, cynical dictator. In the film's most dramatic scene, Silvia, who in the past had admired and fought for Zuwanie, points a gun at his head, trying, before she kills him, to understand what has taken place within his spirit.

It's likely that *nothing* had taken place; there had been no profound changes, nor had any moral mechanism mysteriously deteriorated.

It's likely that Edmond Zuwanie, like Robert Mugabe, was always bad. The heart that beat in the chest of the hero is the same as beats in the elderly chest of the traitor. Wickedness depends on circumstance. There are bad men who never have the opportunity to exercise their wickedness. Mugabe did.

The Zimbabwean leader's exile in Mozambique lasted two years and was beset by problems. Samora Machel, Mozambique's first president and an exuberant, charismatic man, did not like him. He sent Mugabe to Quelimane, a small, historic city in the north of the country, putting him in a closely-watched residence for several months. Machel, who prided himself on his knowledge of human nature, did not think Mugabe possessed the maturity to lead a guerrilla movement against Ian Smith's racist government, much less rule over an independent Zimbabwe. History would prove him right.

Zimbabwe had every chance of becoming a success: a population with a decent level of education and a political culture that was far superior, on average, to other countries in the region; a well-developed agricultural sector, even if in the hands of a white minority (as remains the case in South Africa); a healthy tourist industry inherited from the colonial period; mighty rivers and inexhaustible natural resources.

Mugabe ruined Zimbabwe. He destroyed the economy, yes, but even worse, he undermined plurality of thought, imposing a climate of terror on the country. Hundreds of thousands of Zimbabweans left. Others subjected themselves to decades of shamefaced silence. Like all dictators, Mugabe failed to understand that, by corrupting and weakening the opposition and civil society, he was corrupting and weakening his own party. And the entire country.

As I write these lines, we are still unsure of the outcome of the military intervention which, last Thursday night, disturbed Mugabe's sleep: a coup d'état lacking the courage to assume that name. There are reports of people celebrating the dictator's downfall in the streets, but there are also statements from leaders of the opposition and human-rights activists, who draw attention to the fact that the generals now appearing on television have always supported the dictatorship.

I am not aware of many military coups that have aspired to

democratise a country. There is nothing democratic about an army, much less an army that has always found itself in the service of a dictatorship. The hope is that the Zimbabwean army, in order to gain support both national and international, will be forced to negotiate an open politics with some of the few forces still constituting civil society.

Silvia Broome did not kill Edmond Zuwanie. In the film, as I recall it, Silvia puts down her gun and Zuwanie ends up being arrested and tried for his crimes in an international court. It is what I would like to see happen to Robert Mugabe. Sadly, I don't believe in happy endings.

Bantu Spring

There are those who speak of a "Bantu Spring" in relation to the recent removal of Robert Mugabe in Zimbabwe, and the vigour with which the new Angolan president, João Lourenço, has gone about dismantling the nepotism that had become embedded within the apparatus of the state. However, it may still be too soon to begin warming the drums and sounding the vuvuzelas.

The difference between Mugabe's fall and those of the leaders of Egypt, Tunisia and Libya during the so-called Arab Spring is the surprising courtesy with which the insurrectionist officers treated the deposed president. There was no violence; quite the opposite. There was so much kowtowing, so much deference, that it took the old dictator some time to grasp the army's intentions. Zapiro, a famous South African cartoonist, published a sketch showing Mugabe in his palace, while outside crowds celebrate. An anonymous general explains to an astonished Mugabe: "It's the people, sire. They've come to say goodbye!" To which Mugabe replies: "Goodbye? I wonder where they're going?"

Mugabe has relinquished power, but he will not be made to leave Zimbabwe. He will retain all the privileges due an ex-president, his personal fortune intact, along with reinforced security in response to the overt hostility of the population.

In Angola, João Lourenço surprised everyone by removing Isabel dos Santos, considered the richest woman in Africa, from her position as head of Sonangol, the national petroleum company, which for decades had kept the entire country afloat while at the same time bringing fabulous wealth to half a dozen families connected to the regime.

As well as José Eduardo dos Santos's eldest daughter, the new president has also dismissed two more of his predecessor's children, Tchizé dos Santos and José Paulino dos Santos, who together ran one of the public television channels. The wave of dismissals has also hit the army and the secret services, the directorship of the National Bank and many other important positions in the public sector, and is being received with euphoria by civil society as well as incredulity by the opposition parties. Members and directors of the ruling party, the MPLA, have been equally incapable of masking their surprise and discomfort.

The pro-democracy activist Luaty Beirão, the face of non-partisan youth resistance to the Angolan regime for a number of years, has come out publicly in numerous interviews to praise the new president for his actions. During one of these interviews, Luaty stated that Lourenço had gone further in his first fifty days in government than the opposition would have managed had they won the elections. Few doubt this.

In Angola, we are living through a strange moment – a triumph of the absurd, or of magical realism – in which the elected president is being applauded by members of the radical opposition and regarded with suspicion, or even open hostility, by more conservative sections of his own party. The situation resembles a coup d'état, but is even softer, more cordial and more respectful of the constitution than the one that took place in Zimbabwe.

Sadly, it may still be too early to let off fireworks. It's hard to believe the foxes would raid the henhouse simply in order to liberate the hens. In the case of Zimbabwe, it's not a fox, but a crocodile – the nickname by which Emmerson Mnangagwa, who became President upon Mugabe's resignation, is known. The Crocodile, a faithful ally of Mugabe's for many years, has a reputation as a cruel and violent man who has always displayed a disdain for democracy and human rights. During the civil war in the 1980s, the Crocodile led Zimbabwe's powerful secret police, responsible for a series of massacres and other abominable crimes.

Fortunately, Lourenço doesn't boast such a terrifying profile. There is no record of acts of violence. If he has accumulated wealth, he doesn't like to flaunt it. He has six children, about whom very little is known. His wife, Ana Lourenço, is a highly respected economist who has held important positions both in government and for international institutions such as the World Bank. She was imprisoned in 1977, accused of having supported an attempted military coup. Reintegrated by the regime, she does not like to recall those difficult months. There are some who believe that she should be the one holding the presidency. There are some who believe she is.

In the case of Angola, then, it is not so much the personality of the new president that is in question – it is the integrity of those who surround him. Some of the new ministers and public servants appointed by Lourenço have previously occupied positions in government and face accusations of corruption.

I have already dusted off my vuvuzela, which had been lying forgotten since the 2010 World Cup in South Africa. But I shall not be heading out onto the streets just yet. From my window, I am keeping a watchful eye on the crocodiles.

Brave new world

I turn on the television and see an old Croatian general accused of war crimes take his own life in the middle of a courtroom. I switch to another channel and watch in horror as a report reveals how black Africans are being sold in Libya by white Africans. And then there's Donald Trump. There's always Donald Trump, every day a new scandal. We're living in a time when news bulletins have become more dramatic and more surprising than the best action films – and that isn't good.

In this day and age (and what a frenetic age it is), even the weather has become a topic of heated debate. I've found myself having to reconcile couples on the verge of falling apart because one supports the Treaty of Paris while the other doesn't believe in global warming.

In days gone by, at family dinners, certain topics were considered off-limits in order to prevent your bearded cousin becoming embroiled in a shouting match with your conservative uncle. Even we children knew there were some words that shouldn't be uttered at the dinner table. *Communism*, for instance. Now, it's speaking about the weather that's off limits, and the word "communism" has practically disappeared. Except in Brazil, that is. Brazil must be the last country on Earth where "communist" continues to be used as an insult. In other countries it now resembles an anachronism, like calling someone a rapscallion, a blackguard or a scallywag (though *scallywag*, to be fair, remains an excellent insult).

The general who committed suicide in The Hague during a session of the International Criminal Tribunal for the former Yugoslavia (ICTY) was called Slobodan Praljak, and he stood accused of having ordered the executions of hundreds of Muslim civilians during the civil war that tore the country apart. His death was widely mourned in Croatia, where he is considered a hero by a large portion of the population and the majority of its political leaders. Praljak was a poet and a dramatist. Moreover, he was not the only war criminal tried by the ICTY to enjoy poetry. The most famous of them all, the Serbian Radovan Karadžić, was also a poet.

Karadžić, one of those responsible for the Srebrenica massacre in which 8,000 Bosnian Muslims were murdered, managed to evade justice for over a decade thanks, in large part, to the protection of the Serbian authorities. This long pursuit was the subject of a film, *The Hunting Party* (2008), in which Richard Gere plays the part of an American journalist investigating the whereabouts of a terrible war criminal.

In the final utterance of his dramatic exit, more befitting of his background as a playwright than a soldier, Praljak insisted on his innocence. He did not consider himself a criminal. Nor did Karadžić. I'm always shocked by the fact that murderers can be poets – sometimes even good poets. But it surprises me even more that they see themselves as heroes. And that they could be regarded as heroes by so many others.

Sadly, this has always been the case. In schools all over the world, children are taught to glorify great murderers: Vasco da Gama, for example. It was only after I visited India, speaking to local historians, that I learned the other side of this history. Among the many accounts of the Portuguese navigator's cruelty, an attack on a ship full of Muslim pilgrims returning from Mecca stands out. Da Gama forced the pilgrims, including women and children, into the hold before setting fire to the ship and hanging around to watch the tragedy unfold.

I imagine that, in Libya, modern slave traffickers also have their own version of history, and that they are regarded by their respective clans, families and friends as honourable people.

When I was a child, my grandmother used to tell me the story of a peasant who, having drunk too much the night before, stayed in bed until very late. That morning, a vile, dark rain fell over the region, causing all those working out in the fields to go mad. Upon leaving his home, the man found himself surrounded by a rabble of crazy people with whom he was unable to communicate, and who either assaulted or mocked him. Finally, out of sheer desperation, the peasant himself leaped into a puddle of the dark water. I think about this man as I watch the television.

What can we do when the world around us goes crazy?

We can look for a puddle of water. That is, we can deny global warming in the firm belief that the thing we don't want to happen will never happen; we can switch off the television when it begins to show us the first images of Africans being sold at auctions; we can refuse to see the danger represented by Donald Trump, and by the many little Trumps cropping up all over the world. Or we can clench our fists and join the fight.

The December sky

Many years ago, in Luanda, I interviewed Father Christmas. The broad December sky pulsed, blue and sweltering. I came across the old fellow outside a well-known home-appliances store. His role was to attract and entertain customers, which he did skilfully and with a good deal of sweat. I offered to buy him a beer at the bar opposite. We sat on the small terrace in the shade, observing the anxious crowds.

"My name is Adérito," Father Christmas told me, removing the heavy hat and wiping his face and bald head with a paper napkin. "The beard is real. You can grab it. Go on, pull."

I didn't doubt it. It was a remarkable beard, very white and bushy, tumbling down his chest like a cascade of light. Only the belly was false. Adérito was seventy-five years old, but were it not for the beard, you wouldn't say he looked a day over fifty-five. In his youth, he'd worked as a cotton picker. Later, with the war, he'd come to Luanda. He'd been a postman, a cobbler and now, finally, an artist.

"An artist?" I struggled to conceal my surprise. "What kind of artist?"

"I paint. I do the sort of paintings white people like to buy when they visit Africa: elephants, gazelles, sunsets over the savannah, women dancing in the nude."

Adérito paints all year round. He sells his canvases at a famous open-air craft market, a few kilometres from Luanda. When December arrives, he gives his brushes a break and turns into Father Christmas. I wanted to know what it felt like to sit there sweating under a harsh African summer sun, dressed for the European winter, portraying a character lacking even the slightest link to this country's traditions. Didn't this business of assimilating foreign cultures strike him as a show of disrespect towards our own?

Adérito calmly rearranged his false belly. He asked for another beer. The beer arrived; he poured it and drank. Only then did he answer: "When you eat chicken, my young friend, do you become a chicken? No! The chicken becomes part of you."

I had to agree. To this day, I still deliver his line as if it were my own when wishing to conclude any discussion about cultural alienation, which, in a sense, is just the reverse of so-called cultural appropriation. While in the United States and Brazil there are arguments over cultural appropriation, in African countries, the main debate has always been about alienation.

I wanted to know what present Adérito would choose for himself, assuming he could ask for anything he liked. Once again, his answer surprised me: "A journey through time."

"What?!"

"Yes. I'd ask to go back in time. I made a mistake that changed my whole life. Or rather, it took my life away from me. After that mistake, I lost my way. I've been drifting ever since."

It seemed like a good idea to me, although in my case, I would require a time machine that let me make at least half a dozen trips. I'm someone who is frequently mistaken. Then I remembered all those films and series where people travel through time to correct some wrongdoing in their personal history, or in a world history filled with human tragedies, and end up provoking an avalanche of terrible societal changes. Best not to mess around with time. Adérito, however, was in no doubt: he would travel back to redo a single act, and his life would take a different course, like a wide river, serene and self-assured, that knows where and why it flows.

"I lacked the courage to be happy," he told me. He finished his drink, stood up, placed the hat back on his head and returned to the task of making others laugh, encouraging them to buy. I didn't see him again.

I remember Adérito every time December comes around, with its plague of Father Christmases – in shopping centres, outside stores, in parks, even scaling buildings – and streets crammed with crowds of compulsive shoppers. There's nothing sadder than obligatory happiness.

I like to believe Adérito managed his journey through time. He became young again, over there, in Angola's interior; he was again able to meet the girl who'd seemed so inaccessible to him. This time, however, he offered her his hand, on some porch facing out over a shimmering cotton field, and she squeezed his fingers, and with this gesture all that was clouded became illuminated, and all that was uncertain became infallible. Adérito would be another person now; maybe a rural patriarch, surrounded by children and grandchildren; perhaps a famous painter – but certainly not Father Christmas.

When the lion builds its own cage

In May of next year, the publisher Todavia (the best surprise in the world of Portuguese-language publishing in 2017) will be releasing Kalaf Epalanga's first novel *The Whites Can Also Dance* in Brazil. The book was launched this month in Portugal by Caminho, Mia Couto's publisher, at an event that brought together, in the São Luíz, one of Lisbon's noblest and most beautiful theatres, many of the leading names from Portuguese and African hip hop and popular music.

The presence of so many people with connections to music is not surprising. Kalaf was one of the founders and masterminds behind Buraka Som Sistema, the famous Luso–Angolan electronic-music outfit responsible for the international recognition of Kuduro music. The novel, moreover, aims to tell the story of the birth and development of Kuduro, a rhythm that was born in the *musseques* (shantytowns) of Luanda and ostracised and ridiculed by a large section of the self-proclaimed Angolan intellectual elite before it began conquering audiences all over the world.

The publisher presents Kalaf's debut as a "musical novel". I think that's an excellent definition, not only because the novel includes music as one of its themes, but also because it develops like a song.

In a number of recent interviews, the author has confessed his admiration for Ruy Castro, stating that his reading of *Carnival Under Fire* helped him conceive of and construct his own novel. The first part of the book really does share a certain affinity with Ruy's. It's a kind of biography of Kuduro, with Kalaf himself as the narrator, and presents a series of characters – some farcical, almost caricaturish, others vaguely terrifying – who were involved in the origins and development of this Luanda rhythm. It's hard, during this first part, to distinguish the real from the purely fictitious – a highly entertaining game for those more familiar with the topic. The second part is narrated by a white Portuguese woman, a dance teacher, enamoured of Lisbon's vibrant African universe; the third and final part gives voice to the Norwegian police officer who arrested Kalaf during a working visit the author made to Oslo. The arrest really did take place, although the policeman is fictitious. This third part, the most interesting from a literary point of view, affirms Kalaf in his reincarnation as a writer.

The highlight of the book launch at the São Luíz Theatre was a discussion between the three different presenters, two Portuguese women of African origin – the actress Cláudia Semedo and the journalist and blogger Carla Fernandes – and the Angolan musician and visual artist Nástio Mosquito. Carla runs a podcast, *Rádio Afrolis*, on which "artists and ordinary (and less ordinary) people discuss issues of blackness, racism and identity, revealing facets of Portugal's emerging black consciousness". It fell to her to enliven the discussion by attacking – very courageously, given the stage on which she was sitting – the novel she was supposed to be presenting. For Carla, Kalaf had failed by not offering a voice to black women. Even worse, in her opinion, was his inclusion of a *white* woman who spoke about matters that should have been discussed, first and foremost, by black women.

Kalaf had not anticipated this attack. But, once he'd recovered his breath, he was, as ever, the picture of elegance, thanking the journalist for her forthrightness and explaining that he'd opted for a white woman as a narrator for his book in order to demonstrate, somewhat ironically, the vitality of African rhythms, which had taken the old colonial power by storm – colonising it in turn. (The sociologist Joacine Katar Moreira, also a black woman, published a generally very positive review of the book in the newspaper *Público*, in which she also raised the issue of the absence of black women.)

Like Kalaf, I never imagined the novel would be attacked on this front. For decades, European – or Western – criticism demanded that African and Latin American writers conform to a presumed authenticity. Alongside this came the implicit suggestion that an African writer should only write about Africa, or rather, about what Europeans understood by 'Africa'. There was no shortage of African writers who allowed themselves to fall into this ingenuous trap, a bit like a lion building its own cage. More recent generations of African writers such as Chimamanda Ngozi Adichie, Teju Cole and Sami Tchak, among many others, have managed to break free of this trap: they are writers who have found themselves by assuming their right to observe, and occupy, the entire world.

Kalaf manages this by placing himself inside the skin of a white Portuguese woman or a Norwegian police officer. The greatness of this (now) writer from Angola lies in his ability to transcend his own skin, his intimate sphere, which, naturally, includes black women, and observe the world through the eyes of another.

The sceptical palm reader

What I like most about this time of the year is the idea of new beginnings. First day. Blank slate. What will come next? I am not attracted to the possibility of rescue or forgiveness. What attracts me is the possibility of *surprise*.

If we could peer into the future the same way we look into the past, we wouldn't understand a thing – just as, try as we might, we never do truly understand the past.

This is also the season for taking stock, and for prophecies and predictions. We take stock of the year that has gone by just so we can pretend to organise the past. With prophecies and predictions, we are looking to organise and domesticate the future. There are prophets and astrologers – and also political analysts, economists, etc. – who do get a few of their predictions right. It happens. Pure chance. When that happens, however, we like to believe that *all* of them have made such predictions by leaning on some special knowledge, or on account of a mysterious vocation. That brings us comfort, the illusion of having a certain kind of control over Fate.

As a teenager, I took an interest in the occult, the esoteric, magical and religious African practices, etc. I even enrolled in a parapsychology course led by Father Óscar Quevedo, a Spanish-born Brazilian Jesuit who was devoted to the demystification of miracles and other interventions from the beyond. I was also interested in chiromancy; I learned palm reading. By doing this, I also found out a few things about human nature. For example, that people are ready to believe in any old nonsense. All a good palm reader needs to be successful is a grain of intuition and another of common sense.

Years later, in Brasilia, at the launch of one of my novels, at a lovely bookshop (I remember its name was Rayuela – a tribute to Cortázar – but I believe it no longer exists), I revealed my unlikely talent to one of the booksellers. Very quickly, the queue of people who wanted me to read their palms stretched longer than the queue of people interested in getting my signature. Some would buy the book, would ask for a dedication, but what they really wanted was to get their palms read by me. Even though I kept saying to everyone, "I do this as a joke, you can't really take it seriously", the line continued to grow. I remember a woman to whom I confirmed something from her past, an illness, a broken heart, and she hugged me, teary and happy, after I forecast better days to come.

Despite being a fierce sceptic, I enjoy reading the predictions for the coming year. In fact, I even write my own lists. I never get them right. I think I'd be scared if I ever did. Rereading the list I wrote twelve months ago, I can see that I'd correctly predicted Trump's and Temer's impeachments. I also predicted the fall of Kim Jong-Un. Deep down, this was really a list of wishes, not predictions.

My wish list for 2018 still includes the non-violent dismissals of Trump and Kim. I would like to see free and fair elections in Zimbabwe, as a follow-up to the very soft coup that deposed Robert Mugabe. I would also like to see the emergence, on a global level, of a new way of thinking from the left, unshackled from the errors of the past, connected to the present, which could stand against the conservative wave sweeping the world. I hope, on the other hand, that the feminist movements do not lose momentum, and that they are able to forge a path that is fitting to our times. In Angola and in other African countries, this new feminism has, in the last few months, shaken up something that has lain dormant for centuries. It could become the most important civic movement since the independences.

I hope the 2018 Nobel Prize for Literature will be awarded to António Lobo Antunes, Mia Couto or Rubem Fonseca. I eagerly await the publication of Paul Auster's immense new novel *4,3,2,1*, as well as *Swing Time* by Zadie Smith (translated in Brazil by Daniel Galera), which, like Auster's novel, was longlisted for the Man Booker Prize. In 2018 I still hope to read, in Portuguese, *Mudbound* by Hillary Jordan, a race-themed novel set in the 1940s, the film adaptation of which was acclaimed at the Sundance Film Festival. I also wait eagerly and anxiously for the new (African and feminist) album from Maria Gadú.

For however much evil 2018 might bring us, if I have good books to read and good music to listen to, I can take it.

A Swedish Hell

Christian, the main character in *The Square* by Ruben Östlund, is the chief curator of a great Swedish museum. The film has been referred to as a satire against modern art, and against the increase in value of works whose meaning eludes almost everyone. I watched it, and I was not convinced that this had been the director's intention.

Modern art in *The Square* is mostly an excuse to tell a story about vanity, arrogance and remorse. What is best about the film is perhaps that which, at first glance, would be its main fault: the (apparent) disorder with which it has been built, opening doors that lead nowhere, which can be construed as a subtle metaphor for the life of the protagonist.

Christian is a middle-aged man who, in a succession of clumsy moves, loses control over his own destiny and begins a descent into Hell. This would be a subjective kind of Hell; a Swedish Hell, one might say. If we were to rewrite the screenplay and adapt it to Brazilian reality, for example, the result would be infinitely more violent. To a good part of the Brazilian population, there is a lot of Heaven in a Swedish Hell.

Also, there is a different conversation about modern art happening in Brazil. Brazil is living through such a difficult moment nowadays that even the word *modern* comes as an insult, or as a red flag, to the archaic, ultraconservative way of thinking that the evangelical front has been imposing on the country. The latest great scandals in Brazil surrounding 'modern art' all involve nudity. Evidently, nudity does not scandalise or bother anyone in Sweden. The truth is that the closer we get to Hell, the more of a problem there is going to be with nudity. This should not come as a surprise: in Paradise, after all, Adam and Eve walked naked. God doesn't care at all about nudity. But the Devil does.

The square to which the film's title refers is an installation by an Argentinian artist that the museum where Christian worked was about to exhibit. The idea came from an artistic intervention in the real world: a square painted in front of a museum, a representation of sanctuary, of tolerance and openness. Two people occupying the square simultaneously should pay attention to one another. The piece, which is not shown in the film, serves as an ironic counterpoint to the egotism and arrogance of the main character.

The antagonist is played by a stubborn, angry young boy, the son of Turkish immigrants. It is this young boy who confronts Christian, finally waking him from his lethargic social blindness. Christian's small crime, which so angers the young Turkish boy, will seem insignificant by Brazilian standards. In Complexo da Maré in Rio de Janeiro, or in Alto José do Pinho in Recife – places tormented by ancient negligence and institutional, atavistic and constantly renewed cruelty – this Swedish film might not even be intelligible.

In the 1990s, I climbed up to Alto José do Pinho to write a piece about the punk bands that were shaking up Pernambuco at the time. I remember going to the home of Canibal, lead singer of a band called Devotos do Ódio (Devotees of Hatred). Years later, the name was shortened to just "Devotos". I believe Canibal is still called "Canibal". I wouldn't be surprised, however, if now he were just "Anibal", dressed in a suit and tie, having cut his Rastafarian dreadlocks. There was another band I followed called Matalanamão, whose lead singer, Adilson Ronrona, enjoyed reading Nelson Rodrigues. I think he thought of himself as the Nelson Rodrigues of punk. I watched one of their shows in a small warehouse packed with feverish, impatient fans. Onstage, a young stripper took her clothes off with extraordinary calm as Ronrona spat furious verses and the young men closer to her tried to grab her. Every time a hand came too close to the heroic woman on stage, the drummer would punish this impudence by hitting it with his drumstick.

That night, despite having become almost deaf on account of so much noise, I understood that chaos can be just another kind of organisation. That warehouse, to me, was like the square in Östlund's film: a space of openness to the Other.

One of the strongest scenes in Östlund's film shows an artist performing the role of an ape-man during a sophisticated dinner party. The guests allow themselves to be humiliated by the performance artist, either because his false animality frightens them or, more prosaically, because they are afraid of looking stupid if they were to stand up to him. To those who think that films must have a lesson to teach, here is the most elementary one: if we let ourselves be humiliated by an artist because we're afraid it will make us look stupid, then perhaps we really *are* stupid.

The Queen's blue-collar accent

I really enjoy V.S. Naipaul's books. However, I do not care for the man who wrote them. Insolence might be rather fun on the page; in a person, however, it merely reveals bad manners.

Naipaul is well known for his arrogance, vanity and misogyny, and for collections of borderline racist statements. The Angolan writer José Sousa Jamba interviewed him in London many years ago and describes how, after three or four standard questions, he finally summoned up the confidence to confront Naipaul: "They say you are very successful among white readers because you make prejudiced remarks about black people with which your white readers agree, but are too afraid to admit to publicly."

Naipaul stared at Jamba, furious, and in that moment lost his gloriously posh accent (that of an old British aristocrat), and regressed to the demotic English of Trinidad, the Caribbean island where he was born and where he lived until the end of his teenage years.

Ironically, Jamba, who grew up in an Angolan refugee camp in Zambia, studied in London and is today based in the United States, makes a point of speaking English with an accent not dissimilar to Naipaul's. I remember one occasion when Sousa Jamba visited me in Rio de Janeiro. I was reading, lying in bed, when I noticed a commotion. Looking out the window, I saw my friend admonishing one of the neighbours. Apparently, the neighbour had mistaken him for a thief. Jamba reacted, irritated, addressing my neighbour in the poshest English. Later, I asked why he hadn't addressed the man in Portuguese. "If I'd spoken in Portuguese, he wouldn't have shown me any respect," Jamba protested. "Did you see how he changed his attitude as soon as I started speaking English?"

I thought of Jamba and Naipaul while reading an article about the decline of the British aristocratic accent. According to an American linguist, Jonathan Harrington, even Queen Elizabeth II has been losing – though subtly – the famous 'royal accent'. The youngest members of the monarchy, such as Princes William and Harry, make a point of speaking in more of a cockney accent than a posh one. Cockney – a blue-collar, workman's accent – has become somewhat cool among the younger aristocrats, as they want to feel closer to the people. Then there are some members of the public who have climbed up the social ladder and would like to pass as aristocrats. Those people do insist on that posh accent. In other words, among the young people of the British upper class, social climbers are distinguished from nobility because they speak as if they had been born into it and not from a working-class environment, whereas true aristocrats speak – or try to – as if they were working-class.

The actor Pedro Cardoso, currently based in Lisbon, gave an interview a few days ago to the newspaper *Sol*. In this interview he remembers that 'theatre' actors in Brazil, up to the 1950s, with Nelson Rodrigues, would speak in a European Portuguese accent. European Portuguese was no longer heard on the streets, but it would appear onstage to create a sense of seriousness.

In Angola, this is still the case on television and radio. Some broadcasters still speak in a Portuguese accent, which is so archaic it no longer exists anywhere in Portugal itself. I suppose it only ever existed in the early days of Portuguese radio. Maybe they believe that, by falsifying their accent, the news will sound more authentic.

The idea of falsifying in order to add legitimacy reminds me of the case of the São Jorge castle, in Lisbon. Originally, the castle did not have battlements. However, in the 1940s, António de Oliveira Salazar ordered battlements to be built along the walls just so the building would look more like what most people thought a castle was supposed to look like. Nowadays, the vast majority of Lisboners firmly believe that the castle had battlements to begin with. It would be a scandal if they were ever to be removed.

The fact that the British aristocracy is losing its traditional accent, that the upper-class accent is now coming closer to a working-class accent, says more about the vigour of British democracy than it does about the decline of the British monarchy. Accent is a part of our identity. But a regional accent is one thing, and a social accent something else. That the next British monarch might speak with a cockney accent, even if it's a little fake, a little forced, is probably a good thing.

The moon is not for everyone

Last week, I watched the rising of a giant orange moon just as the sun was setting, from the pier of the Island of Mozambique. Halfway along the pier, which extends for 300 metres into the tepid serenity of an emerald-coloured sea, there is a little bar called, naturally, The Pier Bar. That evening, it was packed with people drinking beer and eating shrimp. There were South African and Portuguese tourists, and some members of the small Scandinavian community that has been living on the island since the socialist revolution over forty years ago. All of them, with mobile phones, turned towards the horizon. Two young boys, of the kind who roam the streets in packs asking tourists for spare change, observed the group with something akin to curiosity.

"What are they photographing?" asked Maninho, a skinny boy around seven years old with tame hazelnut eyes that he employs, with the talent of a great actor, to pretend to be a destitute orphan and tug on the tourists' heartstrings.

"It's the moon!" the other explained while pointing at the perfect round disc that, at that moment, rose over the old walls of the keep.

Maninho squinted at it, doubtful: "Can you eat it?!"

The next day I found out, to no surprise, that the beautiful moon had remained unnoticed by the majority of the population. None of the salesmen knocking on our door during the day, trying to sell us live lobsters, mangoes, bananas or old coins, had noticed the exceptional brilliance of the moon. Or they perhaps had noticed it, but did not assign it any special value. Beauty is worth very little on an empty stomach.

It's normal to hear Mozambicans refer to their country as a poor one. However, driving along the coast, you find a very green country traversed by wide rivers, with one of the most beautiful coastlines in the world. Mozambique's potential, when it comes to tourism and agriculture, is immense. Evidently, potential is not enough. As Eça de Queirós once wrote, every large piece of land has the potential to become a palace. But you need to build the palace.

The British magazine *The Economist* recently published its Democracy Index, an annual evaluation of democracy's advances and regressions around the world. Unsurprisingly, Cape Verde is the Portuguese-speaking country with the strongest, most advanced democracy, three places ahead of Portugal and twenty-six ahead of Brazil. Mozambique ranks 115th, which is still way ahead of Angola, rotting at the bottom of the list among the countries still subjected to totalitarian regimes.

Unlike Mozambique, Cape Verde is an unequivocally impoverished country. Punished for centuries by eastern winds, almost without rain or significant natural resources, it survives solely on tourism and fishing. Poverty all around, and misery out of sight. I am certain that on that same Wednesday, in Cidade da Praia or in Mindelo, people looked at the moon and were able to appreciate its glow.

Looking at the world map published by *The Economist*, it is easy to understand the connection between democracy and development. At the top of the list of countries with most solid democracies are Norway, Iceland and Sweden. In Africa, besides Cape Verde, the nations that stand out are South Africa, Zambia and Namibia.

The index is based on sixty indicators grouped into five categories: electoral process and pluralism, civil liberties, functioning of government, political participation and political culture. The bad news is that democracy has taken a few steps back all over the world. After decades of advances, there is now a confirmed tendency towards a general degradation of civil liberties and pluralism. Freedom of the press, for example, has decreased to its worst rating since 2006, with greater restriction occurring even in some democracies that are considered more robust. Only thirty of the 167 states analysed were classified as entirely free in that area.

With receding democracy, poverty grows; inequality, hatred and bitterness grow. It would come as no surprise if the years to come bring more war and terrorism. Today's crisis stems, mostly, from a breach of trust in democracy itself. Democracies are failing a little all over the world, a crisis mined by opportunists taking advantage of such failings to attain power. I don't know what the solution is to reverse this process. I do know that we must think about it now, as a matter of urgency.

The Macua samurai

An American producer, Lionsgate, is working on a feature film with a screenplay by Gregory Widen, the creator of *Highlander*. It is about Yasuke, the black samurai, an Afro–Japanese hero some historians claim was born on the Island of Mozambique. In France, a book about Yasuke was published in January, authored by Serge Bilé, a journalist from Côte d'Ivoire who specialises in the forgotten histories of black people. He wrote, for example, about black people in Nazi concentration camps. It is an interesting book. As for the film, I don't have such high hopes.

Interest in Yasuke grew in Japan on account of a TV documentary made in 2013. A Japanese team visited the Island of Mozambique, gathered images of the historic city and searched for possible descendants of the ancient warrior. They found none. There are very few people on the Island of Mozambique who know the story of Yasuke.

Some historians argue that the name Yasuke might be a bastardisation of *Iusufe*, a name still very popular in the region today. What is known, thanks to accounts from Jesuit priests and Japanese documents from that time, is that Yasuke arrived in Japan in 1579, in the service of an Italian missionary, Alessandro Valignano, who had been named Visitor to the missions in the Indies, which, at the time, also included the east coast of Africa. The Visitor, a type of inspector, reported directly to the Superior General of the Society of Jesus.

Yasuke's presence, as a black man 1.88 metres tall, a bona fide giant for the time especially by Japanese standards, attracted a lot of attention wherever the Visitor's committee went, to the point of causing great commotion. Oda Nobunaga, a rich and powerful feudal lord, heard of him and arranged a meeting. Not believing that any man could have such a dark complexion, he ordered that Yasuke be given a bath. Naturally, Yasuke emerged from the bath even darker and more resplendent than when he went in. Nobunaga was also impressed by Yasuke's strength, intelligence and refinement, and invited him to live in his castle in Azuchi. It is believed that Yasuke had become fluent in Japanese; Valignano supported the study of Japanese customs, and favoured the adaptation of the missionaries and his servants to the local culture.

Yasuke rose quickly through the ranks of Nobunaga's court, becoming the first foreign samurai in the history of Japan. He fought alongside his lord's army until they were defeated by rebel forces commanded by General Akechi Mitsuhide in 1582. Nobunaga committed *seppuku*, the cruel samurai practice of suicide by gutting, and Yasuke then joined Nobunaga's son, Oda Nobutada. He distinguished himself in combat, but ended up captured nonetheless. In a decision that might have had political motives as well as humanitarian ones, Mitsuhide spared his life and delivered him back to the Jesuits.

Yasuke's story might seem even more extraordinary today than it did to the eyes of those who witnessed it. Back then, in Japan, Africans were seen as a curiosity; however, there are no signs of any racial prejudice. Yasuke was admired as an exotic being, that is true, but his recognition came from his humanity and his qualities as a great warrior.

Today we consider Yasuke with the inevitable weight of centuries of anti-African prejudice. This makes his exceptional story look more exceptional still. We accept with little surprise the white samurai character portrayed by Tom Cruise in *The Last Samurai*, a weak and fanciful film, but it's hard for us to imagine a black samurai, an African samurai. The ideological construct of racism was extremely well executed by the slave-owning system. That system has been dismantled, but the virus of racist thought persists, insidiously, throughout Western societies – even in the more progressive ones.

A film about Yasuke destined for the wider public could be significant, contributing to an idea of Africa and of African people as active agents in the process of the invention of the world. I fear, however, that Lionsgate may not resist the temptation of creating yet another mainstream hero of our times, sort of like Black Panther, instead of attempting to understand the time in which Yasuke lived and the silent drama of a man who found himself compelled to fight and to excel in a universe so distant from his own.

Afterword

As I reread the pieces that make up this *Paradise and Other Hells*, I encounter, with some amazement, even shock, a world that, to a great extent, no longer exists. Brazil, for example, has survived Jair Bolsonaro, even though it is still struggling to reverse some of the after-effects left behind by his misrule. The US has also survived Trump, though, as if in some surreal nightmare, it seems to want to return to this inconceivable past.

The Covid pandemic had not yet shaken the foundations of the civilisation in which we still move, based upon an irrational exploitation of resources. Nonetheless, it was predictable – which was how I was able to predict it.

Many of the concerns that kept me up at night at that time have deepened: the environmental crisis, first of all, as well as the strengthening of a certain antiquated way of thinking, organised around the forces of the most radical right, which feed on bitterness and racism, and which have been slowly growing everywhere.

What is most startling, reading these pieces, which are a little old now, is the realisation that the world is not advancing in a linear, consistent fashion, towards a future of greater intelligence, greater justice, greater equality, greater safety and greater democracy. We are making progress in some areas, while we are regressing in others. If there is one lesson we can learn from these past years, disturbing and difficult and complex as they have been, is that everything is fragile and perishable. No, I'm sorry to say, there are no democracies that cannot be corrupted and toppled. We need to unite around fundamental questions. We need to keep alive the flame of the old ideals – liberty, equality, fraternity – and remain open to dreaming new utopias.

Island of Mozambique, June 2024

Translator Credits

RAHUL BERY

Tuesday, 5 November 2013
Black people in blackface
Death according to Sacks
Literature and identities
A toy for creating marvels
God is sick
In praise of strangeness
Friday, 25 September 2015
On race and justice
On untranslatability
Towards an ethics of spitting
In case of emergency, use poetry
The magicians' reawakening
Before there was blue
Sunday, 15 May 2016
Monday, 16 May 2016
The writer who beat me
Wednesday, 6 July 2016
Manoel and me
The day the Virgin Mary lost her head
The cruel months
A strange fruit
Cannibalism, expanded
A garden of memory
What is truth for?
My new obsession
He's back
Muhamed's choice
After the end

DANIEL HAHN

Note
Wednesday, 20 August 2014
My daughter's hair
Book of titles
A dead boy on the beach
Monday, 31 August 2015
The awareness of Evil
Monday, 21 September 2015
The intelligence of life
Saturday, 3 October 2015
Starting again
On drugs and literature
Tuesday, 9 February 2016
Wednesday, 21 June 2017
Tuesday, 18 July 2017
The book thief
The language of the alchemists
Three divers and a dwarf
A wondrous discord
The Doomsday clock
Afterword

ANDREW MCDOUGALL

Cataloguing monsters
Dead poets' island
All poetry aspires to be song
Sunday, 19 May 2013
Thursday, 4 September 2014
Friday, 5 September 2014
Monday, 8 September 2014
The light of our language
The boys of Porto Mosquito
Non-places, non-people
Saturday, 16 January 2016
Thursday, 21 January 2016
From magical to autophagic realism
Private drama, public comedy
Two views on Brazil
A ghost ship
Magnificent losers
Crazy season
Life's Vanquished, under the sun of the tropics
Castaways in the city
Uninventing the enemy
Almost immortals
The useless beauty of giraffes
Wonderful cultural appropriation
While the Earth shakes
Tiradentes' lice
Thursday, 4 May 2017
Sunday, 7 May 2017
The curtains of censorship
A wolf in the mirror
Fear of nudity
The elegance of silence
On books and revolutions

VICTOR MEADOWCROFT

Friday, 12 June 2015
The oldest tree in the world
An unlikely reader
A false blonde angel
Thursday, 28 April 2016
Thursday, 5 May 2016
Conviction and skulduggery
Tuesday, 12 September 2006
Tuesday, June 22 2010
Monday, 1 June 2015
Monday, 15 February 2016
Something maybe like a forgiveness
That precise instant of glory
Lynchings
Mad not to dream
The zombie's bite
Trained not to smile
The gold of the islands
Hero and traitor
Bantu Spring
Brave new world
The December sky
When the lion builds its own cage

ROBIN PATTERSON

The nakedness of authors
Thursday, 25 June 2015
Friday, 3 July 2015
Thursday, 30 July 2015
Sunday, 2 August 2015
Saturday, 26 September 2015
Love letter to Luaty Beirão
The thinker's silence
Wednesday, 14 October 2015
Thursday, 15 October 2015
Thursday, 29 October 2015
The boy who walked through walls
A river's lament
Books burn well
Black power (or the power to be black)
Beware of the clown
The flooded airplane
Paradise and other hells
Saturday, 24 June 2016
A whole host of whites
Keep calm: it isn't the end yet
The European explorer financed by an African king
The ideal kleptocracy
The end of miracles
Monday, 19 June 2017
Secret authors
Neural lace
Improbable happiness
The art of falling
The secret poetry of chance

FRANCISCO VILHENA

The convulsive solitude of our days
An unintentional anarchist
The extinction of unicorns
The Bar Oficina
The beautiful useless things that save our lives
The death of Cecil
The sceptical palm reader
A Swedish Hell
The Queen's blue-collar accent
The moon is not for everyone
The Macua samurai